ENGLAND

Publisher:	Aileen Lau
Project Editor:	Emma Tan
Assisting Editors:	Aileen Lau
	Catherine Khoo
Design/DTP:	Sares Kanapathy
	Sarina Afandie
Illustrations:	Eric Yeo
Cover Artwork:	Susan Harmer
Maps:	Hong Li

Published in the United States by
PRENTICE HALL GENERAL REFERENCE
15 Columbus Circle
New York, New York, 10023

ISBN 0-671-88283-X

Titles in the series:
Alaska - American Southwest - Australia - Bali - California - Canada - Caribbean - China -
England - Florida - France - Germany - Greece - Hawaii - India - Indonesia - Italy - Ireland -
Japan - Kenya - Malaysia - Mexico - Nepal - New England - New York - Pacific Northwest
USA - Singapore - Spain - Thailand - Turkey - Vietnam

USA MAINLAND SPECIAL SALES
Bulk purchases (10+copies) of the Travel Bugs series are available at special discounts for
corporate use. The publishers can produce custom publications for corporate clients to be
used as premiums or for sales promotion. Copies can be produced with custom cover
imprints. For more information write to Special Sales, Prentice Hall Travel, Paramount
Communications Building, 15th floor, 15 Columbus Circle, New York, NY 10023.

Printed in Singapore

ENGLAND

Text by Christine Pemberton

With contributions from:
Morten Strange

Project Editor:
Emma Tan

Prentice Hall Travel

New York   London   Toronto   Sydney   Tokyo   Singapore

C O N T E N T S

C O N T E N T S

C O N T E N T S

C O N T E N T S

A land of gardens and gardeners rewards itself each spring

and summer with a riot of colour of roses, daffodils, daisies, tulips...

Pomp and ceremony are the order

royal nation.

of the day in this very

City pleasures, modern lifestyles, country

leisure, traditional pursuits, are part of English life.

Just what is it about the simple word "England", that inevitably conjures up tranquil, timeless images, of the Queen, thatched cottages, afternoon tea, city bankers in bowler hats, the chimes of Big Ben, cricket, Oxford and Cambridge, and red double-decker buses. Ask an expatriate Englishman to describe his home country, and almost certainly a nostalgic image will follow. He will wax eloquent with talk of village greens and cricket matches, of country pubs and warm sunny evenings, with never a mention of rainy weather, or the problems of modern society, and you would be forgiven for thinking that England was still locked in some kind of time-warp of the early, Edwardian years of this century.

England is, indeed, all of these things, but of course it is also much more. It is still a country of some gentility, where people shake hands and say "How do you do?" when

The Big Ben in London, one of England's many landmarks.

Introduction

1

Quaint half-timbered houses, part of the charm of the English village.

being introduced, where cars slow down at pedestrian crossings to let old ladies cross – though they are not actually called pedestrian crossings, but more picturesquely, zebra crossings. People still do find time to have tea in the afternoon, and will turn out on Saturday afternoons to watch their village cricket team. But amidst all this "olde-worlde" charm, there is, of course, another facet to the country.

The England that is about to enter the 21st century is a multi-racial, multi-religious, multi-cultural society. A country where more people support football than cricket teams, where the banker is more likely to be wearing yuppie-era braces than a bowler hat. A country where more people live in and around cities, than in country villages and where, after generations of unswerving, unquestioning loyalty to "King and Country", there are faint rumblings of discontent about the monarchy. In short, England is coming to terms with her present, whilst still living with her great and glorious past.

Green & pleasant land

Let us take a closer look at the country which was poetically described by one of her many famous sons, Blake, as a "green and pleasant land". But first of all, we should define exactly what we mean by England. England is just one of the countries that makes up the United

Kingdom (UK), which is not the same thing as Great Britain. Confused? Well, in very simple terms, Great Britain refers to the large island, on which are situated the countries of England, Scotland and Wales. When the six provinces of Northern Ireland are added, the political entity known as the United Kingdom is formed.

It is not always easy to totally separate the identity of England from that of the UK – the Queen, for example, is head of state not just of England but of the whole UK. There are however, still many differences between the four main races in the UK that make up Her Majesty's subjects. History has created separate political identities, different cultures and languages.

Although an Englishman and a Scot both see themselves as British, they do not consider themselves as identical races, and they have separate "national" teams for soccer and rugby, just to prove it. It is a fact that you would never, ever be able to make an Englishman wear that pride of every Scottish man, a kilt! There are distinctly English characteristics, just as there is a separate strand of English history. If you are looking for stiff-upper-lips, cool under-statements and phlegmatism, then you must find not just a "Brit" (slang for British subject), but specifically, an Englishman.

Great institutions

Although England, like any other Euro-

A budding English beauty.

pean country, is increasingly industrialized, increasingly technical and visibly multi-cultural, there is definitely a certain timelessness to it; institutions and social customs remain unchanged, decade after decade.

Thus it is that the children of the country's elite still go to public schools, which, with typical English logic are as private, that is, expensive, as they come – with names such as Eton and Harrow, Winchester and Cheltenham Ladies College. The most intelligent ones will then go on to Oxford or Cambridge, the country's two oldest universities, which are often referred to together as "Oxbridge".

The old school tie, and the old boy network, are still alive and well in the

Leeds Castle, one of the many treasure troves of English history.

An English country garden.

Home Counties (the English counties into which the city of London extends).

Historically, one of England's major, enduring exports has been the English language, and the language of Shakespeare and Jane Austen is spoken, in a range of accents and dialects, over much of the globe. Another, highly successful, though less widespread export, was cricket, which is played avidly, and expertly, in the former colonies of the Caribbean, much of the Indian sub-continent, and Australia.

The head of state of the country is

Fast Facts

Land Area: 50,363 square miles (19 km²).
Geographical Area: Along with Scotland, Wales, Northern Ireland, the Channel Islands, the Isle of Man, the Isles of Scilly, and the Isle of Wight, England is part of the United Kingdom.
Capital city: London.
Head of State: Her Majesty Queen Elizabeth II.
Parliament: Parliamentary democracy consisting of two houses of parliament, the House of Lords and the House of Commons.
Currency: £ Sterling.
Religion: Majority of Christians but there are also sizeable communities of Jews, as well as Muslims, Hindus, Sikhs and Parsis – the majority of the latter deriving initially from countries belonging to the former British Empire.
Race: Majority of white Caucasians, but due to immigration in the 19th and 20th centuries, there is a substantial non-white population, many of whom are third and fourth generation English.
Weather: temperate climate, unpredictable.
Highest point: Scafell Pike, 3,210 feet (1053 m) high.
National flower: the rose.
Main industries: with the decline in coal mining and ship building, the service industries are increasingly important economically; London is a world centre for banking and insurance. Agriculture is still important, and tourism is a big earner.

Queen Elizabeth II, who has ruled for 41 years, after being crowned in an epoch-making televised coronation, in June 1953. Although the majority of her subjects, (who are, by the way, not citizens, but subjects), remain quietly loyal to the Queen and the abstract concept of a monarchy, the unabated gossip and scandals which have swirled around the House of Windsor over the last few years, have done much to damage the prestige of the royal family, and have called into question what kind of role the monarchy should take in the country in the 21st century.

From imperialism to the EEC

Over the centuries, the monarchy has weathered many storms, and the British in the 1990s are far from happy at the notion of a President in place of Her Majesty, but some royal changes have already taken place, and more are certain to follow. What is abundantly clear is that England, and the UK as a whole, must face up to the reality of its post-imperial existence. The British Empire, the pride of the Victorians, has been virtually dismantled and with the loss of Hong Kong in 1997, the sun will have finally set on the imperialist dream, with only a few tiny colonial outposts remaining.

The destiny of the UK, as seen by many of the country's politicians, lies most definitely with Europe, although the average person is not so committed. The average person on the street may accept in his/her mind that Europe makes political and economic sense, but in his/her heart is reluctant to cede an inch of that national identity, to which people attach considerable pride.

The English are unreasonably attached to "English" things such as pints and stones, rather than the standardized European litres and kilograms. There is a robust pride in the absence of

The pomp of England at the Royal Windsor horse show.

national identity cards, and the fact that most policemen are unarmed.

Industrialization & entrepreneurship

The early agricultural vocation of England underwent major changes during the late 18th and early 19th centuries with the advent of the Industrial Revolution, when the country was at the forefront in the development of railways and steamers, and industries such as mining and textile weaving transformed not only the economy, but also the physical appearance of England. The "dark Satanic mills" and the exploitation and poverty depicted in many of the classic novels of Charles Dickens, have long since disappeared, to be replaced with a highly regulated industrial system, and an economy based increasingly on service industries and high-technology manufacturing.

England today is a country where education is important, where qualifications matter, and it is increasingly a meritocracy. It does not matter so much nowadays who you are, and whom you know (although net-working is still rife) for it is also a country where someone from a modest background, with skill and education, can rise as high as they wish, or almost as high. The world of exclusive London dining clubs will almost certainly remain off-limits to the new comer, especially if the new comer is female, but little else will.

Former Prime Minister Margaret Thatcher, represented this culture perfectly: from what the English like to describe as an "ordinary" background – her father was a grocer – she went to Oxford, into politics, and the rest is contemporary history. Single-handedly, she did much to glorify the "yuppie" (young urban professional) culture of the 1980s, where talent and hard work, especially lots of the latter, brought rich rewards.

The world-wide recession of the early 1990s may have done a lot to eradicate the yuppie culture, but a whole generation has seen that ability and work experience pays, no matter which school you went to.

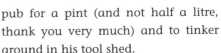
A smiling welcome from a beefeater at the Tower of London.

The English character

So, what is the England of today like? It is a country of traditions, where the guard at the royal palace is changed precisely at of 1100 hours, where most people eat lunch at 1300 hours and drink tea at 1600 hours. It is also a country where tradtitional values are being eroded in keeping with the rest of the western world, society is becoming increasingly competitive and qualifications equal better prospects equal better jobs.

People believe in the work ethos, but this is not a country of Japanese-like extremes: the English worker needs time to mow the lawn, to go down to his local pub for a pint (and not half a litre, thank you very much) and to tinker around in his tool shed.

England is a country of dog-lovers, of ardent "do-it-yourself" addicts, of enthusiastic gardeners and poor linguists, of careful drivers and mediocre chefs, of traditionalists who are firm believers in the need for change, of quiet self-effacing people who will vociferously protect the rights of the underdog.

Writing about the British character, in the early 1920s, a writer called George Santayana accurately summed up the English in one simple sentence: "England is the paradise of individuality, eccentricity, heresy, anomalies, hobbies and humours."

History

Knowledge of English history before the Roman era is largely derived from archaeology, which provides clear traces of cultures and ways of life, but no detail of personalities or specific events; that knowledge comes only with the advent of written records. Thus it is, that pre-Roman English history derives only from archaeological remains.

Originally, England, or, more properly, Britain, was part of continental Europe. Towards the end of the Ice Age, around was a slight cli- 11,000 BC, there matic warming, and gradually tundra was replaced by forest, home to red deer and elk, which were hunted by migrating hunters from what is now continental Europe. Around 6,000-5,000

The English hero Admiral Nelson, who defeated the audacious Napoleon Bonaparte at the Battle of Waterloo.

11

The prehistoric site of Stonehenge.

BC, there was a physical separation from France: the Channel was formed, and the destiny of Britain was transformed. The cutting of the land bridge hampered migration, and Britain developed at a different rate, and in a different manner from her neighbours across the Channel. Her island character, therefore, goes back some 8,000 years.

Visitors & invaders

Visitors and invaders still arrived on the island, of course. Neolithic immigrants introduced agriculture, around 4,000 BC, and brought with them not only their flint tools, but their burial tradi-tions. Early Neolithic man buried his dead in communal graves: in the west of the country, stone tombs were built, and in the east, long barrows, or mounds of earth. There is early evidence of some forms of ritualistic worship and communal celebrations, from enclosures, which would later develop in the third millennium into ditch-enclosed earthworks, known as henge monuments. Some of these, such as Durrington Walls in Wiltshire, are large, and enclose smaller circles.

Invaders from the Low Countries, known as the Beaker Folk, probably arrived around 2,300 BC. Their name refers to their habit of burying a drinking vessel alongside their dead. Later groups brought with them a knowledge

Magna Carta

On June 15, 1215, on a small island in the River Thames called Runnymede, the highly unpopular King of England, John, was confronted by a group of rebellious barons. The barons presented the king with a document known as the Articles of the Barons, on the basis of which the *Magna Carta* was drawn up. The document set out to provide protection not just for the Barons, as one might have imagined, but for all freemen, and attempted to provide guarantees of feudal rights, many of which had been ignored by the Plantagenet kings.

One clause, number 39, promised judgement by peers or by the law of the land to all freemen. The barons, although unhappy with John, did not attempt to undermine nor dismantle the monarchy, nor did they attempt to legitimize rebellion. What they did, was to try to ensure that the king was beneath the law, and not above it.

A series of simultaneous sealed originals – at least 41 – were made; one for each county and the Cinque ports. Today there are only four surviving originals; one is displayed in Lincoln Castle, one is kept in Salisbury Cathedral and two are in the British Library.

The *Magna Carta*, written in shorthand medieval Latin, in immediate terms, was not a success; it was just another stage in a series of attempts to prevent civil war, and John was soon released from any obligations under *Magna Carta* by the Pope who annulled it on the 24 August 1215, after only nine weeks in effect. It was however re-issued in 1216, 1217 and 1225 and was eventually confirmed as English law in 1297. Parts of the *Magna Carta* are still law, namely Chapters 1, 9 and 29, and part of chapter 37.

The surviving copy of *Magna Carta* in Lincoln probably arrived in the cathedral town around 30 June 1215, having been brought there by Bishop Hugh who had been present at Runnymede.

The fact that this is the original can be seen from the back of the document, where the name Lincolnia, is inscribed in the same hand as the Charter; there are also continuous records of it in Lincoln since 1215. It remained in the cathedral office until 1939 and spent the war years in Fort Knox, USA.

of metallurgy, a name which they gave to their age, the Bronze Age. Trade and prosperity were concentrated in Wessex, and the wealthy chieftains built a monument of large, shaped sandstones, known as Stonehenge III.

During the period of the Iron Age (700-400 BC), small groups of migrants continued to arrive, and were absorbed into the community. Gradually a more distinctly British type of settlement evolved, and a Celtic system of farming, with small fields and grain storage pits.

Some time before the end of the second century, tribes from Belgic Gaul migrated to England, establishing more settlements. The southeast of England, especially Kent and north of the River Thames, saw the development of a distinctive culture, whose people used coins, made pottery on the potter's wheel, and created images of their dead.

Roman England

Julius Caesar invaded Britain in 55 BC, bringing the country into contact with a totally different culture. Thirty years after the Roman invasion, there were two principal zones of power in England, one group north of the Thames, and a

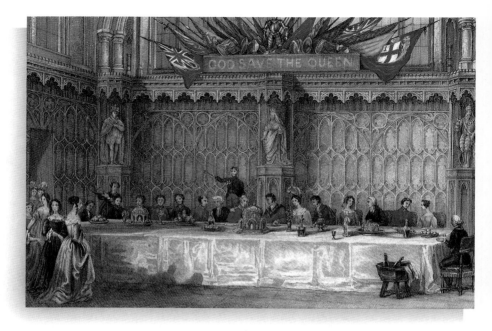

The Lord Mayors' table, London Guildhall, has been the setting for great State occasions for over a hundred years.

second one south of the river. In addition, there were independent tribes, with whom Caesar had established client relationships, as did his successor, Augustus. But tensions existed, and in AD 43, Claudius invaded the island, with the aim of subduing it, landing at Richborough in Kent. The British were defeated in two fierce battles, yet resistance remained, and the Roman Legions advanced into different regions to conquer the local tribes. By AD 47 the Fosse Way had been built as a frontier for the Romans, but it was by no means permanent or totally secure.

One of the last rebellions against the Romans was that of the Iceni tribe, led by their Queen Boudicca, around AD 60. The tribe's land had been forci-

bly annexed, and Boudicca rallied to their cause other local tribes, and together they sacked the three main Roman cities, London, Camulodunum (Colchester) and Verulamium (St Albans). Over the ensuing decades, as the Romans concentrated on subduing Wales and Scotland, troops were withdrawn from southern England, allowing more self-government by the local tribes. In the face of troop withdrawals from Britain back to the continent, and the greater degree of resistance offered by the pastoral hill people, who rebelled against the Roman idea of urbanization, the Romans decided to build a stonger frontier; Hadrian's Wall was the result. The Emperor Hadrian built it between AD122-130, and, marking as it did, the permanent frontier of Roman Britain, it was the most impressive in their empire.

The 4th century was a period of great prosperity in all parts of Roman Britain, yet by the early years of the subsequent century, increasing numbers of Roman troops were withdrawn, leaving the country vulnerable to attacks from the Picts and the Scots. In AD 410, the Emperor Honorius authorized cities to provide for their own defense, in what is seen as the symbolic end of Roman rule in Britain.

Angles, Saxons & Jutes

Over the following decades, in order to combat the troublesome Picts and Scots, the Romans invited mercenaries to settle in England, and the three main groups who came were the Angles, the Saxons and the Jutes. The Saxons settled and garrisoned areas of the east coast, which inevitably led to fighting, the destruction of many of the Roman properties, and such economic hardship that many British emigrated to Brittany, in France. In the second half of the fifth century, the legendary King Arthur is credited with military successes against the Saxons, and the first half of the 6th century was a time of peace.

By the end of the 7th century people considered themselves to be "English", although different kingdoms existed, yet there was a sense of unity, enforced by the acknowledged overlordship of a single chief, who governed over all the kingdoms south of the River Humber. He was known as a "bretwalda", the first of whom was Aelle of Sussex. When Saint Augustine arrived in England from Rome in AD 597, the bretwalda was Aethelberht of Kent, who had a legal code written down, and Kent was the first county in England to be converted to Christianity.

Both the influence of and the proponents of Christianity gradually found their way into the Anglo-Saxon system of kingship, and within a century of the arrival of Augustine in Kent, England was in the forefront of Christian scholarship, producing such great writers as the Venerable Bede (AD672-735). There was a famous school centred around Canterbury, but the centre of scholarship was Northumbria, where the beautiful illustrated *Lindisfarne Gospels* were made.

The Vikings

The 8th century was the golden age of the Kingdom of Mercia, a small kingdom in the northwest under the rule of King Aethelbald and his successor, King Offa. Offa was an immensely powerful ruler, treated on equal terms with Charlemagne, he regarded himself as king of all England up to the Humber. He is remembered today principally as the architect of Offa's Dike, which marked his frontier with Wales.

After Offa's death in AD 796, the

Elizabeth J's fiery half-sister Mary, Queen of Scots.

Upon Alfred's death in 899, he was succeeded by his son Edward, who continued his father's work, advancing into the Danelaw, or Danish held territory in England. In AD 980 the Vikings made a second advance, fighting raged wih the English for the next 30 years, until the exhausted and impoverished English accepted a Danish king, Sweyn, in 1013. His son, King Cnut (or Canute), fought to subdue England, and led campaigns in Scotland, and Scandinavia. After Cnut's death, his unpopular sons succeeded, followed by Edward the Confessor, whose reign was the prelude to one of the major events in English history, the Norman invasion of 1066.

King William & 1066

No English records survive, only Norman ones, but these claim that Edward the Confessor may well have promised William of Normandy the English throne. Whatever the truth, the historical fact remains that the Norman King, William the Conqueror, with the support of the Pope, invaded England in 1066, defeated and killed the English king Harold at the Battle of Hastings, and on Christmas Day 1066, William was crowned king of England.

hitherto small, scattered Viking raids became more frequent and more successful. The Danish Vikings came intent on conquering England, which they did. East Anglia, York, and Wessex were in turn the scene of conflict. King Alfred the Great drove the Vikings out of Wessex in 877, and after spending the winter of 878 in the Somerset marshes, Alfred defeated the Danes at the Battle of Edington, forcing their king to convert to Christianity, and to retire to East Anglia, where they settled. King Alfred's victory was a major one, for it prevented the Vikings from ever governing the whole of the country. He went on to capture London in AD 886, and was accepted as king by all the English outside the Danish held areas.

The Norman Conquest of England was not achieved immediately, and for the next ten years, William had to fight to quell uprisings against his rule. He introduced a feudal system of governing, and carried out the Domesday Sur-

The new National Gallery, Trafalgar Square, London.

vey; an attempt to list all the properties and agricultural holdings in the country. Under William and his sons, England forged greater links with continental Europe, especially Normandy in France.

Two of William the Conqueror's sons ruled England, whilst still fighting their wars in France, and on the death of the youngest son, Henry I, England was plunged into a 20 year succession crisis, since the only legitimate heir, his daughter Matilda, was not a popular choice. Henry's nephew Stephen sailed from France to England, claimed the throne and was crowned in 1135. Four years later Matilda arrived in England to stake her claim to the throne, and civil war raged in the country until, in 1153, Stephen recognised Matilda's son Henry as his heir, and he succeeded to the throne as Henry II in 1154, the first of the Plantagenet kings.

The Plantagenets

Henry II was king of England and inherited vast areas of France, through his father, his brother, Stephen, and though his marriage to Eleanor of Aquitaine, who brought with her most of southwest France. It is from this date that the long English involvement with Bordeaux and southwest France originates.

One of the things for which Henry is remembered is, sadly, the murder of Saint Thomas à Becket, the Archbishop

The Roman walls, London.

of Canterbury. Henry's wish to be rid of Becket, uttered in anger, was taken literally by four of his knights, who murdered the Archbishop in Canterbury Cathedral, which became one of the country's major pilgrimage sites almost overnight.

Henry was succeeded by his son Richard the Lionheart, who spent most of his reign abroad fighting the Crusades, and when his brother John came to the throne in 1199, resentment against the Plantagenet kings was high. King John has the unenviable reputation of being one of the most detested kings in English history, who managed to lose all of his Norman possessions, except the Channel Islands, and when his unpopular and expensive attempts to regain his French possessions failed, he was forced by his disgruntled barons to sign a document called *Magna Carta* (see Box story p13).

For the next hundred years, under the long reign of Henry III and then Edward I, the identity of England became progressively more established, and under Edward, the concept of parliament grew, initially drawn from representative Knights of the Shires who met with the king on a regular basis. Wars against the Welsh, the French and the Scots consumed much energy, manpower and finance, and when Edward II came to the throne in 1307, he inherited not only an ongoing war with Scotland, but a huge treasury deficit - some £200,000.

Edward II was almost certainly homosexual. His reign was an unsuccessful, troubled one. His favourite, Piers Gaveston was murdered, as was the king himself, in Berkeley Castle in 1327. His son Edward III inherited the throne when he was 14 years old; he a popular king and ruled for a successful 50 years.

The "Hundred Years War"

Edward III's claim to the French throne, through his mother Isabella, and Anglo-French trade rivalries, plunged the two countries, in 1337, into The "Hundred Years' War". Initially the war was inconclusive, despite the English invasion of Normandy in 1346, the Battle of Crécy and the siege of Calais. By 1360, a truce had been negotiated, under which Edward dropped his claim to the French throne, on receiving guarantees of the sovereignty of English possessions in France. In 1348, there was an outbreak of plague, known as The Black Death, which killed between a third to a half of the population. There were further debilitating outbreaks in 1361 and 1369.

When Edward III died in 1377, his 10 year old grandson Richard II came to the throne, and almost the first crisis he had to face was the 1381 Peasant's Revolt. Crushed by the huge expenses of the war with France, impoverished and weakened by successive outbreaks of plague, the peasantry rose up against the king and the government, under their leader Wat Tyler, who was himself killed during negotiations with the king.

In the light of the subsequent alteration of many documents from this period, it is still not clear how Richard's reign ended, but he is alleged to have abdicated in 1399, when his cousin Henry Bolingbroke ascended the throne as King Henry IV. He successfully crushed a Welsh uprising, as well as defeating supporters of Richard, and the latter's son. Henry V only ruled from 1413-1422, but his brief reign is remembered for the English successes in the wars with France, especially the Battle of Agincourt, which, with a little dramatic help from Shakespeare, has become a major symbolic event in English history.

Henry VI ruled from 1422-1471, but, during 2 bouts of mental illness, Richard, the third Duke of York ruled as protector. Rallied by Joan of Arc, by 1453 the French had recaptured all their French possessions, except Calais.

Henry VIII

All monarchs leave an impact, however fleeting, on their country's history and destiny, but few can have left such a lasting legacy as Henry VIII, larger than life, married six times, and the founder of the Church of England, the country's main religious denomination today. Six unhappy women, and their overwhelming husband, changed not only the country's religion, but also shaped the future relationship of the kingdom with Rome; even today, a Roman Catholic by law can not be Prime Minister of Great Britain, nor can he or she, sit on the throne.

The Royal divorce

Henry inherited the throne in 1509, when he was 18 years old. Together with his Lord Chancellor, Cardinal Wolsey, he helped to make England one of the centres of Renaissance learning. Henry's wife, Catherine of Aragon was seven years older than the King, and had given him only one child who managed to survive beyond infancy, the future Queen Mary. She was also the widow of his brother, and it was this fact which Henry used, despite a papal dispensation at the time of the marriage, to seek annulment of his marriage to Catherine. Henry quoted from the biblical Book of *Leviticus*, in support of his request for an end to his marriage: "If a man takes his brother's wife, it is impurity: he has uncovered his brother's nakedness, they shall be childless." And the fact remained that every male child born to Catherine and Henry had indeed died, and there was no male heir to carry on the Tudor line.

The break with Rome, over the Pope's refusal to grant the annulment was not a quick decision. Diplomatic means were tried over a number of years, to solve the impasse. There were various compromise suggestions: that Catherine become a nun, to allow Henry to re-marry, or that Mary be married to Henry's illegitimate son. Cardinal Wolsey died in 1529, just in time to escape being put on trial for treason, and Henry moved inexorably towards a break with Rome, a church which was itself going through something of an identity crisis, in the face of internal corruption and the rise of Lutheranism.

Reformation & re-marriage

Henry convened the so-called Reformation Parliament in November 1529, and for seven years it passed a mass of legislation, much of it crucial. The King was proclaimed the supreme head of the church "so far as the law of Christ allows", but the Pope had still not come round to Henry's way of thinking, so when Anne Boleyn became pregnant, the King hastily married her in January 1533. Henry was left with just a few months to solve the problem of his first marriage to Catherine, or risk the charge of bigamy, and yet another illegitimate child. Events moved rapidly. In April 1533, it was decreed that "this realm of England is an empire"; in May, a compliant English archbishop annulled Henry's first marriage; in June, Anne was crowned Queen; and in September, a child was born – not the hoped for son, but the future Queen Elizabeth I. A remarkable woman, stronger than most men, Elizabeth was to reign over a golden era in England But her bitterly disappointed father was not to know this. He was, however, confident that Anne would have a son.

The Wars of the Roses

The Wars of the Roses, were a dynastic struggle between the houses of York and Lancaster, two family branches which both descended from Edward III. This long civil war owes its name to the symbols of the two houses, the white rose of York and the red rose of Lancaster. The Duke of York's legitimate claim to the throne, backed by his time as

By the end of the following year, the break with Rome was irrevocable, and by the Act of Succession, Henry was decreed to be the Supreme Head of the Church of England. This time the rider about being according to Christ's laws was dropped. Once the legal and moral existence of the Roman Catholic Church in England had been destroyed, it was inevitable that its physical destruction would follow, which soon happened with the Dissolution of the Monasteries. Henry's new Lord Chancellor, Sir Thomas More and Bishop John Fisher both refused to recognize the new church, and were executed. They have both been canonized as saints in the Roman Catholic Church.

The struggle for a son

Henry VIII was omnipotent, and with the death of Catherine of Aragon in January 1536, and Anne Boleyn's continuing failure to produce a son, Henry felt secure enough to send Anne to her execution in the Tower of London, and 11 days later, to re-marry. Jane Seymour gave Henry a son, the future King Edward VI, a sickly child, but an heir nonetheless. Jane died in childbirth, and Henry's next Queen was Anne of Cleves. Within a year, he had divorced her, and executed Thomas Cromwell, who had engineered the marriage. On the day of Cromwell's execution, he married Anne Boleyn's cousin, Catherine Howard, but 18 months later, she was also executed. His sixth wife, Catherine Parr, nursed and cared for her husband, who was by now a sick old man. Henry VIII died in January 1547, survived by the third Queen Catherine, an unhealthy 9 year old son, and 2 daughters.

protector, during the king's insanity, was side-lined by the birth of an heir to Henry VI, and civil war broke out.

After Richard's death at the Battle of Wakefield, his son Edward IV was still committed to fight the House of Lancas-

ter. He was briefly deposed, on at his death in 1483 he two minor sons, Edward and Richard. Left to the protection of their uncle, Richard, Duke of Gloucester, they were imprisoned in the Tower of London, where, according to popular history, their ambitious uncle had them murdered. Richard was then crowned King Richard III, and has had a consistently bad press ever since. He was killed in battle two years later, at the Battle of Bosworth Field, during the course of which, Henry Tudor, the sole male claimant to the House of Lancaster defeated not only the unpopular king, but also the Yorkist cause.

The Tudors

The Tudor dynasty came into being on 22 August 1485, when Henry Tudor left the Yorkist King Richard III dead on the battlefield at Bosworth and, as Henry VII began what would be 118 years of Tudor rule. Henry VII's claims to the throne were not overly strong, for his Lancastrian blood was tainted by illegitimacy twice over, but might won over right, and his victory at Bosworth Field, followed by marriage with Elizabeth of York, ensured his position.

The England over which Henry VII ruled, was slowly recovering from the demographic disaster of the Black Death plague, helped economically by the rapid development of the woollen industry. Henry VII was successful in battle, and his efficient regime helped secure a permanent dynasty. But Arthur, his eldest son, died and it was his second son, Henry VIII who inherited the throne. Henry VIII's marriage to Arthur's widow, Catherine of Aragaon – more specifically his divorce from her – was a most significant event in English history, sparking as it did the Protestant Reformation in England; a split with the Pope and the Roman Catholic church, the foundation of the Church of England, and the dissolution of the monasteries.

Despite his six marriages, Henry VIII produced only one legitimate son, Edward VI, who died of consumption after a short reign. Desperate, the Lord Protector tried his hand at king-making: he persuaded the king to declare his half-sister, Mary, illegitimate, and make a Protestant cousin (and the Lord Protector's daughter-in-law) his legal heir. On his death, Lady Jane Grey ruled for nine days, before being despatched to the Tower, along with the Lord Protector, where they were both executed.

Mary I, Henry VIII's daughter by his first wife, was a passionate Roman Catholic, but her vision of Catholicism was already outdated by the time of her accession to the throne. Her conviction that Catholicism could be restored by the persecution and torture of its opponents, led to hundreds of Protestant martyrs being burned at the stake. Her marriage to the King of Spain was unpopular and childless, and dragged England into a war against France, during the course of which England lost her last French possession, Calais.

Elizabethan England

The country was relieved by Mary's death, and greeted the accession of her half-sister Elizabeth I with joy and relief. In 1558, Elizabeth was 25 years old, highly intelligent, magnetic like her father, without being ruthless, and opposed to religious bigotry. There was an energy and dynamism about the young queen which influenced the mood of the country; this was the era that produced Shakespeare, Marlowe, Donne, Spenser and Bacon. English sailors set out to discover the world, chief among them Sir Francis Drake and Sir Walter Raleigh.

Elizabeth's reign was not trouble free. Her apparent refusal to marry not only left the succession unclear, but added impetus to the plots of her Roman Catholic cousin, Mary, Queen of Scots – Elizabeth herself was a staunch

A memorial to Queen Victoria's beloved Albert, Kensington, London.

Protestant. Mary had been forced to abdicate the throne of Scotland in favour of her baby son James VI, and in the eyes of many Englishmen, she was the rightful ruler of England. Elizabeth was put under considerable pressure to deal with Mary, but instead she had her held in nominal captivity, where scheming continued unabated. Mary was finally executed in 1587, when England was at war with Spain. The spectacularly dangerous Spanish Armada arrived at the shores of England in 1588, to be efficiently defeated.

Queen Victoria and Albert

Queen Alexandrina Victoria was born in 1819, the only child of the Duke of Kent, and ascended to the throne at the age of 18. On October 10, 1839, her German cousin, Albert of Saxe-Coburg-Gotha, paid his first visit to her court, at Windsor. Five days later, the smitten Queen proposed to her "so extremely handsome" cousin, noting in her diary her gushing first impressions of him: "Albert really is quite charming, and so extremely handsome...my heart is quite going."

A few months later, in February 1840, the Queen married her beloved Albert, or, to give him his full name, Franz Albert August Karl Emanuel. Victoria had, from the very first days of her reign, aligned herself politically with Lord Melbourne and his Whig party, despite the dangers of such political partisanship, and so very few Tories were invited to the royal wedding. They, in turn, rejected the Queen's request that her husband should be second in rank only to herself. This snub caused a suitably impassioned royal outburst, "Monsters! You Tories shall be punished. Revenge! Revenge!"

From their nine children are descended many of Europe's royal families today, current and deposed. The eldest, Victoria, known as Vicky, was born in the year of their marriage, 1840, and the Prince of Wales, the future Edward VII in the following year. Victoria was a grandmother at forty, and a great-grandmother at sixty.

The kingly prince

The Queen was totally and utterly devoted to Albert, the Prince Consort, who became effectively her private secretary and privileged councillor, and she relied implicitly on his advice; Victoria did not even wear an outfit unless Albert approved. Initially, Victoria had not wanted Albert to have any share in government, but only six months after their marriage, Albert was allowed to start seeing dispatches, then to be present at the Queen's meetings with her ministers, and as Victoria progressed from one unhappy, unwanted pregnancy to another, Albert's role in the affairs of state grew, as did the Queen's dependence on him. By

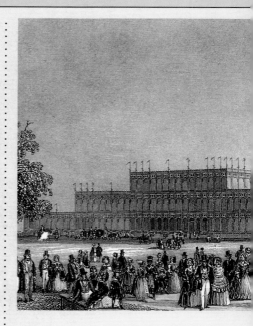

1845, one royal watcher wrote of Albert, "He is the King to all intents and purposes".

Doubtless due to an anti-German feeling in the country, Albert was personally unpopular, undeservedly so, but what was undeniable, and clear for all to see, was that the Queen and her Prince Consort were very, very happy together, giving a degree of stability to the monarchy which was absent at Victoria's accession.

Family values

It was the Queen's increasing dependence on Albert that characterized their years together, years during which she loathed pregnancy and child-bearing, despite (or, most likely, because of) her nine offspring. When her eldest daughter was going to be married at 18 to the Crown Prince of Prussia, Victoria, whose reign had come to symbolize an idealized image of the family and motherhood, described today as "Victorian", had distinctly un-Victorian advice for her daughter: "What you say of the pride of

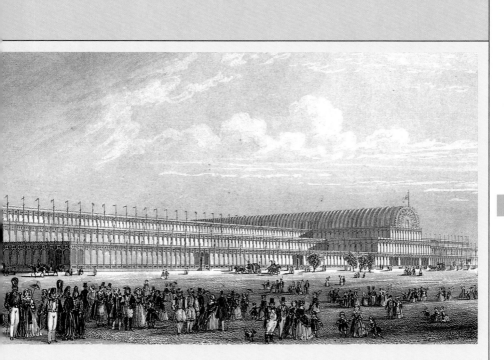

The Great Exhibition, of 1851 was Albert's showpiece and Victoria's proudest moment.

giving life to an immortal soul is very fine, dear, but I own I can not enter into that; I think much more of our being like a cow or a dog at such moments."

As well as influencing Victoria's wardrobe, Albert changed her views on social life, and from a party-loving young woman, she became an avid country lover, despising London life. Albert acquired and designed their two principal retreats, Balmoral Castle in Scotland, and Osborne House, on the Isle of Wight. Balmoral was the Queen's favourite, and she became fonder of Highlanders than any other of her subjects.

The Great Exhibition of 1851, with its specially constructed show-piece, the Crystal Palace, was Albert's project, and, as she noted in her diary, in what would appear to be a constant capacity to adore Albert "I do feel proud at the thought of what my beloved Albert's great mind has conceived."

The shadow of death

Victoria was devastated by Albert's death from typhoid fever in 1861, which she blamed on her eldest son. Albert had gone to see his son at Cambridge, to sort out some princely indiscretion, and returned ill. Victoria never forgave the Prince of Wales, for the loss of her "dear one", and was later to resent the Prince's popularity.

Victoria remained in mourning and partial retirement until her own death in 1901. Throughout nearly 40 years of widowhood she managed by basing any necessary decisions on what she thought Albert would have done. Her devotion to her beloved husband would never weaken. Every night, Albert's clothes were laid out, and every morning, a servant would put fresh water in Albert's basin. Finally on Victoria's death in 1901, the couple were reunited, being buried side-by-side at Frogmore, near Windsor.

Bath was one of the Romans' favourite cities where they built
a complex of baths.

Constitutional crisis

Elizabeth died in 1603, to be succeeded
by King James I of England (James VI of
Scotland), the son of the ill-fated Mary,
Queen of Scots. Given the centuries of
hostility between England and Scotland,
James, who had been King of Scotland
since 1567, was initially viewed with
some suspicion by his English subjects.
James was tolerant in matters of religion, but the failed Gunpowder Plot of
1605, when a group of plotters, led by

Guy Fawkes planned to use dynamite to blow up the Houses of Parliament during the King's visit, forced James to be less lenient and tolerant than he would have wished – the event is celebrated bonfire style in modern England by Guy Fawkes day, every November 5th.

Negotiations to marry James's son Charles, to the Spanish Infanta, had floundered ostensibly on grounds of religion, and his marriage to the highly unpopular French, Roman Catholic Henrietta Maria, did little to help the destiny of Charles I, who ascended to the throne in 1625. He inherited a war with Spain, and an unstable domestic situation, and within two years England was also at war with France.

Relations between the King and Parliament had become increasingly strained, and he dissolved it several times, and governed for a period without it. Peace was made with France and Spain to end the seemingly pointless, but exorbitantly expensive wars. Against a background of religious upheaval, Charles convened Parliament in 1640, but within a month he had it dissolved, earning the nickname "the Short Parliament".

The Scots invaded England, forcing the King to re-convene Parliament, and "The Long Parliament", which lasted from 1640-1653 limited the king's constitutional authority, in order to protect its own existence. In 1641, a long list of grievances against the king was prepared in the "Grand Remonstrance", but by now the political situation was at crisis point, with wild rumours flying in both directions. On 4 January 1642, Charles went to Parliament, intending to impeach five members of the House of Commons and one member of the House of Lords, but the six men had fled.

Within months, the queen and her children had left the country, Charles had abandoned London, and headed north, and on 22 August 1642, the king raised his standard against Parliament, and England was embroiled in the Civil War.

Cromwell & the Civil War

The Civil War pitted the Royalists against the Parliamentarians, the former flamboyant "Cavaliers" and the latter, increasingly, austere Puritans, known as the "Roundheads", because they eschewed the long wigs of the Cavaliers. In 1645, the Parliamentarians formed themselves into the New Model Army, one of whose leaders was Oliver Cromwell.

The New Model Army defeated the royalists decisively at the Battle of Naseby, on 14 June 1645, and the following year, the king surrendered to the Scots, fighting alongside the Parliamentarians, erroneously believing he would be able to negotiate with them. In January 1647, the Scots returned Charles to English custody, and he was blamed for a bloody renewal of fighting. Two years later, in January 1649, Charles was put on trial, charged with treason, found

Edward VIII and Mrs Simpson

On the death of King George V in January 1936, his son ascended the throne as King Edward VIII. Edward was born in 1894, and as Prince of Wales, was handsome and charming, a most eligible bachelor, who had become well-known and well-loved by the British people. His extensive visits to the Empire had also earned him the affection of many people well beyond the British Isles, and he was thought to be everything a King should be. But, unknown to his loyal and admiring subjects, Edward was in love, and, unfortunately, with a woman who was unsuited to be Queen.

Mrs Wallis Simpson was an American, and a divorcee, the latter of which disqualified her from becoming Queen. However both the king and Mrs Simpson – who divorced her second husband in July 1936 – were determined to marry and Edward was faced with the dilemma of love against duty; to the delight of romantics he chose the former, and the nation suffered the sad loss of a most gentlemanly King.

Abdication & exile

On December 10 1936, the King submitted his abdication, and the next evening, he spoke to his former subjects via the radio. This radio broadcast, explaining his abdication was not only moving, it was also unprecedented. No British monarch before – and to this date – had ever voluntarily relinquished the crown. He explained his dilemma to his subjects, in heartfelt language: "I have found it impossible to carry the heavy burden of responsibility and to discharge my duties as King, as I wish to do, without the help and support of the woman I love." The former King, created the Duke of Windsor the following day by his younger brother, left England immediately, for what was to become a virtually permanent European exile. His younger brother succeeded to the throne, as King George VI, the father of the current Queen Elizabeth II.

Intrigue & the war years

The Duke of Windsor married Mrs Simpson on June 3, 1937, in France, and although she became the Duchess of Windsor, Mrs Simpson was never allowed to be addressed as "Royal Highness", a snub which apparently hurt her husband very much. The couple lived in France, and visited other European countries, including Germany, where the Duke met with Nazi officials and even Hitler himself.

At an early stage of World War II, there was a rather bizarre Nazi plot to re-establish him as king, and to use him against the British government. Sir Winston Churchill, displaced the idea by appointing the Duke as Governor of the Bahamas from 1940-1945, where he spent the remainder of the war years away from the fanciful plots of the Nazis.

guilty, and beheaded on 30 January 1649, an unprecedented event that aroused hostility in Europe, and, rather surprisingly, in England itself.

The Commonwealth was declared, the Monarchy and the House of Lords were abolished, and Oliver Cromwell continued the fight against the royalists in Ireland. In 1650 Charles II landed in Scotland, and Cromwell again defeated the royalists. After the Battle of Worcester in 1651, Charles II barely escaped with his life. Over the next few years, religious and political wrangling continued, and it was only the force of Cromwell's personality and will that kept the regime and what was known as the "Rump Parliament" together; with Cromwell's death in 1658, the situation disintegrated and in February 1660,

After the war years, the Duke and Duchess lived in Paris, with rare visits to England – for his brother's funeral in 1952, and his mother's in 1953. In 1967, the couple made their first official public appearance in England, in the presence of other members of the Royal Family. The Duke died in Paris in May 1972, and is buried in the grounds of Windsor Castle, next to the Duchess.

Historical mystique

Who was Bessie Wallis Warfield, ex-Mrs Spencer, ex-Mrs Simpson, the woman whose relationship with the King changed the direction of history. What was her power and charisma? Married at 20, divorced at 29, remarried at 32, divorced at 40, remarried to the Duke of Windsor at 41, she outlived him, and died in Paris, a few weeks short of her 90th birthday in 1986. Wallis Simpson was neither young, nor in want of wealth.

She was not conventionally beautiful, and even her much touted sense of style was questionable. In the late 1980s, when her jewellery went on auction in Geneva, there was much criticism of the flashy vulgarity of the pieces, expensive though they were. An innate sense of sober taste was not a facet of Mrs Simpson's character. She has one truly memorable line to her credit: "One can never be too rich or too thin."

Parliament dissolved itself, paving the way for the Restoration.

Restoration of the monarchy

Charles II returned to London, a shrewd political realist, who instantly issued the Declaration of Breda, offering pardons and religious tolerance, but unfortunately he left the details of implementation to parliament, and repressive religious measures followed.

Within 5 years, England was at war with the Dutch, and despite the economic success of these wars, the country faced major problems. The Great Plague of 1665 was followed by the Great Fire of London in 1666, two major human and economic catastrophes.

In 1670, Charles allied himself with Catholic France against Protestant Holland, agreeing by a secret clause to profess his conversion to Catholicism, in exchange for a large financial settlement from Louis XIV. Most of the country, and Parliament remained resolutely anti-Catholic, and the king was forced to sign the Test Act in 1673, by which only Anglicans could hold national office.

Anti-Catholic feeling was exacerbated by the debauchery of court life, with the king himself acknowledging 17 illegitimate children, and no legitimate heir. There was a general feeling of malcontent.

As part of a move to weaken the French link, Mary, the eldest daughter of James, the Duke of York, was married to the Dutch king, William of Orange. In 1678, rumours of a Popish Plot were rife. They were also false, but there was a hysterical outcry against Catholics, harsh laws against Catholics were introduced, and by the Second Test Act of 1678, only Anglicans were eligible for Parliament.

The impressive structure of Hadrian's Wall marked the frontier of Roman Britain.

The following year, a bill was introduced into Parliament, to exclude the Catholic Duke of York from the throne. Charles dissolved Parliament, called for elections, and when the new Parliament voted to bypass the Duke of York in favour of his daughter Mary, Charles dissolved it again.

The threat of civil war was again brooding and after the execution of various leading Whigs – as the opponents of the king and his brother were called – the balance of power swung back towards the king.

The country stabalized again in 1685, when Charles died. He was however, succeeded by his brother James II whose 3-year reign was again one of rebellion and confusion.

1688 Revolution

The first challenge James II faced was from the Duke of Monmouth, whose rebellion was however a fiasco; he was executed, and hundreds of his supporters were hanged or deported in brutal reprisals, known as the Bloody Assizes. James's determination to repeal the Test Acts, and to reintroduce Catholics into public life created such dissent, that an appeal was made to his son-in-law William of Orange to come to England.

William landed in England in the winter of 1688, Anglicans flocked to his cause, but the Revolution of 1688 was a brief affair, for James II fled to France. Parliament met in early 1689, declaring that James had effectively abdicated, by his flight overseas, and William and Mary were declared to be the sovereigns. A Bill of Rights of the same year stated that only a Protestant could become the British monarch – a rule that still applies today.

William of Orange & Mary

In 1690, James II resurfaced, with French support he invaded Ireland, initially defeating the Protestant forces. William III however came to the rescue personally leading an army, which defeated the Catholic troops at the Battle of the Boyne, an event which is still commemorated every year, amidst the troubled politics of northern Ireland.

Amidst the Nine Years' War, which pitted James II's French-backed forces against an Anglo-Dutch alliance, the question of the succession loomed. William and Mary were childless. Mary's sister, Anne, had only one surviving child, the Duke of Gloucester, from her 18 pregnancies, and on his death, the situation became even more complicated.

The 1701 Act of Settlement named the grandchildren of James I as heirs to the throne, namely Sophia of Hanover and her son George. Meanwhile, Louis XIV had placed his grandson on the Spanish throne, and had recognized James III (the son of James II) as the rightful King of England.

Queen Anne inherited the throne from her brother-in-law in 1701, along with the War of the Spanish Succession, which was to last for the 13 years of her reign. During her rule, English party politics became more firmly entrenched between the Whigs and the Tories, who generally stood for the Anglican Church. One of the dilemmas of the day, for the Tories as much as anyone else, was the issue of the succession, and there were many who hoped that James III might convert to Protestantism, thus allowing him to inherit a throne which many felt was rightfully his.

The beginnings of the empire

Britain's succession dilemma did nothing to quell her overseas activity, and successful military campaigns led to the capture of Gibraltar in 1704, Minorca in 1708, and there was much colonial activity in Canada and the Caribbean. Union with Scotland took place in 1707, and upon Anne's death in 1714, George I, the elector of Hanover became the King. Domestic reaction to George was bitterly divided, but the country was strong, prosperous and a leading Imperial power.

George I, with a more European outlook than many of his subjects, favoured the Whigs, regarding the Tories as too insular, and after the Scottish uprising in favour of James III, known as The Old Pretender, which was supported by some Tories, George was even more suspicious of them.

There was another plotted uprising in favour of James III, but it was uncovered: the Jacobite (that is supporters of James) cause was not dead, however, and would continue to unsettle George's successor, his son George II, who came to the throne in 1727.

Bonnie Prince Charlie & the Stuarts

Britain was dragged into the War of Austrian Succession, with France on the opposing side. The time was ripe for another Jacobite plot. The French supported the invasion of Scotland by The Young Pretender, or Bonnie Prince Charlie as he is universally known. Prince Charles Edward Stuart, the Catholic son of James III, landed in 1745, defeated a British force, and marched south as far as Derby, 150 miles from London.

The bulk of the British Army was in Europe, fighting the Austrian wars, but, curiously, the Jacobites did not march on London, retreating instead to Scotland. The rest of Bonnie Prince Charlie's tale, despite the romantic stories that have always surrounded him, is far from impressive.

The Jacobite Army was defeated decisively at the Battle of Culloden in April 1746, the last major land battle ever to take place in the country. Charles escaped to France, where he died in 1788, much the worse for alcohol.

George III came to the throne in 1760, and would prove to be one of the most controversial of the country's rulers. Governments resigned in quick succession, and in the American Declaration of Independence of 1776, the king was condemned as a tyrant. American resentment against taxes was the last straw, leading to the American Revolution (1775-83), in which Britain humiliatingly lost control of one of her major colonies.

In 1780, William Pitt the Younger entered Parliament, aged 21, destined to become a minister by the age of 24. As the King suffered increasingly from bouts of insanity, Pitt, by then Prime Minister, governed the country with success: he signed a Triple Alliance with Prussia and Holland, passed the India Act, and the Canada Constitutional Act. Meanwhile, across the Channel, France was in turmoil.

The French Revolution of 1789 had seen the monarchy overthrown, and by 1793, war had broken out between England and France, the latter led by a rising young general by the name of Napoleon.

The Napoleonic Wars

The Napoleonic Wars were on a massive, hitherto unknown scale, both geographically and financially, as well as in terms of manpower – the wars lasted from February 1793 until June 1815.

France was stronger on land, Britain on the sea; 1797 saw British naval victories, and in 1798, Admiral Nelson won the Battle of the Nile.

In 1803, the British captured many Caribbean islands, and in 1805, at the decisive Battle of Trafalgar, defeated the French fleet, and prevented the planned French invasion of Britain – Pitt died a few months later in 1806. Despite British victories, Napoleon's successes continued, and it was not until 1809 that the tide of the war began to turn in Britain's favour. June 1813 saw Wellington defeating the French army in Spain, and the final defeat of Napoleon at Waterloo.

The blossoming of an empire

Britain's success in the Napoleonic Wars was matched by her growing imperialism, and in the period from 1793-1815 Britain gained 20 colonies. By 1820, when George IV ascended the throne, a quarter of the world's population was governed from London. Post-war England saw the passing of the Corn Laws in 1815 which taxed imported grain, and increasing pressure for the removal of many of the bans against Roman Catholics.

On the death of George IV in 1830, William IV became king, and during the 7 years of his reign, a number of social measures were passed - the Reform Act and the Poor Law. In 1837, the young Queen Victoria came to power, and was to reign for over 60 years, overseeing a period of unprecedented change and expansion.

The Empire was at its apogee, the country was rich, industrialized, successful, and supremely confident. The country produced coal and iron, developed railways, built steamships, and governed over its wide empire, over which it was reputed, the sun would never set. The age of Victoria produced many quintessential "Victorian" values, chief of which was The Family. (see box story on Victoria and Albert p24).

"the white man's burden"

Imperialism was a key element of Victorian policy, and it was not only the financial aspect of the Empire that mattered – there was also the notion of the prestige accruing to the crown, along with that archetypal 19th century notion of "the white man's burden", a term coined by Rudyard Kipling.

However, by late Victorian times, measures of self-government had been granted to white colonies such as Australia and Canada, whereas "the brightest jewel in the British crown", India, was held under very firm imperial control, increasingly so, after the 1857 Indian Mutiny.

In 1901, Victoria's son, Edward VII, became king, at nearly 60 years old, and with markedly different views and values from his mother..

Government

35

Entering the 20th century, Britain was faced with the reality of two horrific world wars, which had long-lasting implications for most of the world, beyond the sheer carnage and destruction which they created. Neither war was fought on British soil, although the Germans conducted bombing raids on British cities during World War II, in both wars however, the British lost thousands of lives, and millions of pounds. People thought that life would improve after the war, but severe economic depression and mass unemployment hit the country in the 1930's, whilst the hardships of the British people in the decade following World War II, led to the creation of the welfare state. The 20th century also hailed the end of the great British Empire.

The pride of England, the Union Jack, flies high.

The humiliations suffered by the hard-pressed British in the Far East, at the hands of the Japanese during World War II, were a key factor in the Empire's downfall. Britain was, for the first time, seen by the natives of the colo-

nies to be vulnerable and she was definitely impoverished. One by one over the ensuing years, colonies attained independence, and the British Empire was virtually dismantled as Britain began to concentrate on domestic affairs.

The English constitution

A concise definition of the British system of government is that the United Kingdom is both a constitutional monarchy and a parliamentary democracy. The ruling monarch is the head of state, currently Her Majesty Queen Elizabeth II who plays a constitutional role and the head of government is the Prime Minister (PM). The prime minister is the leader of the political party which can command a majority of votes in the House of Commons.

Parliament consists of 2 houses; the lower house is the elected House of Commons, and the upper house is the House of Lords; both are situated in Westminster, London.

After the Act of Union of 1707, England became the centre of government for the entire UK, with the Scots, Welsh and the inhabitants of Northern Ireland, sending Members of Parliament (MPs), to Westminster; it remains thus, to the present day.

Party politics

All those who are eligible to vote may exercise their franchise once they are 18 years of age, and they may vote in general elections, as well as local elections. The principal political parties are the Conservative Party (also known as the Tory Party), the Labour Party, and the Liberal Democratic party. By-elections take place between general elections, generally due to the death or resignation of an MP. The largest opposition party is always addressed as "Her Majesty's Loyal Opposition".

By and large the English are not extremists, distrusting Communists and loathing the ultra right-wing National Front in equal measure, and so the extreme left-wing elements that were active in the Labour Party in the 1970s and early 1980s did much to favour the fortunes of the Social Democratic Party (SDP). This party was founded in 1981 by four right-wing members of the Labour Party, universally referred to as "the gang of four", who broke away from Labour, to form a new party, which initially met with an almost euphoric degree of enthusiasm and success. In the same year as the SDP

The legal system

The British constitution is only partly written, and is quite flexible. Unlike many countries, which have a formalized, definitive statute book, many legal and judicial matters in the UK rely on tradition. What is written and codified are, generally, those laws which have been passed by Parliament. The other half of the country's legal system is judged under "common law", which is the traditional unwritten law of England. Common law is based on judges' decisions, rather than on parliamentary ones. What this means in practice, is that judges will refer to similar decisions made by their predecessors: they may decide to follow precedent, or not, as they see fit. It is from this mix of systems that the flexibility and facility for modification arises. The Scottish legal system differs from that of England, Wales and Northern Ireland, since it is based on Roman Law.

Making law

Although the monarch has the right of veto, over laws, this has not been used since the 18th century. The legislative role of the House of Lords was reduced in 1911 to that of delaying legislation, with the exception of the Law Lords. These peers, and therefore members of the House of Lords, sit as the country's highest court of appeal, and include the Lord Chancellor, and any peers who have held high judicial office, or who have themselves been Lord Chancellor.

The courts alone declare the law, but any Act of Parliament is automatically accepted by the courts as part of the law. A court could never declare an Act of Parliament invalid. Under the British legal system, a person is presumed innocent until proved guilty.

The legal profession

Solicitors work in offices, in legal partnerships, and carry out legal work such as the drawing up of contracts and wills, they administer the paperwork connected with house sales and purchases, and they also offer advice to clients on legal matters. Solicitors act in many court cases, but if a case has to go before a higher court, then the matter is handled by barristers. These are the people who feature in court, wearing horse-hair wigs and long black gowns – the wearing of wigs is currently being mildly called into question, and may one day be phased out. A lawyer who has been "called to the bar" – which has nothing to do with drinking, and everything to do with the court room – is called a barrister. Barristers must belong to one of the four Inns of Court, legal societies in central London, which have existed since the 14th century. These Inns are: Lincoln's Inn, Gray's Inn, the Inner Temple and the Middle Temple, and today they function mainly as offices, known as chambers, although a handful of barristers do still reside in the Inns.

was founded, it entered into an alliance with the long-standing third party in British politics, the Liberal Party, which had always enjoyed moderate success, but since the World War I cabinet of David Lloyd-George, had had no more than a handful of elected MPs. Voters, disillusioned with the two major parties, voted for the new Liberal & SDP, Alliance Party, in numbers which gave the party cause for optimism. However, a combination of political infighting, and a re-thinking of strategies by the Labour and Tory parties, led to the disintegration of the SDP. Today the Liberal Party stands alone, as the Liberal Democratic party, but is again enjoying enough support to make feasible, the possibility of a Liberal government in the not to distant future.

There are many other political parties, some with substantial regional sup-

The Houses of Parliament, Westminster.

port, like the Scottish Nationalists and the Plaid Cymru, (Welsh Nationalists), and others which verge on the frankly eccentric, such as the Monster Raving Loony Party, regarded as nothing more than a bit of harmless fun, in the otherwise deadly serious game of politics.

The House of Commons

Six hundred and fifty elected MPs make up the House of Commons, of these 523 represent English constituencies, 72 represent Scotland, there are 38 for Wales, and 17 for Northern Ireland. Basically, the main purpose of the Commons is to make the laws of the land, by passing various Acts of Parliament. Parliament is elected for a maximum term of 5 years, after which a general election must be called.

Thus in the last year of a government's tenure there is always much speculation as to when the next election will be called; will the Prime Minister choose to go on until the last possible day before he or she must call elections, or will an early election be called, bolstered by a particularly favourable economic climate, or a successful piece of world diplomacy?

Of the ruling party's MPs, about 20 are selected by the Prime Minister to form the Cabinet, and they exercise supreme parliamentary control, as well as co-ordinating government departments. Whichever party is in opposition forms the "shadow cabinet" – the team of ministers in the opposition who would probably form the cabinet, if their party were to win the next election. They therefore "shadow" their opposite number,

dealing with appropriate matters, and keeping abreast of the issues, in the hope that if elected, they can take over the portfolio which they have been shadowing. Although you will hear of the Shadow Chancellor and the Shadow Minister of Defence, you will not hear of the Shadow Prime Minister, for he or she is always called the Leader of the Opposition.

The House of Lords

The upper house, the House of Lords, consists of over 1,000 non-elected members, who technically belong to one of two groups, the Lords Spiritual or the Lords Temporal. The spiritual lords are the Church of England bishops who sit in the house, while the lords temporal consist of everyone else.

A further classification of the Lords are those who are hereditary peers and those who are simply life peers, which makes for a totally undemocratic institution with a fascinating mix of people. Hereditary titles often belong to the

Churchill and World War II

Statue of Sir Winston Churchill, Parliament Square.

Sir Winston Churchill, the son of an English aristocrat and an American heiress, was born in 1874, at Blenheim Palace, Oxfordshire, and was, during the course of his long and eventful life, variously a soldier, a war correspondent, a writer, and a politician. He was most famous as the latter and particularly for leading England as Prime Minister through the grim years of World War II, by his grit, astuteness, and inspirational words.

Having spent much of his life moving in and out of politics, his bold genius which had led to his falling out with all the political parties in turn, at last rewarded Churchill. In May 1940, Prime Minister Chamberlain resigned, to be replaced by Churchill, the only politician capable of uniting the country.

The War Cabinet

Churchill immediately formed a coalition government, headed by a War Cabinet, a judicious mixture of himself, his Foreign Secretary, two Opposition leaders and a Trade Union leader – the latter a particularly clever move, as it guaranteed the co-operation of the labour movement in the war effort. Churchill himself took on the portfolio of Minister of Defence. Although the individual members of the War Cabinet changed over the years, its basic balance did not. It remained throughout the war years capable of rapid decision making, and representative of all the different groups in Parliament. Churchill delegated, but remained keenly aware of most of the details.

Stirring speeches & hard times

Some of Churchill's most memorable lines were prompted by war. On his first appearance in the House of Commons as Prime Minister, he said, in a phrase which countless admirers have since plagiarized, "I have nothing to offer but blood, toil, tears and sweat." For Churchill, his vision of the war aim was simple: the enemy was Hitler's Germany, which was to be defeated at all costs. Anyone, Communist, American, whoever shared this aim, was an ally. Anything which could serve the national interest, the defeat of the Nazis, was acceptable, even if it involved trampling a few national icons underfoot. Thus it was, that a staunch anti-Socialist like Churchill, within a few weeks of assuming power, passed

landed gentry, whose titles have been passed through the family for several centuries. Trade Union leaders, and former politicians, are often given life peerage, though some, like Margaret Thatcher, have hereditary rights. It is often these dyed-in-the-wool politicians, turned peers of the realm, who are the

a law placing all "persons, their services and their property" at the Crown's disposal, a remarkably sweeping measure.

In the face of the collapse of France in 1940, and the British evacuation of Dunkirk, Churchill desperately tried to keep France in the war, even proposing an Anglo-French Union, but when all his efforts failed, and the prospect of a German invasion of Britain became very real, the Battle of Britain began. The popular image of Churchill dates largely from this time, when he tirelessly visited coastal defences and the sites of bomb damage, his trade-mark cigar clamped tightly in his mouth, giving his "V" for victory sign.

The British respected him, admired him, and listened to his spell-binding speeches, whose stirring rhetoric can move people even today, 50 years ago:

"We shall defend our island, whatever the cost may be, we shall fight on the beaches, we shall fight on the landing grounds, we shall fight in the fields and in the streets, we shall fight in the hills; we shall never surrender".

The stirring language of Shakespeare's Henry V, echoed down the centuries as Churchill thundered to Parliament in June 1940: "Let us therefore brace ourselves to our duties, and so bear ourselves that, if the British Empire and its Commonwealth last for a thousand years, men will still say: 'This was their finest hour.' " And in one of his more moving speeches, paying tribute to the Battle of Britain pilots, whose bravery still impresses today, he said: "Never in the field of human conflict was so much owed by so many to so few."

The Grand Alliance

Churchill oversaw the war in Europe, including disasters like the evacuation of Crete in Greece,

and simultaneously forged alliances with the north Americans, culminating in the Atlantic Charter of August 1941. When Hitler invaded Russia in June 1941, despite Churchill's distrust of Communism, he pledged aid to the Russians. The Japanese attack on Pearl Harbour, in the closing weeks of 1941, galvanised Churchill. The grand alliance with the United States of America, under the leadership of President Roosevelt came into being, with a pooling of British and American resources, both economic as well as military, joint chiefs of staff, and a unity not only of command but also priorities in the war effort. The priority remained the German defeat.

During 1942, the Grand Alliance came under both domestic and Russian pressure, but survived. In 1943, as the Americans were planning an invasion of Burma in 1944, Churchill was planning Operation Overlord, the invasion of France across the English Channel, and, worried that their joint resources would be over-stretched, met with Roosevelt in November to urge him to give the European invasion priority. Stalin became a party to the meetings between Churchill and Roosevelt, and Churchill was outvoted on the issue of the Allied offensive in southern Europe.

At the Yalta conference in February 1945, Churchill was deeply worried about the effects of the power vacuum left behind in eastern Europe, following the German defeat, and urged that the Allies move quickly to fill it, before the Soviets did. The Americans did not agree.

Britain was in the throes of an election, and although Churchill the victorious war leader was popular, Churchill the Conservative Party leader was not, and the Conservatives lost the elections. Churchill, an unenthusiastic Leader of the Opposition, returned to his writing. A truly great PM, he was to be the role-model for many a politician.

most active in the House of Lords, whose work is largely complementary to that of the House of Commons. The Lords examines and revises bills which are

sent up from the Commons, and the upper house also acts in a legal capacity, as a final court of appeal, called the Law Lords.

Lady Thatcher the "Iron Lady".

Thatcher days

A recently elevated peer is Margaret Thatcher, the Prime Minister for 11 years, before her controversial ouster as leader of the Conservative Party. As Lady Thatcher, she now attends the House of Lords, where she is active and as eloquent as in her days in the Commons.

"Maggie" Thatcher was almost a cult figure during her years as PM (Prime Minister) with as many detractors as fans, but since her departure in 1991, her successor has appeared to be distinctly lack-lustre, and many people now regret Mrs Thatcher's political demise. She may have been lampooned by all and sundry, notably by a highly popu-

lar satirical TV show called *Spitting Image*, but at least, the argument now goes, people knew what Mrs Thatcher stood for: a strong Britain; a strong pound; monetarist economics. The current drift towards greater union with Europe, a topic which many people still regard with misgivings, was a hot issue for PM Thatcher, who vehemently opposed a single European currency and many European social bills.

Thatcher was given a number of nicknames by the press, among them, "Nanny", as in "Nanny knows what's best for you", and the "Iron Lady", both of which make reference to her domineering and determined character. Thatcher seemed able to master a man's world. One of the great victories of her

A monument to American troops killed while training for D-day, World War II.

era, was a re-stirring of British patriotism in the Falklands War, from which Britain emerged victorious over Argentina, securing Maggie a few more years in office.

The Irish question

One of the thorniest problems which faces every British PM, is that of Northern Ireland. Trying to explain decades of mistrust is not easy, but essentially the six counties of Northern Ireland, or Ulster, owe their separate identity from Eire, or southern Ireland, to a deep and bitter religious division, which has become entwined with politics.

Essentially a Protestant area, Ulster was created as a self-governing state within the UK in 1920, and from that date on, there has been a pattern of political unrest with the southern, Catholic part of Ireland. The troubles, increasingly violent and bloody, have spilled over to mainland Britain, with the Irish Republican Army (the IRA), carrying out a number of isolated bombings and shootings, particularly in the areas of London and Liverpool, with the purpose of drawing attention to the Republican cause. It is impossible to discuss Ulster without reference to the long civil war that has raged there, a war which hinges, essentially, on the issue of union with, or separation from, Britain. The Protestant majority in Northern Ireland known as the "loyalists" wishes to remain British, whilst the Roman Catholic minority, the "republicans", want union with Eire, whose constitution acknowledges that Eire is rightfully her's. It has been a long, violent civil war, with many Republican and Loyalist deaths, and many prayers on both sides, lie with hopes of peace.

Royal ups & downs

The Royal Family is one of the country's major institutions, and has long been revered in a quasi-religious manner. Certainly, in the 1970s and 1980s, whatever other major social upheavals were taking place, the existence of the monarchy was simply not an issue to be called into question.

The subjects of Her Majesty have traditionally been unquestioningly loyal, the Queen or a member of her family's visit to a town was sure to draw crowds, whilst hundreds were prepared to sleep out on the street for a night, to see the bride arrive, at one of the fairytale royal weddings of the 1970s and 1980s.

There have no doubt always been critics of the monarchy, who opposed the expense of the royal family's not inconsiderable upkeep, but always the criticism was more for the institution of the monarchy and rarely for "the royals" as individuals.

In the 1990s however the issue of persona, has become prominent. The well-publicized break-up of the marriages of 3 of the Queen's 4 children, including that of the Prince of Wales, the heir to the throne, has dismayed the public. People are now beginning to question the right of a handful of people to lead lives of great luxury and privilege, whilst failing to set an example in the sphere of morality. This slump in royal morals, has moreover, coincided with a severe economic recession. Thus the tax-payer's anger when he thinks of his money subsidizing the expensive clothes and holidays of members of the royal family, whose very function has by many, been called into question.

The future of the monarchy

The constitutional implications of the marital separation of the Prince and Princess of Wales presented a more thorny issue. As the head of the Church of England, could a divorced Prince Charles one day ascend the throne? Attitudes to divorce have changed immeasurably since the days of the Abdication crisis (see box story p28) but the idea of the coronation of a couple who no longer live together, is somewhat progressive. An unfortunate personal rift, has, in the case of the royals, long-term ramifications.

The acrimony which surrounded the separation of the royal couple, did much to damage their prestige and integrity. Nineteen ninety two, was a particularly bad year for the royals, with the collapse of the marriages of two of

Head of State and the Church, Queen Elizabeth II.

her sons and the fire at Windsor castle, the Queen summed the year up with undisguished honesty as a *"Annus Horribillis"* (a truly horrible year).

The future of the monarchy meanwhile, stands in doubt. The Queen has vounteered to pay tax on her private income, whilst her much favoured Commonwealth of Nations is unstable with the Australian PM calling for the end of the establishment of a Republic. Many church leaders have also called for the dis-establishment of the Church of England... many questions remain.

Economy

Until the 18th century, the English economy was mainly agricultural, but, with the Industrial Revolution, the country gradually evolved into an urbanized, industrialized region. The late 18th and 19th centuries were periods of growth and change for England, as the country's then abundant coal and iron-ore deposits were exploited. Iron and steel, textiles and shipbuilding, were centred in the northeast of the country, close to natural deposits, the foundations were thus laid for many of the large industrial cities of Yorkshire, Lancashire, the Midlands and Tyneside. In the 1980s it was these industrialized areas which were most affected by the shift away from mining and heavy industry, as reserves depleted and mines were closed down. The northern part of the country especially, became economically severely depressed, as the means to a livelihood disappeared.

47

An offshore oil rig in the North Sea.

The rewards of industrialization

During the Industrial Revolution, English scien-

The Channel Tunnel

At some point in the not too distant future, a family in London setting off for their annual French holiday, will pile into their car and drive down the M20 motorway to **Folkestone** in Kent. There, instead of driving their car onto a car ferry, as they have always done, they will drive through toll gates, manned by French speaking staff, through a terminal, and straight onto a train.

The crew on the train will be fluent in both the French and English languages, and as the train carries our English family under the English Channel and in the direction of the **Coquelles terminal** on the French coast, during their 35 minute journey, they will be able to chat with some of the other 800 passengers on their shuttle.

The verge of reality

Well, that is the theory, at least, although the centuries-old dream of linking the French and English coast is still incomplete albeit tantalizingly close to fulfillment. A provisional opening date have been constantly pushed back, and it may even be in 1994, or even 1995. But the Channel Tunnel, or "Chunnel" as it is nicknamed, will open. It is virtually finished, with the terminals built, the tracks laid, and the first test trains have already run. What still needs perfecting is the smooth running of the system, including all the vitally important fire and evacuation tests, as well as all the highly complex control and signalling procedures. With passenger trains running every 15 minutes during peak hours, as well as main-line trains (meaning London-Paris direct) and numerous freight trains, there could potentially be a train entering and leaving the Channel Tunnel every 3 minutes.

Although it is on the verge of realization, the project has been a long, massively expensive one, and fraught with problems. Cost over-runs are stupendous, and as the boom 1980s petered out into the recession hit 1990s, both the British and French partners faced cash constraints.

On the English side of the Tunnel, there are still years more work needed, to upgrade the regional train network in Kent, to enable the high speed trains racing out from under the Channel to mesh efficiently into Network South East's busy, and much slower, lines. British Rail's Network South East is currently one of the busiest train networks in the country, catering to huge numbers of daily commuters to London, and it is estimated that it will not be until the turn of the century that both the railway network and the London terminal, will be completed.

The *Eurostar*, the first Channel Tunnel express train, started undergoing engineering and late-night operating tests in the autumn of 1993. These highly sophisticated trains do not come cheaply, each one costs £24 million. The 19th century London station of **St Pancras** has been chosen as the site of the future terminal for the London Channel Tunnel high speed trains, but a lot of work is needed, to convert this high Victorian mix of pseudo-medieval Gothic and Italianate terracotta, into a terminal for the 21st century. In the interim, **Waterloo**, a frantically busy commuter station will be used.

So, looking yet further ahead, to the early years of the 21st century, the scenario should be as follows: a family from Manchester, or even further north in Edinburgh, will travel to St Pancras, remaining in their train, which will then join the new line that goes through to Paris, and onto their holiday destination. Passengers boarding a *Eurostar* train in London, can expect to be in Paris in less than 3 hours.

tists and craftsmen pioneered the development of the railways and the use of iron in building steam engines and power looms. As the late 20th century visitor travels around, he will see many reminders of the country's industrial past:

The **Ironbridge Gorge** in Shropshire has been transformed into a colourful museum which tells the story of

An open-caste mine.

the world's first iron bridge, constructed in the late 18th century and the effects of industrialization on the region (See Western Borders p324). In Derbyshire, you can visit the first factory in the country, also from the 18th century. The north of England, in particular, is taking a vigorous pride in its architectural heritage.

The era of the Industrial Revolution was a glorious time for England; while industry was growing and expanding back home, the country was also looking beyond its shores, and explorers and colonial adventurers were raising the Union Jack over what was to become an enormous Empire. The Empire created a guaranteed international market for British goods, and most significantly provided access to a seemingly endless supply of raw materials. Rubber, cheap Indian cotton, gold and silver, textiles, each of the colonies had some product which could be put to use back in England. Industry, a spirit of exploration and the prevailing political situation, all combined to make the England of the 18th and 19th centuries a major economic power.

Energy for the future

Today, though, the picture looks very different. Faced with the economic strength of many Asian countries, England is having to re-think its future, and adapt to a new world order. The future

Colourful pageantry in England's capital, an attraction of the tourist industry.

of English mining, for example, is currently under review, since it is becoming increasingly expensive to extract coal, tin and iron ore. Iron ore is mined in Humberside and Northamptonshire, whilst tin ore, used to make china clay, is mined only in Cornwall. Clay and salt are found in the northwest of the country.

The decline in the coal mining industry, has been partly influenced by the discovery of useful reserves of natural gas and oil in the North Sea. Nuclear power is still a controversial issue in England, but it is in use, perhaps most famously at the **Sellafield nuclear power station**, which has been opened to the public in an effort to persuade the populace that nuclear power is a safe and efficient energy for the future. Post-Chernobyl Europe, remains somewhat cautious.

Targets for growth

Although some economic sectors of the country are experiencing problems and retrenchment, others are steadily flourishing, and overall the economic balance is shifting from heavy industry towards light industry and the service industry. More than two thirds of people who work in England, now work in the service industries.

London, of course, is a major financial, banking and insurance centre, but there are other major regional centres such as Cambridge, Ipswich and Norwich, all three important service and high-tech centres. Given the high costs of working and living in London, there is an increasing trend towards the decentralization of some civil service and central government functions, and more companies are deciding to re-locate outside of London.

Tourism plays a significant role in England's economy, and the millions of annual visitors earn substantial income for the country. Although not an economic world leader, England is the base for some of the world's leading art auction houses, including names like Sotheby's and Christie's.

The financial markets in England are concentrated in London, where centuries of tradition and expertise mean that even with the globalization of trading, and 24-hour foreign exchange dealing rooms, London is still a vitally important hub.

Making hay while the sun shines, part of England's farming tradition.

Manufacturing

Nearly a quarter of English workers are employed in manufacturing, producing an enormous range of goods. In the north, the principal industries include food processing, brewing (in the Burton-on-Trent area) and the manufacture of chemicals, textiles, computers, cars, aircraft, clothing, glass, and paper. The Southeast is home to pharmaceuticals, computers, micro-electronics, aircraft parts and cars.

One shining light in the gloom which otherwise surrounds such a recession-prone industry as car manufacture, is Land Rover, 45 years old in 1993, and a world-beating car company, even in the midst of a global recession. Land Rover is currently recording record sales and profits, and bucking the near-universal European trend of laying-off workers.

In fact, Land Rover is steadily increasing production. One thousand and three hundred vehicles a week roll out of the factory at Solihull in the West Midlands, earning the company a £60 million profit in 1992.

Agriculture

The topography and natural resources of England make it the most successful part of the UK, in terms of agriculture. The English countryside, has a large

The domestic market absorbs most of British beef.

area of lowlands, with good quality farming soils.

Most English farms are small, in the number of acres they cover, but they are all highly mechanized. Wheat is grown in the east and south of the country, where it is relatively sunny and dry. Potatoes are grown in the clay soils of Humberside, and the fens of Lincolnshire, Norfolk and Cambridgeshire. Kent and the Vale of Evesham are the country's principal fruit and vegetable growing areas.

Like Wales and Scotland, the most important sector of English agriculture remains livestock husbandry and dairy farming in particular. Dairy farming is important in just about every English county, although the main concentra-

tions are in western England. Domestic production supplies most of the country's beef breeds.

Sheep farming is centred in hilly areas such as Yorkshire, the Pennines and the Lake District, where the animals are bred more for meat than for wool.

The fishing industry is currently going through a period of turmoil, as European directives limiting the number of days per year on which fishermen may work, is adversely affecting the country's many fishing fleets. The European Commission has imposed catch quotas, with the perfectly laudable aim of conserving dwindling stocks in the North Sea, but it is a move which has angered British fishermen.

For a relatively small country, England has a diverse landscape, with a variety of land forms ranging from the mountains of the Lake District to the flat plains of East Anglia, from the fertile, fruit-producing Vale of Evesham, to the windswept, deserted Yorkshire Moors.

Geologically, the oldest part of the country is in the southwestern tip, in Devon and Cornwall, and the alluvial soils covering the East Anglian fens are the most recent. Between these two extremes, are hills which show evidence of volcanic activity – notably in Cumbria – and glaciers from the Ice Age.

Formerly, parts of central and southern England were submerged below sea level, until hills were formed during the geological upheavals which caused the formation of the Alps in Europe. From

The picturesque Lake District, one of England's popular holiday areas.

Geography & Climate

The perfect beginning for a walk, Farndale, in the North Yorkshire Moors.

Tarn Howes, Cumbria.

this activity emerged the Downs and the Cotswolds of southern England.

At one point, the country was physically attached to continental Europe, however, once the ice caps melted, the sea levels rose and gradually the land-link became submerged.

It was in this way that the island of Great Britain was formed. As an island Britain's flora and fauna became more distinct.

Mountains, lakes & fens

The Pennines are the backbone of England, dividing the north of the country, along a west-east divide, and notably separating Yorkshire and Lancashire, the two large counties, which have always been traditional rivals. The Pennines rise to 656-984 m (2,000-3,000) feet, and are largely wild moor land,

The horizontal wood

Aggressive conservation is the name of the game these days, if the business at a wood in Kent is anything to go by. **Sladden Wood**, which probably dates back to prehistoric times, is situated in the Alkham Valley, between Dover and Folkestone. It contains a wide variety of trees, including beech, ash, hornbeam, oak, field maple, elm and cherry. In 1951, the wood was declared a site of special scientific interest, for it has an unusual variety of soil types, giving rise to a wide range of flora and fauna. The wood was renowned for its orchids, and had long been home to dozens of bird species.

The disappearing trees

At dawn, on 23 November 1977, a fleet of bulldozers and a chain-saw gang moved into Sladden Wood, since the landowner wanted the hillside cleared for arable farming, orchids and wild birds notwithstanding. However, because of its age and its importance to wildlife, the wood was protected by law, and the District Council hastily made an order for the preservation of the trees. If it had not been such an ecological scandal, it would have been funny. When the preservation order was presented, Mr Bachelor, the landowner, hid behind the remaining trees until he was eventually cornered. When the order was given to him, he claimed not to have his reading glasses. So the order was read out to him, to which he answered with the

immortal line, "what trees?"

Whilst all these theatricals were taking place, Sladden Wood had actually been reduced to a field of stumps. Not to be out-witted, the Council argued that a stump, because it still possessed roots (unlike a fully uprooted tree) was alive, and therefore subject to protection. So the horizontal wood, as the locals named it, was left to grow again.

Growing into life

The trees at Sladden had traditionally been coppiced, or harvested at ground level, every 15 to 20 years. By this system, each year in rotation, a small area of the woodland was cut and the timber used for firewood, for fencing and as building material for wattle and daub houses. What Mr. Bachelor had just done, amounted to wholesale coppicing, rather than sectional coppicing, and his drastic action had left all the woodland at the same height. The lack of tree cover would adversely affect both the natural habitat and the variety of wildlife.

If there was ever to be any hope of bring back Sladden's former wealth of wildlife, proper management was needed. So, the Kent Trust for Nature Conservation bought the wood. Fifteen years later, the trees are now 20 feet tall, and strong enough to begin to coppice them again. Muscular conservation won the day – eventually.

where, even today, you can walk for hours without meeting anyone, surrounded only by heather and flocks of sheep.

The North Pennines, a vast landscape which straddles the counties of Cumbria, Durham and Northumberland, gives rise to the great rivers of the north, the Tees, the Tyne, the Derwent, and the Wear, all of which have their source high up in the moor lands. The

remote North Pennines, once the wealthiest lead-mining centre in Europe, are today a wildlife haven, where hen harriers breed, and where merlin and other rare species can be seen.

West of the Pennines are the Cumbrian mountains, known as the Lake District, where **Scafell Pike** the country's highest point, towers at 1053 m (3,210 feet). The Lake District is a stunning combination of lakes and

The rugged cliffs of Cornwall, at Treen, near Penzance.

mountainous hills, and even its 20th century tourist popularity has not been able to diminish its beauty: once you leave the busy shores of **Lake Windermere**, you can hike through virtually deserted peaks.

At the opposite end of the spectrum, and also the country, the eastern regions of Norfolk, Suffolk and Cambridgeshire are flat territories drained by straight, man-made canals. This Dutch-like area, dotted with lock-gates and windmills, is home to the country's flower and bulb growers.

Coastal scenes

The English coastline is some 1243 km (2,000 miles) long. In general, it is highly indented, with high cliffs, sheltered fishing villages, and beaches. The "white cliffs of Dover", immortalised in wartime songs, are just one section of a white chalk structure that stretches from the Isle of Wight east to **Dover**.

Erosion is taking its toll on some of the highly indented coast-line, and in June 1993, in a highly spectacular and publicized landslide, a luxury hotel in the north Yorkshire resort of Scarborough, slipped slowly over the cliff-head and into the sea. The first to disappear were the gardens, and after everyone had been safely evacuated from the Victorian hotel, the building itself gradually collapsed into the sea.

The **Goodwin Sands**, which lie

The Lake District

The poet William Wordsworth had reason to praise the Lake District, for he lived there; but even allowing for a certain amount of vested interest, his comments on his birthplace were, and still are, fulsome; he described it as "sublime and beautiful". The rugged beauty of this area of northwestern England charmed not only Wordsworth, but also his contemporaries Southey and Coleridge. John Ruskin lived on the shores of Lake Coniston, and Beatrix Potter, from her cottage near Windermere, created some of the best loved characters in childrens' literature, including Peter Rabbit and Jemima Puddle-Duck.

Preparing the land

The Lake District covers 340 sq km (880 square miles), and is England's largest National Park, and also the most visited. The combination of glaciated valleys and mountains, of volcanic rocks and lakes, makes the area equally popular for mountain climbers, trekkers, water-skiers or budding landscape painters.

The area was, for a long time, physically isolated from the south of England, hemmed in by moor-land, bogs, and forests, but gradually communications were established. The Romans built two roads across the area, and the Norse invaders started to clear the forest. Sheep farming followed by iron-ore smelting and lead and copper mining, all involved further clearance of the tree cover, but today there is little industry in the area, and during the last century much re-forestation has taken place.

In 1951, the Lake District became a National Park, and as tourism increased, so did the popularity of this region, aided significantly by sailing and climbing enthusiasts, whose sports were becoming more and more accessible to a wider range of people.

Lakes & mountains

The Lake District has, of course, many lakes, ranging from the well-known **Lake Windermere** to the smaller, less visited **Wast Water**. There are also mountains: **Scafell Pike** (1,052 m (3,206 feet)), is the highest point in England, closely followed by **Helvellyn** (1,023 m (3,118 feet)), **Skiddaw** (1,002 m (3,054 feet)) and **Saddleback** (934 m (2,847 feet)).

Lake Windermere, the longest lake in England, is ten and a half miles long, with the busy little town of **Windermere** and the next-door village of **Bowness-on-Windermere** on its western shore, and the pretty town of **Ambleside** to the north. The lake is very popular with sailors and water-skiers, and there are many steamers making trips across the lake.

The Wordsworth home

To the west of Windermere is **Coniston Water**, on the eastern bank of which, is **Brantwood**,

about 6 miles off the Kent coast, bring forth one of the characteristics of the English – their mild eccentricity.

Most of the time, the shifting sandbanks of the Goodwin Sands are submerged by the English Channel, but when they do surface, they become the site for pot-holing, cricket matches and, most recently, a run, celebrating the 39th anniversary of Sir Roger Bannister's 4 minute mile.

Access to the sand banks is by hovercraft, and once the race has been run, or the cricket match played, with the number of overs necessarily limited by the tides, the participants return to Dover in the hovercraft, and the impromptu sports ground disappears again, to resume its treacherous role as a place of shipwrecks.

the home of John Ruskin. From his study in a turret, there is a beautiful view of Coniston Water with the peak of The **Old Man mountain** 263 m (801 feet), reflected in the water. A little to the north are two delightful lakes, Grasmere and Rydal Water, beautiful enough in their own right, but with the added charm of the Wordsworth connection, they have an irresistible appeal to the visitor.

The Wordsworth family lived together in **Dove Cottage**, their most famous son William, later taking a house at **Rydal Mount** where he lived from 1813 until his death in 1850. Various members of the Wordsworth family are buried in the churchyard of the little 13th century village church. You can always find William's grave – it is the one which almost always has a bunch of daffodils on it, placed by an admiring visitor, doubtless with childhood memories of learning by heart the most famous of this Poet Laureate's poems, "I wandered lonely as a cloud..."

Before Stonehenge

Further north is **Thirlmere**, which is now used exclusively as a reservoir, hence the absence of boats and steamers. **Castlerigg Stone Circle**, older than Stonehenge, lies near to the town of **Keswick**, where Coleridge and Southey used to share a home. To the southeast of Thirlmere, is the town of **Kendal**, an attractive town, which grew up around the wool industry.

Weather worries & tales

Making jokes about the English weather is a national past-time, and a sense of humour is most definitely an asset, in coping not merely with daily changes in climate, but hourly ones too. One thing is certain, you can never rely on the English weather. In May it can snow (it

The silent beauty of winter snow.

did in 1993) and September and October can be unseasonably warm and sunny.

England's reputation as a green and pleasant land has to have a logical reason, and its recipe for success comes from the country's diet of rain and yet more rain. It definitely does rain a lot in England, which is why there are so many trees, beautiful lawns and flower beds, but, in point of fact, it does not rain excessively; it is just the sheer unpredictability of the rain, that makes it seem so. In the northeast of the country, annual rainfall is less than 40 inches, and some parts of the southeast are blessed with less than 8 cm (20 inches) a year.

The higher parts of the country have snow cover for perhaps 50 days a year,

Robin Hoods' Bay, North Yorkshire.

and yet many summers will see drought conditions, with restrictions placed on the use of water; a source of anger for those to whom all those beautiful lawns and gardens belong.

October 1987 saw the country ravaged by violent gales, and there was an unprecedented loss of tree cover. Five years later, areas of Southeastern England still show very visible scars, with fallen trees and wrecked undergrowth. The off-shore Isles of Scilly, suffered badly during the 1987 gales, and later in January 1990, when further violent storms

Derwent Water in the Lake District National Park.

damaged many of the islands' famous tropical gardens.

The sheer unpredictability of the English weather has had a very definite impact on the national character. The English love to talk about their weather. In England, when two strangers meet, there is never an embarrassing silence, nor a desperate search for something to talk about, for they can always resort to mutual chat about the unseasonable rain, or heat, or snow, or fog, or how it rained at Wimbledon, or how it never snows any more at Christmas.

Weather wear

Now, the moral of all this is, in England, you should never take the weather for granted. Never go out without a raincoat or an umbrella. Dress in layers, so that you can peel off or add on the sweaters, depending. Never presume anything about the English weather; just because it is October, there is no reason for it to be cold.

The converse is also true; just because it is summer there is no reason for it to be sunny or even warm. On the day of the Queen's coronation in June 1953, it was a grey, damp day. Forty years later, as people were half-heartedly commemorating the day, trying to re-live the splendour and re-capture some of the magic, only one thing required absolutely no effort – the weather. It poured with rain. Be prepared.

The English countryside is pretty and green, dotted with small farms and villages, and lots of trees. This gently rolling countryside is, in fact, a composite of many different elements, including woodland, agricultural land and hedgerows. England has a profusion of wild flowers, and in the spring and summer, as you drive down winding, narrow, country lanes, you can be literally surrounded by grass and flowers, as the hedgerows tower above you, lining both sides of the lane.

The national flower, which, by any other name smells just as sweet.

Flora & Fauna

65

The country's lungs

Historically, England has always been a land of forests and woodlands. In the Middle Ages, large tracts of land were royal forests, and the contemporary status symbol was to own a deer park. In time, developments such as the increasing industrial working of the land, overuse of timber in the early days of the iron and ship-building industries, rapid urban development,

The Chelsea Flower Show

Every year, in London, in late May, hundreds of people start queuing in the early morning, to gain admission to the grounds of the **Royal Hospital** in London's Chelsea district, home since 1913 to the annual Chelsea Flower Show.

Sights & smells

If you have ever been tempted to dismiss gardening as an unexciting weekend chore, then a visit to this horticultural high spot of the year, will be a revelation. For four days, huge crowds throng the Royal Hospital grounds, where they can admire the award winning designer gardens or the latest in garden furniture; check out the newest hybrid plants, or browse through the latest coffee-table books on flower arranging.

The focal point of each flower show is the Great Marquee, reputedly the world's biggest tent, where exhibitors display anything and everything to do with gardening. At the 1993 show, for example, exhibitors ranged from a bonsai specialist to the Carnivorous Plant Society, from 150 different varieties of rhubarb on one stand, to (reputedly) the world's oldest garden gnome – 2.4 cm (6 inches) high, 150 years old and insured for £1 million.

People visit Chelsea, as the Flower Show is usually known, for many reasons: to see the Royal visitors delicately sniffing new varieties of tube roses; to buy a specialist piece of equipment; to get ideas for their own gardens; or simply to drink in the sights and perfumes of such a unique display of flowers and plants.

Pure, unadulterated floral beauty is much appreciated by the English, who are a nation of keen gardeners. It is not even hype, but the truth, when the organizers of the Chelsea Flower Show, claim that gardening is the country's most popular hobby.

Medals of merit

Chelsea has moved with the times: when attendance rose to uncomfortable levels in the late 1980s, it was decided to limit the daily attendance, to ensure that everyone present could enjoy the show to the fullest. Members of the Royal Horticultural Society, who organize the show, have their own private viewing sessions, and there is now a Royal Gala charity preview, held on the Monday evening of Chelsea week, which raises funds each year for a different charity.

There are a welter of awards, medals and certificates up for grabs at Chelsea, including such delightful categories as Certificates of Preliminary Commendation for "new plants of promise". Giving almost human dimensions to plants, there are further awards for "plants of great excellence" and "plants which are meritorious".

Garden creations

Although specialist visitors to Chelsea will automatically head off to their own area of interest – be it displays devoted to African Violets or the

and the mis-use of pesticides, all took their toll on the richness and variety of the countryside and its flora. However, a vigorous conservation and "greening" policy has long been under way. Nature reserves and National Parks are constantly being established, offering protection to both wildlife and vegetation. Huge stretches of desolate moor-land in

Yorkshire, for example, are deliberately left untouched, home only to flocks of sheep, wild horses, and the last vestiges of the tundra of the Ice Age.

England is a very densely populated country, so naturally enough, pressure on the countryside, especially for building, is intense. Undue attempts to encroach on the much needed country-

National Collection of Erodiums – the magnet is, without question, the gardens. Newspaper groups, charities, garden centres – they all create exquisite gardens from scratch, solely for the enjoyment of the 4 days of Chelsea. Plants, lawns, running water and fountains, all give the appearance of mature gardens, and it is one of the major triumphs of the show that these short-term gardens create an illusion of permanence.

Amongst the gardens landscaped especially for the four days of the 1993 was a garden designed specifically for sufferers of asthma and hay fever, by, not surprisingly, the National Asthma Campaign. Here, the emphasis was on plants which produce low amounts of pollen. Yet another garden was designed to demonstrate how to make a garden safe for a blind or a partially sighted person; interesting and very colourful ideas.

Images of the ideal

Whether your horticultural interest stretches no further than trying to add a little colour to your apartment window box, or whether you secretly harbour fantasies of undertaking a major landscaping of your country estate; Chelsea will definitely give you ideas, will most probably make you despair a little in the face of such elegance, and will almost certainly make you jealous of the merit of plants to which your own garden varieties hold not a semblance of identity. Never mind you could always come back and compare, next year!

side are controlled by a series of conservation measures. There are a range of conservation categories, such as: green belts, generally sited around towns to provide much needed "lungs" for city dwellers; officially designated "Areas of Outstanding Natural Beauty" with special conservation rights; stretches of the coast line have been designated as "her-

itage coasts"; and there are the National Parks such as the Lake District and the Yorkshire Dales.

The National Trust

One of the major influences in the business of conservation has been the National Trust, a charity founded in 1895 with the aim of preserving places of historic interest and natural beauty. Today, the National Trust is the largest private landowner and conservation society in Britain.

Open any map of England, and in addition to the host of National Trust properties, such as castles and stately homes, you will see "NT" marked on many areas of moor-land, forest, coast and even entire villages. In order to pay for the huge cost of conservation and preservation, most National Trust land is open to the public at all times, the only constraints being the requirements of the resident farmers, or the need to protect wildlife.

A factor that the National Trust has had to take into consideration, is the need to strike a happy medium between allowing reasonable access to an area, and preventing damage through overuse. This is the problem currently confronting another beautiful northern area, the Yorkshire moors and dales. High crags, vast heather-covered moorlands, and sheltered meadows, have provided a home and a way of life for generations of farmers. Yet, sadly, the

Kew Gardens, the botanical mecca, houses a spectacular collection of national and international flora.

landscape that 20 million visitors come to enjoy each year is in danger. There are various threats: the decline of traditional hill farming and the constant danger of unwelcome development, but, the moors are significantly affected – somewhat ironically – by the harsh tram-pling of those 20 million pairs of feet who come each year to appreciate their beauty.

Dry stone walls and field barns are as much a part of Yorkshire's traditional landscape as they are part of its livelihood. But neglect and wear-and-tear

gritty – repairing tumble-down walls and barns, caring for woods and meadows, protecting rare plants, birds and animals – but the end results are worth it.

An English country garden

Gardens are an intrinsic part of the English scenery, and wherever you go in the country, you will find beautifully manicured lawns and well-tended gardens, ranging in size from little more than a pocket handkerchief, right through to the sumptuous formal gardens belonging to the large estates. Whatever their size, most will be lovingly tended, and much appreciated. Gardening is indeed the nations' prime hobby and is taken very seriously indeed, with regular radio and television chat-shows and phone-ins taking place to give the ordinary gardener a chance to quizz the experts, on a whole range of gardening issues. Middlesex University is even offering a degree course in gardening, a clear indication that "green" issues are here to stay!

Famous gardeners & their gardens

The English love affair with their gardens really started in Elizabethan days, with the formal patterns of the knot gardens, where small beds were laid out, planted with herbs or flowers, and

have taken their toll. A worrying number of barns are on the brink of collapse, and many of the 50,000 miles of dry stone walls in the Yorkshire Dales will have to be repaired soon. Here again, the National Trust, one of the largest land-owners in upland Yorkshire, has a programme of essential countryside maintenance. The work is hard and

Daffodils, the hope of spring.

surrounded by low, clipped box-hedges in a formal stylized pattern. In the 17th century, the essential form of the garden was still geometric, but on a larger scale. Tall hedges separated the garden into "rooms" with flower beds of different varieties, these hedges then opened out, to reveal a vista, such as a fountain or a lake.

It was in the 18th century that the English passion for gardening was at it apogee, and the art of landscape gardening was born. Lancelot "Capability" Brown (1716-83), who used to talk about his work as being to improve the "capa-

bility" of a site – hence his nickname – revolutionized the appearance of the garden of the English country-house. He removed formal boundaries between house and garden, abandoned the hedges and formal patterns, choosing, instead, to fuse all the elements at his disposal – house, garden, and surrounding countryside – into an idealized representation of nature. Statues, lawns, woodland and lakes were all part of Capability Brown's palette, which created such marvels as the gardens of **Blenheim Palace** and **Stourhead House**, as well as scores of lesser gardens and estates all over the country. William Kent (1684-1748) had earlier invented the ha-ha, an open ditch which allowed the garden to merge naturally with the surrounding countryside, whilst effectively preventing cattle and deer from straying in.

If the 18th century gardener introduced such follies as "classical" temples and grottoes to decorate his garden, the 19th century gardener literally set out to find rare species for his. Victorian families would finance expeditions, especially to bring back rare plants for their gardens; greenhouses and conservatories were built to raise these alien species, and some of the country's most spectacular plant collections grew up this way. In Staffordshire, the **Biddulph Grange Garden** is an example of this Victorian passion for both gardening and exotica. The garden was designed to display the owner's extensive exotic plant collection, and is decorated with 19th century interpretations of the Great Wall of China, with an Egyptian temple-like monument, forming a background to the plants.

The rose & the oak

England is not a country which places much store on the visual symbolism of national flowers, or birds, or trees. However, the rose, throughout the world, is instantly associated with the country, and the term "English rose", is sometimes used to describe pretty young women. English oak or brown oak, was formerly used for carving and ship-building in England, and in a well-known 18th century song, there is a much-quoted line about English gentlemen - "Heart of oak are our ship, heart of oak are our men."

Bird life

Several animal species such as wolves and bears are threatened with extinction. However, a similar threat to bird-life, especially to large birds of prey, seems to have been avoided by such policies as laws restricting the collection of birds' eggs. Education has also helped

The Blackbird, a common English garden bird.

Birding in England

It was in England that modern concepts of birdwatching began, largely out of a concern for animal rights. As recent as the1930's, local birds were kept in cages and used for popular singing contests around the Regent's Park area in London, just as they are all over Asia today; but in the years subsequent to World War II, such practices quickly changed. Today in England, it is illegal to keep European birds in cages, although rather illogically this ruling does not apply to overseas birds.

Bird crazy

In recent times this interest and concern for wild birds and nature in general has exploded into something like a national obsession. Over 1 million Britains today are members of a birdwatching organization, the largest one being the Royal Society for the Protection of Birds (RSPB). The watching and protection of nature has turned into a big money-spinning industry and expensive hobby: bird-feed, bird-tables, books and magazines about birds, computer software, pictures, sculptures and souvenirs, equipment for watching and photograhing birds, outdoor clothes and camping gear, birding tours and holidays, are just some of many buys available to tempt that budding ornithologist. In England when a rare species is sighted news spreads quickly and birdwatchers venture out

The coot, a common English Park bird, feeds its juveniles.

The Pochard is a resident duck in England.

with eager eyes, sometimes in such large numbers that the traffic police have to be called in to divert passing traffic away from the site.

The BBC and other independent broadcasting companies have also contributed to the bird craze, the excellent quality and number of their documentaries have opened the eyes of people the world over, to the wonders of the natural world.

The bird scene

Despite the enormous local interest in birds, England is not naturally blessed with a rich avifauna. As an island state the diversity of resident birds does not equal that of parts of continental Europe. Some families, such as the woodpecker, are very sparsely represented. Even when the UK and Ireland are taken together as a region, the area has only approximately 200 regularly breeding bird species – about 30 more have been known to breed on occasions. There are however, a large number of passage migrants, winter visitors and vagrants from other places – mostly northern and eastern Europe – with quite a few stragglers flying in across the Atlantic from the American region. With all the keen eyes watching nowadays, more and more of these are spotted and added to the checklist. These visitors almost equal the number of breeding birds, bringing the total number of species

Wood pigeons, often seen in parks, are surprisingly tame in England.

occuring up to 480.

What English birds lack in diversity however they gain in density. The country has a varied scenery of woodlands, moors, marshes and coastlines, thus it caters well to diverse birding habitats; even in the populated areas the landscape is quite bird friendly, with low intensity farming and plenty of parks and small gardens in the urban areas.

Birdwatching in London

The idea of going birdwatching in a city may appear odd to you, but then again even the non-ornithological visitor to London will notice a great number of birds, especially in the parks, many of them tame. **St James's Park** near Buckingham Palace, is a good example; some of the birds here are ornamental species, exotics with clipped wings introduced to brighten up the place, but most are wild birds who have settled there out of their own choice. Here you will find **Coots** nesting in the open right near the footpath, their nest lined with plastic bags and drinking straws. **Moorhens** and several species of duck prefer to nest on small islands off the bank, but they will come to humans with their young – so close you can almost touch them. Thirty years ago the **Wood Pigeon** was a retiring forest bird that would fly off if you came within 91 m (100 yards) of it; today it comes

into the park and sits on people's heads trying to beg food just like a feral pigeon. Again, even more recently the **Magpie** and the **Herring Gull** used to be extremely shy, here they are to be found hopping amongst people's legs on the lawns.

In nearby **Regents Park**, several pairs of the once endangered **Great Crested Grebe** can be seen nesting in the lake. About 50 different birds nest inside the London city district and yet of these only the **Feral Pigeon** – which feeds it juveniles on a milk secrete – can live solely on man-made food. All others need insects or fish to feed their young, some like the swifts and the swallows do not scavenge at all.

There is a reason for the amazing quantity and tameness of these London birds. Environmentally, tough legislation in the early 1970's has meant less air pollution, a higher degree of sunshine penetration, a consequent increase in vegetation cover and thus more insect food for the birds. The water in rivers and lakes is also cleaner today. The attitudes of humans have also changed dramatically; the birds are being left in peace and genetic alterations may even have taken place in the birds when the tamer individuals proved better able to survive.

Around the country

If you are looking for somewhat wilder species

A Mute Swan family.

...Birding in England

The Little Tern from Germany is a common coastl resident.

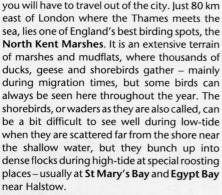

Common Winged Plover.

you will have to travel out of the city. Just 80 km east of London where the Thames meets the sea, lies one of England's best birding spots, the **North Kent Marshes**. It is an extensive terrain of marshes and mudflats, where thousands of ducks, geese and shorebirds gather – mainly during migration times, but some birds can always be seen here throughout the year. The shorebirds, or waders as they are also called, can be a bit difficult to see well during low-tide when they are scattered far from the shore near the shallow water, but they bunch up into dense flocks during high-tide at special roosting places – usually at **St Mary's Bay** and **Egypt Bay** near Halstow.

The **Dee Estuary** on the west coast near Liverpool, is another well-known location for crowds of tens of thousands of shorebirds. Also quite near London at **Minsmere** in Suffolk, is a bird sanctuary managed by the RSPB, permission to enter the reserve must be obtained from the society. There are a wide variety of habitats

in this 600 hectare site and a greater variety of birds can be seen here in one day than anywhere else in England. The **Cley district** in Norfolk is a better choice for rarer sightings; here there are locations for both waterbirds and landbirds; vagrant species have also turned up here unexpectantly on a number of occasions.

In the west Midlands on the river Severn lies the **Slimbridge reserve**, a legendary waterbird location and a great birding destination open to the public. The reserve is owned by the Wildfowl Trust, which specializes in research and management of wetland ecosystems. Some of the thousands of birds living here are released, but most are wild birds attracted by the management practices of the trust.

More information

The country where birdwatching began, is also the place on earth where it is best documented. Any English bookshop will have several titles on local birdlife and specialist shops will have dozens. Every nook and cranny of the place has been searched over and written about. But perhaps most important of all for the birdwatcher is a good field guide to identify the birds that you spot; here Collins' *New Generation Guide to Birds of Britain and Europe* by C Perrins, 1987 is regarded by many as the most useful one currently on the market.

For finding good birding locations *Birdwatching in Britain* is a site by site guide by N Redman and S Harrap published by Christopher Helm, 1987. For the latest information there are several periodicals available in the bookshops, *Birdwatching Magazine* is the most popular and contains all the information you might require about equipment, locations, rarities, tours, accomodation, books etc.. *British Birds* is slightly more scientific and *Birds* is published by the RSPB, which can be contacted at The Lodge, Sandy, Bedfordshire, SG19 2DL, UK.

and such centres as the **Yorkshire Dales Falconry Conservation Centre** at "Crows' Nest", near Giggleswick in North

Yorkshire, has helped to increase public awareness of the threat of extinction that faces many birds of prey. The cen-

Sheep are a common sight, in England's green fields and meadows.

tre has a programme of captive breeding, and you can see vultures, eagles, hawks, falcons and owls.

England is a good place for bird-watching, lying as it does along the path of bird migrations, bird life is unusually varied here. Even in such a busy, noisy city as London, about 100 different bird species are recorded each year.

Livestock farming

Livestock husbandry, and in particular dairy farming, is one of the main focuses of English agriculture, and although dairy farming is found in most parts of the country, it is especially predominant in the west of England. Higher

yielding dairy breeds, such as the Frisian and the Ayrshire, are the most common stock.

Much of the wealth of 18th and 19th century England derived from the woollen industry, and sheep farming is still important in the north of the country, though the emphasis is increasingly on breeding for meat rather than wool.

Animal friends

The English have always bred horses, and bear a great affection for them – it is rare to find an Englishman who will eat a horse's meat! Many keep them as pets or ride them in shows and as you travel round the country, you will see

English dogs & the English

From man's best friend, to "mad dogs and Englishmen", there has always been an English love-affair with dogs. Even the Queen is regularly photographed with her corgis, and feeds them herself – if the gossip columns are to be believed! The English love dogs, be they champions worthy of Crufts Dog Show, or some unidentified mongrel. Most are merely pets, but some are also trained as sheep dogs, guide-dogs to the blind and as police dogs; patient and intelligent they are reputedly, an Englishman's best friend.

The Old English Sheep Dog

Of all the breeds of dog with the name "English", the best known is almost certainly the **Old English Sheep Dog**, an appealing cuddly-looking animal, whose pretty appearance effectively belies its origins as a working dog. The breed was developed in the early 18th century, and they were employed mainly to drive sheep and cattle to market. They have shaggy, long coats, with hair flopping into their eyes and a shuffling gait. Do not be surprised if you hear them referred to as "Dulux" dogs: a tremendously successful advertising campaign for Dulux® Paint, using an Old English Sheep Dog, has identified the dog and the product – though most people would be incapable of telling you anything about the campaign, other than the canine star!

Canine aristocrats

Despite its name, the **English Toy Spaniel** apparently originated not in England, but in Japan or China, but made its appearance in England in Tudor times, since when it has been consistently popular. Mary, Queen of Scots kept English Toy Spaniels, as did King Charles II, from whom they derived their better-known name of King Charles Spaniels. They are little, pretty looking dogs, with long, floppy ears, and large, dark eyes.

The **English Setter** is a beautiful looking hunting dog, with an aristocratic profile, and a gentle temperament. Like his companions, the Irish setter and the Gordon Setter, the English Setter is trained to work in partnership with man, to find birds, then "set", or lie down, until the birds can be caught. Irish Setters have a distinctive russet colour, whereas English setters can be all white, black and white, or black, white and tan. Smaller than the Irish setter, the English setter has the same feathery coat along its legs.

everything from wild, tiny New Forest ponies, to the massive Shire horses, which were once used to pull heavy carts carrying beer from the breweries. Nowadays, these massive dray horses are more frequently used for nostalgic PR campaigns. Bass brewery in the Midlands, at one stage had over 200 Shire horses stabled in the Burton-on-Trent area. The horses have for 11 years been appearing in many fairs and exhibitions.

One must not forget the eternal English love for their dogs, who all have a very good life in this dog-mad society. Most people walk their dog at least once

The English Setter, a gorgeous and much-loved hunting dog.

a day, whatever the weather, day or night, and they bring them in their cars on family outings and even on holiday. A dog is seen as a member of the family, a faithful companion and a friend.

Protection & propagation

In order to combat the threat of extinction to certain animals species, a protectionalist society, English Nature, is running a Species Recovery Programme, aimed at helping preserve the most threatened species in the country, either by captive breeding for birds and animals, so as to re-introduce species, or via seed germination under controlled conditions, to protect delicate flowers.

Current projects include propagating seeds from the only remaining Lady's Slipper Orchid plant in England, and protecting the Common Dormouse whose habitat is being destroyed. The organization is also trying to breed the Red Squirrel, and the Red Kite, the latter of which is extinct in England, surviving naturally in only one place in Wales.

Finally, as the antithesis to talk of threatened species, how about trying out a brand new fruit? Why not try the Guernsey Babaco, the brain-child of the experimental station of the Guernsey Horticultural Advisory Service, in the Channel Islands. For those with adventurous tastes, this completely new fruit combines the flavours of strawberries, melons, grapefruit, lemons and peaches.

People

"**N**o one can understand the nature of England or of English politics who does not realize that this island of ours is and always has been covered with a kind of beautiful cloud. No one can be a good critic of England who does not understand fogs. And no one can be a really patriotic Englishman who does not like fogs."

GK Chesterton wrote this delightfully tongue-in-cheek portrait of the English, nearly 90 years ago, and it is reassuring to know that even then, the weather was bad enough to be seen as the key to unlocking the English psyche.

The moment you set out to define anyone in terms of national characteristics, it is all too easy to fall into the trap of readily identifiable generalizations; such as those which portray all French-

Facing up to school.

A happy pair.

men as wearing berets, all Americans as being charmingly naive, and all Indians as being unworldly mystics. Most stereotypes are clearly far too simplistic, but very often they do contain a certain grain of truth. Bearing this in mind, what should one expect from the stereotyped "English Gentleman"?

Wearing a "stiff–upper–lip"

The first thing to look out for in the English is that renowned "stiff-upper-lip", for the English do not easily betray their emotions and certainly not in public. However sad he may be, an Englishman will not cry in public, nor will he hug his friends, no matter how happy he may be to see them. However hassled and provoked, he will try not to shout too much, and will do all he can to avoid public embarrassment. An Englishman will never kiss or hug a male relative – though a woman will do so regularly – as an Italian would; nor would he be so extreme as to kiss a lady's hands, as a polite Frenchman would. Generally the English do not make noisy scenes in public, unless they are of a rare breed that does not care about embarrassment.

Attitudes are changing among some people – footballers are regularly seen to kiss and hug each other and you will see the odd passionate couple on the street – but generally such exuberant behaviour is regarded as "continental", the English themselves having a quiet dignity which is often refined.

The down-side to all this restrained behaviour, especially as it seems to more outgoing people, is that the English can appear to be far too reserved. They are cool and calm and unflappable, often to the point of appearing phlegmatic – at least, that is what the French have to say on the subject, but, as any good Englishman knows, the French are far too excitable anyway! Part of the English reserve stems from the country's traditionally conservative nature – and that, by the way, has absolutely nothing to do with politics and the Conservative party.

The English are bred on tradition; ritual and history play a part in the day-to-day life of many of the country's

The old school tie

Every society has its own form of net-working, where contacts and influence play an important role, but one of the more subtle ways of "making friends and influencing people" in England, is the "Old Boy" network. "Old Boys" are one time members of a school, if this school is a good one, the old school tie will metaphorically, be a passport to enter societys' elite. By virtue of this important status symbol, you can be carried into the circles of the rich and influential, and the connections which this creates, may be the means to the establishment of a most desirable career.

"Public" schools

First of all, a word about schools in England. The main thing to be aware of, is that a "public school" means the exact opposite. It is actually an independent fee-paying private school, usually a boarding school, for children from 11 or 13, through to 18 years of age. Many of the country's public schools are long-established, and are seen to be exclusive, snobbish places, which they probably are to some extent, but since on average they also produce good academic results, places in them are much sought after, and hard to obtain. Stories abound of fathers sprinting straight from the delivery room, to draft a letter putting Junior down for his old house at school, and there is a certain, albeit exaggerated, truth in it. The most famous of the boys' public schools are **Eton**, **Harrow**, **Westminster** and **Winchester**, whilst for girls, who were traditionally sent off to public school less frequently than their brothers, the best known schools are **Roedean** and **Cheltenham**.

After the child's name has been put down for school, he or she will have to cross the hurdle of Common Entrance, the admission examination set by all public schools when the child is 11 or 13. To prepare for this examination, the child is therefore sent off to the appropriately named "preparatory school". Also an independent, fee-paying boarding school, preparatory schools, or "prep school", often have very strong ties to a particular public school, and some even form a junior department to a public school.

The old school tie connection, therefore, can sometimes go back to the age of 7, making it a formidable weapon. Since, even in these days of the much touted "classless" Britain, and Citizens' Charter, the majority of the "Establishment" were educated at public school, there is a very strong net-working system in place, and it stays in place all the way up the professional ladder.

The Oxbridge connection

The other great net-working system is that mysterious institution called "Oxbridge", which is actually the name for the joint phenomenon of Oxford and Cambridge universities, the two oldest and most prestigious in the country. Traditionally a high percentage of Oxbridge students, have been educated in public schools, perpetuating the designs of net-working. Nowadays, however there are more and more projects to encourage applicants from government funded schools, though many of these candidates are not given the specific Oxbridge entrance training that public school pupils receive.

Net-working is indeed still rife in England, it is dauntingly exclusive, and a years-old tradition hard to break in one fell swoop. Yet, since one of the over-riding English characteristics is a sense of fair play, people will always be accepted for their ability, though life is tougher and has to be fought for. You have to be a bit thick-skinned, but eventually, if you make it, you too might become one of those desirable connections!

great institutions: the age-old monarchy with its strict propriety and etiquette; the legal sytem with its bewigged judges and barristers; old universities with archaic traditions; religious foundations dating back nearly a 1,000 years; ancient customs and celebrations; all these leave trace elements in the national

City punks may give you some surprises.

psyche, their adherence to form and manners making the English by nature, conservative and traditionalists.

Class consciousness

One thing for sure, the English are not closet revolutionaries. How could they be, in a society where people calmly describe themselves as being "lower middle-class" or "upper middle-class", without a trace of irony? The English class system is, by and large, alive and well, despite the levelling effects of education, the affluence of the 1980s and the recession of the early 1990s.

Trying to explain the class system is

not an easy task, for its nuances are often difficult to pin-point, and even if non-English people have had the system explained to them, it is not always easy to classify people into a particular social group. People are born into the different strata of society, upper, middle and lower, and although the differences between the 3 classes are not as pronounced as they were generations ago, many people are still aware of their place in society, and, especially, that from which they came.

This class system does however have a degree of security since no one ever moves down in society. A middle class person, however down on his luck, will never "become" working class, nor will an impoverished aristocrat be considered as middle class – he will simply be a poor aristocrat! The two usually accepted means of self-improvement are via wealth and education, with the latter bestowing much more social acceptance than untutored wealth alone. Someone of modest means, who has won a scholarship to Oxford, will be more easily assimilated into upper-middle and upper-class England, than a factory worker who wins a fortune on the football pools.

Distinctions of class

Distinctions are gradually being blurred, and the harsher defining lines between the different elements in society are being slowly eroded through such dispa-

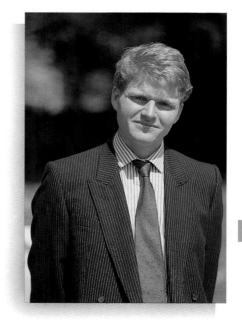

Yuppie Englishman.

rate means as the country's growing multi-racialism, and the age-old honours system. England has a small, but prominent, community of ethnic minorities – mainly Indians, Pakistanis, West Africans, Caribbeans, and Hong Kong Chinese – some of whom have been here for 3 and 4 generations. Initially, perhaps, the children and grandchildren of traders and immigrants, they are now, by and large, assimilated into mainstream English life. They speak, dress and think like any other English youngster, and their parents have the same educational and financial ambitions as any English parent. There are Asians in Parliament and in the upper levels of the judiciary, Caribbean members of the policeforce, and rich Chinese

The English Look

You can still see hippies wandering along London's **Carnaby Street**, and amazingly enough they are not nostalgic 40-somethings, but energetic teenagers, for fashion has come full circle, and platform shoes and bell-bottoms are back in vogue.

English fashion is a creature of extremes. On the one hand, there is the archetypal City banker, in his virtual uniform of a very dark navy-blue or black pin-striped suit, black leather shoes, usually Church's, and a copy of the *Financial Times*, to round off the ensemble. It is increasingly rare nowadays to see the final touch to this outfit, a black bowler hat, but you may just be lucky, and spot one of the few that are still worn religiously to work every day. The majority of children in England still wear school uniform, those from public schools even wearing straw boaters in the summer, and dark hats in the winter.

Funky fashion

The flip side to this sober, uniformed tradition, are the funky street fashions that will hit you as you explore the country. It is not just the youngsters of London who wear sometimes weird and wonderful clothing – you can find punks and rockers in the tiniest of villages, but London is prime street fashion territory. One thing to remember about the English is that they are, generally, a polite people, and not out to create

scenes nor make waves. The same reticence that prevents old friends from hugging and kissing, also prevents them from remarking on strange clothes and even stranger hair-dos. So, the weirdest creations wander by, with hardly anyone batting an eyelid. The English stiff-upper-lip syndrome is still alive and well.

The punk era is a little past its prime, but there are still many punks to be seen – London's **Covent Garden** is a favourite place – and some of the brightly coloured, spiky hair-styles are definitely modern works of art. English teenagers, like their counterparts the world over, seem to live in jeans and tee-shirts, and never forget that Britain is, after all, the country that has produced the punky, funky fashion designer Katherine Hammett, who put slogans on tee-shirts onto the world's fashion cat-walks.

Dressing English

Alongside the tee-shirts and the designer running shoes, there is the classic, timeless "English look". For a man, if he works in The City, his week day office clothes will consist of a smartly cut suit, (and never, heaven forbid, a blazer and flannels like the French), a good cotton shirt, and a not too loud tie. In the winter, this may be topped off by a suitably dark, discreet overcoat – though English men are experts in the art of shivering in the winter, rather than wrapping up warm. At weekends, our English man will

businessmen.

All of these communities now live together in a country that gives titles to its worthy citizens, be they dignified civil servants, or the village nurse; soldiers, sportsmen or industrialist contributors to political coffers; all sorts of people from many different walks of life, who, in the eyes of the Queen and her advisors have made a significant contribution to the good of society. Twice

a year, at New Year, and on the Queen's birthday, an Honours List is issued in which hundreds of men and women are given honours which they collect personally from Her Majesty. Some of these honours are fairly nebulous, such as being able to write the letters "OBE" after your name, meaning Order of the British Empire – a historical notion, if ever there was one. Some chosen few on the Honours List will receive a peerage, wear slightly baggy, misshapen cords, in a sludge green or dark brown colour, a brushed cotton shirt, and a comfortable pull-over. The general impression will be one of casual comfort, of someone who has just returned from walking the dog, or pottering in the garden – which is exactly what he will have been doing.

Our typical English woman - let's make her also a City worker - will dress smartly for work, but definitely not as "chic"-ly as her French counterparts, nor as adventurously as her New York opposite number. She will be elegant, for sure, but definitely not at the cutting edge of fashion. A suit, or a skirt and blouse, a good silk scarf, and, despite whatever she may secretly think about clichés, she will possess a string of pearls - even though the "twin-set and pearls" image may well have been relegated to grandmothers.

Outside the office, she, too, will have that indefinable "country" look, even if she lives in town. A sensible skirt, a Barbour jacket, and if it is winter, or wet, even a pair of green gumboots, known universally as "wellies".

Green wellies are one of the give-away signs of those who really do live in the country, and those who secretly wished they did. People clambering out of a spotlessly clean Range Rover vehicle, wearing dark green wax jackets and green wellies, probably live in Chelsea. If the boots and the car are splashed with mud, they probably live in Suffolk. The Queen is famous for her green Hunters "wellies".

A healthy and happy retiree.

which means that they can then call themselves "Lord" or "Lady". However, as with many traditions in England, nothing is as straightforward as it seems. If you are awarded a life peerage, the title is only applicable to you and your spouse, whereas a hereditary peerage can be passed on to your descendants. Theoretically this means that in time the sons of worthy working class families will sit as equals in the House of Lords, with the sons of aristocratic families – but since everyone knows what kind of title you possess, the distinctions still remain. All very conservative, very confusing to the outsider, and, of course, frustrating for the seriously ambitious!

One of the elements that make up the whole attitude to class is accent. Everyone knows how the Queen's English, or Oxford English should sound, but there are as many permutations on that accent as there are counties. A Yorkshire sheep farmer and a London stock-broker may very well both speak the same language, but there will be many variations of pronunciation and vocabulary, which identify the speakers not only geographically, but also socially. In the media, there is a growing

British youth and college days.

trend away from the hitherto received wisdom that the standardized sound of "BBC English" is somehow "better" than regional accents. Paralleling this however, the BBC has recently announced a drive to weed out "Americanisms", clichés and jargon generally in their programmes, aiming to return to a more authentically "English" voice.

Conversation points

The English are generally a polite race,

ers but that is not necessarily true, for once you leave the relative impersonality of London, a villager in Dorset is every bit as chatty and helpful as his counterpart in Northumberland. What you will discover, though, is that nearly everyone in the North, from a shopkeeper to a policeman, will address you as "love". Once you realize that this is neither informality nor forwardness, but simply a way of speaking, you will quickly get used to it.

One conversational gambit that never fails in England, is to talk about the weather, and after only a few days in the country, the visitor will understand why. The English weather is a fool-proof way of always having something new to talk about, for it varies not only from day to day, but several times within the same day.

Possibly because they live with such an idiotic climate, the English have a notable sense of humour. Although obvious, slap-stick humour, such as that found in pantomimes and circuses, is quite popular, generally what really makes an English person laugh, is something much more ironic and clever.

Satire is popular – witness the cult series of the 1970s and 1980s, *Monty Python's Flying Circus*, and its worthy successor, the wildly popular television series, *Spitting Image*, in which every icon of society is parodied by a rather grotesque puppet image; charcters range from the venerable Queen Mother, through to politicans and football players.

though travellers in London's rush hour may be forgiven for failing to notice it. Still, as a general rule, people are courteous to visitors, happy to give directions and to explain things, and will always take the time to smile and say "good morning".

Northerners consider themselves to be friendlier people than the Southern-

The love of nature and animals is nurtured from a tender age.

National characteristics

The English have a very pronounced sense of what is or is not "fair play", and will often use the expression "that's not cricket" to describe something that is not exactly, fair play. They also have an equally pronounced sense of justice, and a feeling that one should always support the deserving underdog, rather than a more charismatic character.

An ideal place to see this trend in action is during the Wimbledon tennis tournament, when the crowd will stoutly cheer on the losing player – not just if he or she is British – with the encouraging ethic that he or she is at least making a go of it. The English like nothing better than true grit.

The English have a strong aversion to drawing attention to themselves, either through their actions or their words, which means that they do not relish a public altercation or a shouting match, nor any form of excessive behaviour. If you feel like striking up a conversation on the London Underground train with a complete stranger, you almost certainly will not be rudely rebuffed but just politely, though rather coolly, answered.

This reticence has a positive side, for it leads to a degree of tolerance born, admittedly, out of shyness. The Mohican haircuts of the punk rockers of Covent Garden, and the dancing processions of head-shaven Hare Krishna devotees

Pre-teen English children.

along Oxford Street, may not be everyone's cup of tea, but the English firmly believe in live and let live.

Mad dogs & Englishmen

Any form of boasting is considered as being in poor taste, people tend to play down their achievements, and frank discussions about money are considered a little vulgar. Most English people do not have the faintest idea how much their closest friends earn, nor would they ever dream of asking.

This instinctive dislike of pomposity and overt showing-off, combined with a very healthy sense of humour and self-ridicule, means that "poseurs" are laughed out of court. In France, being an intellectual is a recognized role in life; in Paris, people will seriously introduce someone as an intellectual; the English would rather run a mile than be introduced thus. Better to be an amateur, than thought to be pretentious.

A very mild dose of eccentricity is another English characteristic, how else can you explain the whole "mad dogs and Englishmen" attitude. In the 18th and 19th centuries for example, generations of intrepid explorers charged off to the remotest corners of the earth, built cricket pitches and English gardens and drunk tea in the heat of the afternoon sun; after all such "civilized" activities were thought – and still are – to be the quintessentials of Englishness.

E ngland today is definitely a multi-religious country. The religion that has had the most influence on the country today, is Christianity, since it has occupied a place in English life, history, architecture, music and literature, for nearly 1,400 years. Today, although the majority of the population are Protestant Christians, most are not regular church goers. There are also a number of non-Christian religions, including Islam and Sikhism, these religions are prevalent among the immigrant communities, but have few converts among those of the European race.

Choir boys sing the church's praise.

Religion

91

The mission of St Augustine

When Saint Augustine landed in Kent in AD597, with a mission to convert England to Christianity, the country had a vital heathen culture, and the change to the beliefs and practices of Rome, was a slow one. Not only did converts return after a while to their former beliefs, but there were also two, par-

A typical English country church.

allel conversion missions – one to the Church of Rome, and the other to the Celtic Church. Initially, there was little friction between the two groups, but gradually differences grew into controversies. One such issue was the different date on which each group celebrated Easter, an issue which was settled by the Synod of Whitby in 664, which ruled in favour of the Church of Rome. The Church of Rome gradually came to dominate the country. By the end of the 7th century, England was a Christian country.

much contact between Northumbria and Celtic Ireland, and simultaneously, many scholars were sent to Rome, so the kingdom saw a fusion of Celtic and classical learning.

Many important abbeys were founded in the north, including **Wearmouth**, **Ripon**, **Whitby** and **Jarrow**, where the Venerable Bede spent his life, and Lindisfarne, from where the beautiful *Lindisfarne Gospels* originated. This series of illuminated gospels was written in the 7th or 8th century, and they are a fusion of Irish, classical and Byzantine influences. They are kept in the British Museum.

Throughout the 8th century, the hold of Christianity on the country increased, as parishes were founded, monasteries were built, and scholarship flourished. Although monasteries continued to flourish during the 9th century, a strict monastic rule was not always enforced, which led to increasing support for a monastic reform movement. This movement gained momentum in the 10th century, when King Edgar ascended the throne. He promoted the chief reformers, had secular priests evicted, and there was a resulting intellectual revival. Latin and vernacular literature flourished, as did manuscript illumination and production.

When William the Conqueror invaded England in 1066, he brought with him his own clergy, and after re-organization, awarded most of the parishes to continental clergy. These closer continental links led to the founding of new

Scholarship & intellectual revival

The century following Augustine's arrival in England, saw the country quickly achieving a high standard of religious scholarship, the undoubted centre of which was Northumbria. There was

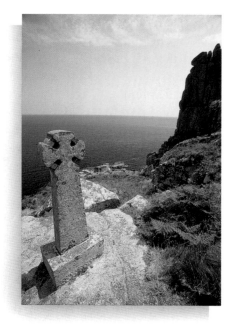

A Celtic cross marks England's early Christian tradition.

religious orders. The first Cluniac house was established in 1077, the Cistercians came in 1129, and many Augustinian houses were founded in the early 12th century.

The murder of Thomas à Becket

In 1162, King Henry II appointed Thomas à Becket as Archbishop of Canterbury, a militant defender of the church against royal interference, a power struggle ensued, culminating in the murder of Thomas in 1170. The king, in a fit of rage, asked for someone to "rid me of this turbulent priest". Four knights, taking their king at his word, murdered

Thomas in the north transept of Canterbury Cathedral. His shrine became a place of pilgrimage almost overnight, and it was the stories recounted by just such a group of pilgrims that became the basis of Chaucer's *Canterbury Tales* (see box story on Canterbury Cathedral p95).

Over the following centuries, political struggles and wars continued unabated, whilst the church remained relatively unaffected. Churches and cathedrals were built, many schools and colleges were founded in the 15th century, some of them linked to religious institutions.

Protestantism & the Reformation

This existing state of affairs was to be torn apart by Henry VIII (see box story p20). Henry's insistence on producing a son was stalled by the ban on divorce by the Catholic church, and the Pope's refusal to annul the marriage, leading to years of wrangling and bitter dissent, and the martyrdom of such leading figures as the Lord Chancellor, Sir Thomas More. Henry broke spiritually and intellectually with Rome, and founded the Church of England, which is still the country's official religion today. When Henry dissolved the country's religious institutions, it was a further physical symbol of his break with Rome, and a consolidation of the Reformation in England.

Canterbury Cathedral

Canterbury Cathedral, the Archbishop's seat of power.

the Cathedral after the fire of 1067, his successors added and remodelled certain parts of the church, and fire destroyed much of the structure in 1174. The murder of Thomas à Becket in the north transept of the cathedral, made Canterbury into the most important pilgrimage centre in northern Europe, and the cathedral was rebuilt to reflect this status. Today, only parts of the Great Cloister date from the 11th century. The choir and Trinity Chapel are 12th century, and the nave and cloister are mainly 14th and 15th century.

Inevitably, with such an important religious monument, there are always hoards of visitors in Canterbury Cathedral, and you can easily lose a sense of quiet calm, as you are swept along by multi-lingual crowds. Try not to rush round the cathedral. Take it slowly - it is huge - and switch off from the babble of voices around you.

London is unquestionably the financial and political capital of England, but **Canterbury** is the country's ecclesiastical centre. Saint Augustine preached in the city in AD 597, and was consecrated as the first archbishop. The original cathedral was burnt down in 1067, and in the light of recent archaeological findings, the history of Anglo-Saxon architecture may well have to be re-written. Excavations being carried out while the nave is currently being repaved, show that there was a huge cathedral on the site in the 10th century, contradicting the prevailing view that the Anglo-Saxons built only small churches. Excavations have shown that this nave was as wide, as long and almost as high as the present one, built by the Normans.

In such a magnificent cathedral, there is so much to see, but one of the most striking things is the shrine to Saint Thomas. On the spot where the saintly archbishop was murdered on the orders of the king, there is a strikingly stark, modern sculpture, dedicated in 1986. The original shrine was destroyed in 1538, during Henry VIII's Dissolution of the Monasteries. There are beautiful medieval stained-glass windows as well as some in modern glass. The cathedral contains two important tombs, the brass effigy of the Black Prince and that of the only English king to be buried in the cathedral, Henry IV.

Pilgrims & tales

Lanfranc, the first Norman archbishop re-built

After the death of Saint Thomas, pilgrims flocked to Canterbury, and in 1380 Geoffrey Chaucer wrote the wonderful series of tales, *The Canterbury Tales* in which a group of pilgrims making their way to Canterbury entertain each other with a series of stories, many of which are as fresh and hilarious today as they were 600 years ago.

From Druids to Hare Krishna

Among the more interesting manifestations of the famed English eccentricity is a ritual that takes place each year at the pre-historic site of **Stonehenge** in Wiltshire, when a group of Druids celebrate the summer solstice. The sight of white-robed figures, arms stretched out to welcome the dawn, is one of the perennial images of the early English summer. The number of Druids in England is small, but they are an accepted, if not a totally understood, lot. There are currently 12 Druid orders in the country, with such stirring names as the Order of Bards, Ovates and Druids.

Motorway's & dragons

There is a fairly strong sense of environmental awareness among these groups. For example, concerned that a wood in southeast London would be destroyed if a proposed six-lane motor way was constructed, a group called "The Dragon" is taking action in a decidedly unconventional way. The Dragon, an umbrella group consisting of witches, Odinists, druids, magicians and other neo-pagan groups, has a plan of action which involves throwing a protective ring of magic around the wood. They hold energy raising sessions under a full moon, and use symbolic spells and potions. Quite what the Department of Transport thinks about all this is difficult to say, but if "The Dragon's" magic and potions can arouse public interest in the cult and/or their concerns, they will be happy.

Hare Krishna devotees

As well as these "indigenous" groups, which have links, however tenuous, to ancient British mythology and history, there are many other religious splinter groups, including a flourishing Indian import, the Hare Krishna movement. Young people in pink robes, their heads shaven but their feet often incongruously wrapped up in woolly socks and boots, are a familiar sight in London. Sometimes they ask passers-by to sign petitions, at other times they dance in a peaceful procession down **Oxford Street**, their Indian musical instruments competing with the din of the traffic. In July 1993, the London Hare Krishna movement celebrated its 25th birthday in typical style, staging a *rath yatra* (chariot-procession), through the streets.

The Catholics never truly regained influence in England, despite staunchly Catholic monarchs like Henry's eldest daughter, Mary, and figureheads like Mary Queen of Scots and the Stuarts. Under King James, an authorized translation of the Bible was made in 1611, still in use today, and universally known as the *King James Version*.

In the second half of the 17th century, fears that there might be a Catholic heir to King James II prompted a group of leading Protestants to invite the Dutch leader, Prince William of Orange to come to England. The king fled, and in 1688, the Protestant monarchs William and Mary became king and queen. In 1689 a Bill of Rights was passed, establishing the principle that only a Protestant could be crowned. This is still applicable today.

The Church of England today

There are more parish churches than pubs in England, yet many are rarely used, and are kept open mainly for tourists. On Sunday mornings, many

Stonehenge has been interpreted by some as a temple to the sun.

people are more likely to head off to the hyper-market to do the weekly shopping, or to a car-boot sale to rummage around for bargains, than attend their parish church. Most people are however married in church and the great majority have a christian funeral, such that the church remains an important institution. Geographically many churches which were originally built in busy working class areas during the 19th century, may today be stranded in the middle of slum clearances or new traffic developments, their original congregations long since dispersed.

There are various solutions to the fate of these unused buildings. One is the Redundant Churches Fund which was set up by law in 1969, to preserve churches that are no longer needed for regular worship, but are of historic, architectural or archaeological importance. The Fund's churches are still consecrated and in most respects indistinguishable from churches in regular use. They are scattered widely throughout England, and range from charmingly simple buildings in lovely settings to others of greater richness and importance.

All however, lack congregations. For buildings not protected by this fund, the Church of England actively looks for alternative uses for churches which have to be closed, occasionally accepting their conversion to restaurants, art galleries, concert halls, and, increasingly, into homes.

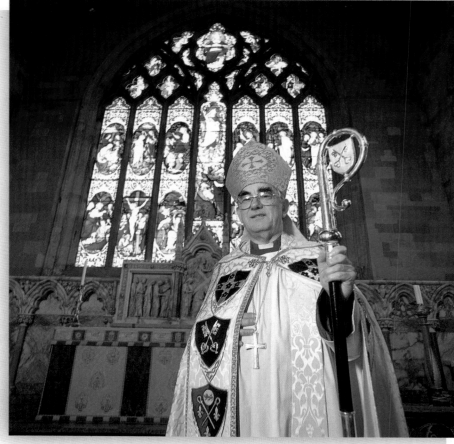

A Bishop in his vestments.

Women priests?

Although the Church of England is still the established church, with the monarch at its head, it is currently in the throes of one of the most divisive controversies ever. Anglicans, as followers of the Church of England are called, are bitterly divided over the issue of the ordination of women, which the General Synod of the Church voted in favour of in November 1992, to be confirmed by the Parliamentary Ecclesiastical Committee in July 1993. Although there is no doubt in the minds of most English people over the equality of women, yet there are some Anglicans who are so bitterly opposed to the notion of female clergy, that they have chosen instead to leave the Church of England, and convert to Catholicism.

Many Anglican priests have contacted the Roman Catholic church, to discuss their future, in what has been described as potentially the biggest schism in western Christianity since the Reformation.

Meanwhile, the issue of female ordination will be further debated by both houses of Parliament, as well as the General Synod of the Church of England, but by 1994, the first women priests will be ordained.

Beyond the established church

Nearly three out of four Britons believe in God, and a third believe in the devil - that is, of course, if you believe in opinion polls. Yet "established" religions are on the decline.

Only 1 in 5 religiously active people is an Anglican, and even though there are actually more active Roman Catholics, between them the two churches only account for 40 percent of the population. Besides this there are the other protestant denominations of Methodist and Baptist, there are also immigrant religions and various cults and charismatic churches.

The main religions of the Indian sub-continent, Islam, Hinduism and Sikhism, are all strongly implanted in England. The early immigrants brought their faiths with them, and given the high birth rates amongst Britons of Asian origin, these religions are flourishing. In cities with large ethnic communities you can find mosques, temples and gurdwaras, alongside churches and synagogues. Of all these faiths, Islam is the fastest growing, new mosques open regularly, and there is an increasing demand for separate Muslim schools.

Charismatic churches tend to emphasise the miraculous, spiritual side of the Christian Bible, rather than dwelling on sin and dogma. Although nowhere near as established as in the American Bible Belt, there are pockets of England, especially in the south, where there are thousands of followers of these independent Christian churches.

The New Age movement & neo-paganism

The New Age movement is rather difficult to define. It is not exactly a religion, nor is it a cult, since adherents do not follow a particular leader or belief. Rather, the New Age movement is a non-mainstream amalgam of various ideas and beliefs, all pointing in the general direction of transformation. The movement believes that people should get in touch with their spirit and with their emotions, via a fusion of Christianity, Buddhism, Hinduism, and environmental awareness, making use of crystal balls and alternative medicine. There is a small, but growing neo-pagan movement in England; most English would however describe themselves as agnostic and rarely as atheists.

Festivals & Celebrations

101

By and large, the English are not an ostentatious people and as such they are not given to public displays of behaviour, even when it comes to celebrations. As a result, most English festivities tend to be low-key, rather private affairs. Christmas, the major festival of the year is a decidedly "family" and indoor affair. Morris-dancing and may-pole dancing, do take place every spring, but they are minority events, as is the colourful spectacle of the Notting Hill Carnival. This absence of public celebration is, to a certain extent, replaced by the celebration of certain events on the social calendar; the races, for example, or the cricket season.

The magic of Christmas.

Bank holidays

The country's public holidays are known by the somewhat strange name of "bank holi-

The Royal Procession at Ascot.

days". Bank holidays were designated as such under the Bank Holiday Act of 1871, a Victorian attempt to reduce the number of holidays on which banks were closed.

The lucky bank employees of the early 19th century had 40 saints' days and anniversaries as holidays, but to-day's bankers have far fewer – only 8 days. These coincide with the major Christian festivals of Christmas, Good Friday and Easter, as well as May Day, Boxing Day (26 December), New Year's Day, and two other days – the last Monday in May and the last Monday in August.

Today, though the name remains, bank holidays are in no way limited only to banks, in fact most working people are "off work" on these days. A typical calendar of public holidays and social fixtures throughout the year is outlined below.

The New Year

The year opens on a holiday note, as **New Year's Day** is a public holiday. The night of New Year's Eve is the real time of celebration when it is especially popular to go to the pub. The New Year is usually hailed Scottish fashion with the fraternity song "Ald Lang Syne" and the alcohol but without the bag-pipes. This is also a popular night for balls, discos and of course, watching TV. Thus New Years' Day is for most a recovery day and a time to think of the traditional New Years' resolution; perhaps giving up smoking or being nice to your mother-in-law.

The more energetic will however head off to find bargains in the many **January sales**. These department store sales are big events, and every year you will read stories in the press, of people camping outside Harrods or Selfridges for 3 days, their sights set on a fur coat at a give-away price. Huddled in their sleeping bags, they talk longingly of their great bargain-to-be, ignoring the cold weather and the competition.

Remembering loved ones

St Valentine's Day on 14 February is the occasion for sending cards, flowers or perhaps even chocolates to your loved one; cards are traditionally unsigned, so as to mystify the recipient. This is there-fore a very exciting time for the unmar-ried who may be alerted to a secret admirer, or perhaps the disappointment of a friend playing a joke. **Mother's Day**, falls around March – much earlier than the American one – this is another day for sending cards and bouquets of flowers as a token of appreciation to "mums" and "grannies".

Easter & Lent

Shrove Tuesday, often called "Pancake Tuesday", heralds the beginning of the

The Easter egg symbolizes new life and it is often a yummy chocolate one.

pre-Easter Lenten period. In order to use up all the rich ingredients that would be banned during the austere days of Lent, housewives made pancakes – a tradi-tion which survives to this day, although few people actually fast during Lent anymore. Pancake races – where people race with frying pans and toss pancakes – are held in many towns.

Every year, on **Maundy Thursday**, (the Thursday preceding Easter Sunday), the Queen goes to Westminster Abbey, where she distributes Maundy Money. The monarch distributes alms to poor people, a ceremony which has evolved from an older tradition of the monarch washing the feet of the poor. Special silver coins have been minted for the occasion since 1662, and a penny is

Morris–dancing

Origins of a dance

Morris-dancing is thought by some, to be derived from the formal dances of the Moors, and may have been brought to England by King Edward

For an art form that is the closest thing England has to a national dance, morris-dancing has consistently aroused the wrong kind of emotions. Hilarity and a slight sense of the ridiculous accompany any reference to this ancient dance form. For the stiff-upper-lip style of most English men, the notion of dancing about, clashing sticks and wearing bells on your shoes, is unthinkable. So the few adherents which this traditional dance has, soldier on, misunderstood and used to gentle teasing.

III. An alternative theory as to the dance's origins is that the name Moorish came about because the dancers blackened their faces as part of their ritual disguise. Whatever its true origin, it has been part of the celebration of May Day in rural England, since the 15th century.

Protest dance

The issue of morris-dancing was brought to the attention of the public in the spring of 1993, when, in protest at the abolition of the May Day holiday, 200 morris-men and women danced outside the Houses of Parliament in London. It was probably the most agitated protest concerning May Day since 1648, when Oliver Cromwell tried to ban the holiday. People died in the riots. The 1993 protest was calmer, though Cromwell's statue was roundly booed.

Partnering a Morris man

Today, a decidedly minority past-time, 10,000 dancers are nevertheless affiliated to the Morris and Morris Federation. The organization is currently involved in a major internal quarrel, over the issue of female morris dancers. Along with a handful of London dining clubs, the Morris Ring, the largest morris dancing organization in England, is a male-only preserve. So, the country's 1,000 or so female dancers have set up rival, women-only dancing groups. In language worthy of a bitter political fight, a spokesman for the male-only Morris Ring said "If we say it's OK for women to dance, we'll split the organisation down the middle. It's a minefield." Strong words for a folk dancer.

given for each year of the monarch's reign.

    Easter usually falls in the early spring, and is not only a major religious

festival, but it is also one of the first long weekend holidays – there are bank holidays on Good Friday and on the day following Easter Sunday.

For devout Christians, **Good Friday** is a day of prayer, for the less religious minded, it is usually a day of horrendous traffic jams, as everyone heads off to the beach or the countryside for the long weekend.

On **Easter Sunday**, children indulge in chocolate eggs, the egg being intended to symbolize the new life which has come into being with the resurrection of Christ.

St George's & May Day

The twenty-third of April is St George's Day. Saint George was a 3rd century Christian martyr, most famous for his heroic deed of rescuing a maiden from a dragon – an act much popularized by medieval art. His cult was revered by the crusaders and during the reign of King Edward III (1327-77) he became the patron saint of England, but no festivities or celebrations take place to remember the saint today.

May Day is a strange sort of day in England, for it is both a recently introduced public holiday that is in the process of being abolished, and at the same time, a day for traditional celebrations, in which hardly anyone participates.

The May Day bank holiday was established by the Labour government in the 1970s, but is scheduled to be axed. The last May Day bank holiday will take place in 1994. Therefore those people who have always celebrated May Day in traditional style, are understandably unhappy. For the Morris dancers of England May 1 has always been a special day, the decision to end the holiday therefore led to mass protests and a number of Morris-men journeyed to the Houses of Parliament to stage a demonstration, but to no avail.

Another May Day tradition takes place every year in the most unlikely venue of the roof of an Oxford college tower. Every May Day, at dawn, the choristers of Magdalen College climb to the top of Magdalen Tower, and at 0600 hours, welcome the spring morning with a Latin hymn, *Te deum*.

Tradition has it that the young choristers used to sing a much longer selection on May Day morning, but some 200 years ago, on 1 May 1773, tired and soaked to the skin by the downpour that greeted them, the young choristers cut short their programme, substituting *Te deum* instead, and the hymn has remained ever since. Get there early as the crowds are usually big.

Colour & exuberance at the Notting Hill Carnival.

Summer socials

The only public holidays between May and Christmas, are two bank holidays, which do not celebrate any event in particular, but are always the occasion for long week-ends.

The last Monday in May and the last Monday in August, are both known, logically enough, as Bank Holiday Mondays. These are good days to stay at home for mass exoduses out of the major cities cause major traffic jams.

The August bank holiday sees the world famous **Notting Hill Carnival**, the second biggest street carnival in the world. This is an extremely colourful event in the diaries of British west-Indi-

Henley-on-Thames regatta, a big event on both the sporting and
the social calendar.

Christmas

Christmas remains the most popular celebration in England, and although it has deep religious significance for practising Christians, commemorating as it does the birth of Jesus Christ, it is, above all, a family celebration. For most people in England Christmas is a time to be with their family, to exchange presents, to eat well, and to enjoy the pleasures of home.

The race to Christmas

Preparations for Christmas seem to begin earlier and earlier each year, as shops and businesses try to make the most of this present buying extravaganza. Most of a family's time and money is lavished on its children, for whom Christmas remains a magical event. Department stores have elaborate window displays for Christmas, and grottos, where children can meet benevolent "Father Christmas" (Santa Claus), sit on his lap and tell him what they hope he will bring them this year.

Other preparations include making Christmas cakes and puddings, ordering the turkey and sending Christmas cards. These cards are an all important part of this season of "good will", often being the only time in the year when distant friends keep in touch.

Decorations & nativity scenes

In the weeks preceding Christmas, groups of carol singers visit homes, singing traditional songs, known as Christmas carols, usually to raise money for a church or a charity or a school. Shortly before Christmas Day, a Christmas tree is set up inside the house, and decorated with lights and baubles; a fairy is usually placed on the top-most branch of the tree. A miniature crib may be set up in the home – a model representing the manger in Bethlehem where Jesus was born, populated by those who witnessed the great event. Holly and mistletoe are also used to decorate homes.

Schools stage Nativity plays and carol concerts and by the time the school holidays arrive, the children are getting more and more excited, whilst the adults shop for last-minute presents and food.

The magic of Christmas

On Christmas Eve, before going to bed, children hang up their Christmas stockings, convinced that some time after midnight, Father Christmas (historically St Nicholas) will visit their home and fill the empty stocking to the brim with presents and sweets. Many people go to a midnight church service on Christmas Eve, and for Roman Catholics, midnight mass is very popular.

Christmas morning passes by in a frenzy of present opening, and preparations for the huge Christmas lunch, which is usually a large, late, family affair. Turkey still holds pride of place on the Christmas Day menu; it is often stuffed with chestnuts, or sage and onions, and is served with a bread sauce. Accompanying the turkey

ans but does not affect the country at large.

Although public holidays might be thin on the ground over the summer, this is still the busiest time of the year for holiday makers and socialites alike. Since schools close during July and August, these are naturally the peak months for family holidays.

The summer is also the time for some of England's most enduring rituals, usually sporting events, which are celebrated with much tradition, pomp and style. Events such as the Wimbledon Lawn Tennis championships, racing at Ascot, the Henley regatta, and

are roast potatoes, Brussels sprouts, peas and, especially in a household with young children, all of this will be served to the accompanying sound of Christmas crackers. These paper crackers make a loud, explosive sound when pulled apart by two people.

Inside can be found little gifts, paper hats, and an all important motto or joke written on a slip of paper. So, paper hats on, the turkey carved, and the meal moves on towards its triumphant conclusion; Christmas pudding, one of the misunderstood gems of English cuisine. A rich, dark-brown, suet-based, alcohol soaked pudding, it is delicious served with brandy butter. If anyone is still hungry after such a mammoth lunch, mince pies (small pastry shells filled with mixed fruit), and Christmas cake, (a rich fruit cake, iced and decorated with Christmas themes) will be served during the afternoon.

Greetings from the Queen

At 1500 hours, another seasonal ritual takes place, the Queen's Christmas Day message, to her subjects at home and overseas. The day winds to a sleepy, happy close, the children playing with their new toys, the adults dozing off peacefully, knowing that the next day, Boxing Day, is also a holiday.

Most people also know what will be on the menu for the 26th and for the next few days, turkey, and yet more turkey. By the time New Year's Eve comes, no one can bear the thought of yet another turkey sandwich!

yachting at Cowes in the Isle of Wight, are classics in the English sporting and social calendar.

June is the month to be in England, and never mind the weather, for Wimbledon, Ascot and Henley follow hard on each other's heels. July sees Cowes Week, and 12 August, better known as

"The Glorious Twelfth" is when the grouse shooting season officially opens. For non-sporting types, there is the open-air opera at Glyndebourne and concerts at London's Kenwood Park.

The Christmas break

The winter is dominated by the big build-up to Christmas, a festival celebrating the birth of Jesus nearly 2,000 years ago, but increasingly dominated by the spirit of commercialism celebrated by non-Christians too. The 25th of December, **Christmas Day**, is very much a family day, when parents, grand-parents and grand-children get together to eat, and exchange Christmas presents.

Unique to the UK, the 26 December, **Boxing Day**, is also a public holiday, and provides a much needed opportunity for rest after the excesses of the previous day. The origins of Boxing Day lie in the 19th century, when the custom arose of giving tips to servants and maids in the form of "Christmas Boxes", hence the name.

Nowadays, Boxing Day is a day for working off the excesses of the previous day's lunch, and you can see families out for long walks, the children excitedly trying out that new bicycle or pair of roller-skates that Santa Claus brought them on Christmas Day. New Years resolutions are traditionally made on 1st January, for many people after a season of eating, this understandably means going on a diet!

nglishmen can justly claim that one aspect of their country's artistic and literary history has had a wide-reaching influence, far beyond the national boundary, namely the English language. Without entering into a debate on the rights and wrongs of history, it is probably true to say that England's cultural influence is inextricably linked with the country's former colonial status, which explains why, today, so many millions of Indians and Africans speak with such fluency, "The Queen's English". The language of Chaucer and Shakespeare may well have been altered virtually out of recognition by its many speakers, both inside as well as outside the country, but it is one of the world's truly universal languages – perhaps the only one.

The Royal Albert Hall, the venue for the annual Promenade concerts popularly known as "The Proms".

Architectural aces

England has an extremely rich and varied architectural heritage, from the Neolithic sites of **Stonehenge** and **Avebury** in Wiltshire, **Hadri-**

The Tate Gallery, London, has the finest collection of modern art.

an's Wall, in Northumberland, built by the Romans, through to the glories of the medieval cathedrals, via functional Victorian terrace housing, and on to avant-garde developments, such as the London **Docklands**. The country is literally chequered with history. There are castles, some ruined some still inhabited; stately homes, some run by outside agencies, some still lived in by their traditional families; there are priories, monasteries, cathedrals, museums and art galleries with top class collections.

This historical legacy, as well as the busy theatre and music scene, attracts visitors, millions of them each year. Britain, as opposed to just England, is one of the world's top 5 tourist destinations, earning a cool £25 billion in tour-

ist money, a year. In 1992, there were 18.1 million visitors, a 9% increase over the previous year, and they spent £7.6 billion.

Culture throughout the country

Although London undoubtedly dominates the country's cultural scene, with its long-established legacy of art collections and museums, there is a very welcome, growing tendency towards decentralisation. Other cities in England are energetically claiming their share of the country's cultural heritage, and increasingly, visitors to England will come across major collections in many different cities, which certainly lessens the risk of cultural indigestion in London. There are definite advantages in decentralising collections, for space is more plentiful, and less expensive, the further away from London you go. To borrow jargon from the computer industry, museums are becoming increasingly "user friendly", with more flexible timings, and a judicious balance between allowing greater access to exhibits, whilst at the same time protecting them.

The Yorkshire industrial town of Bradford, for example, is home to the **National Museum of Photography, Film and Television**. It has proved immensely popular and successful (and not only because admission is free), and amongst other things, you can see films projected there as they were originally intended to be seen, from silent movies to Cinemascope projections.

Yorkshire is also home to three extremely successful museums, all in the ancient city of York, and covering a wide spectrum of interests. The **National Railway Museum** is the kind of museum that parents ostensibly visit "for the children", and then proceed to clamber enthusiastically in and out of the old steam trains on display. These include a replica of Stephenson's *Rocket*, and, much more up-to-date, a section of the Channel Tunnel.

The **Jorvik Viking Centre** is a highly innovative museum, for it not only displays the Viking history of York, but also exposes visitors to the sounds and smells of York, 1,000 years ago. You sit in "time

A young artist dabbles on a painting.

cars" that take you through a reconstructed Viking village, which is on the site of the actual archaeological dig, and the "drive" through the museum takes you through the dig itself, where you can see many of the objects, exactly where they were found, and as they were found. For those with a taste for archaeology, York's other innovative museum is the **Arc**, the country's first "hands-on" archaeology centre. Arc stands for Archaeological Resource Centre, and visitors are encouraged to handle old objects recovered from digs, as well as work with the archaeologists on their inter-active computer displays.

At the opposite end of the country, the pretty fishing village of **St Ives**, tucked away on Cornwall's rugged, northern

London architecture

The magnificent interior of St Paul's Cathedral.

A few years ago, His Royal Highness the Prince of Wales made a frank comment on a new building in London. He called it a "carbuncle", and his choice of words not only outraged the poor architect, but it also provoked much debate in the country about the role of modern architecture, on the nature of urban construction and on what is, or is not, aesthetic architecture. It is an on-going debate, and one to which there will never be a definitive answer, but people now are much more vocal in their opinions on architecture, and how they want their cities, and especially, their capital city, to look.

London has architecture dating from the Romans to the present day, often cheek by jowl. The Roman excavations along the City's **London Wall**, are a stone's throw from the new Nat

West Tower, the new Lloyds building, and, a little further away, the controversial Docklands development (see chapter on London p123). London has glorious architecture, as well as some unmitigated aesthetic disasters. Amongst the former, there are **Westminster Abbey** and **St Paul's Cathedral**, and amongst the latter, the Centrepoint office block at Tottenham Court Road, a highly expensive flop.

Part of the excitement of a massive project like the development of the unfashionable East End and the dock area of London, was that old warehouses and factories were revitalised, and the potential of a relatively under-developed area was realised. Yet it has been dogged by controversy since the outset. The need for an integrated transport system was clear, but its financing was less so. The recession that followed hard on the heels of the free-spending 1980s, has jeopardised the success of certain sectors of **Docklands**, notably that of the huge **Canary Wharf** development.

"Traditional" London architecture includes a whole panoply of buildings, all eminently suitable for a capital city. There is **Buckingham Palace**, the London residence of the Queen, as well as the smaller **St James' Palace**. There are 3 cathedrals, many churches of all denominations, and the 1977 **Regent's Park Mosque**. Between Holborn and the River Thames are the Inns of Court, the ancient, traditional system of legal colleges, whilst the Houses of Parliament are further down the Embankment.

A happy and successful synthesis of old buildings with new functions, is the **Covent Garden** area, which, ever since the former fruit and vegetable market moved out, has been home to restaurants, shops and wine bars. The area has been revitalised, and is one of the city's more popular districts, where serious opera goers rub shoulders with punks, where you can sit outdoors and eat, and watch mime artists and fire-eaters perform against the backdrop of **St Paul's church**, designed by Inigo Jones in the early 17th century.

coast-line, is an out-post of the London **Tate Gallery**, which opened its latest

collection there in June 1993. St Ives has attracted artists for generations, begin-

A Cambridge treasure

King's College Chapel, Cambridge, one of the true greats of English architecture.

Of all the beautiful colleges in the magnificent university city of Cambridge, **King's College** is the most outstanding. Henry VI granted King's College its charter in 1441, and laid the foundation stone of its chapel in 1446, but work was halted by the Wars of the Roses, and it was Henry VIII who eventually completed it in 1515.

Although King's college itself is splendid, and naturally has an impressive academic history and pedigree, it is **King's College Chapel** that is the glory of the college. The chapel is vast, 248 m (289 ft long), 30 m (94 ft) high and 13m (40 ft) wide, yet has an ethereal delicacy about it. Delicate columns soar 26 m (80 ft) high towards a magnificent fan-vaulted ceiling. The intricately carved screen and choir stalls are fine examples of Renaissance craftsmanship, and date from the mid-16th century. After the chapel was finished in 1515, Flemish craftsmen spent 26 more years putting in the glass of brilliant reds and blues, and subtle greys and yellows. The chapel's stained glass forms the most complete set of Renaissance windows to survive in any church in the country.

The chapel's treasures keep on increasing, and in 1962, the college was presented with a Rubens painting, *The Adoration of the Magi*, which is on display in the chapel. Every Christmas the chapel is the setting for the Festival of Nine Carols and Lessons, which can be heard on national radio.

ning with the English landscape painter, Turner, who first visited the village in the early 19th century, to be followed later by Whistler and Sickert. The early decades of the 20th century saw the village becoming the focal point for an influential group of artists, including Ben Nicholson, Christopher Wood, and Barbara Hepworth, the sculptor whose name is most closely associated with St Ives, where she lived and worked from 1949 until her death in 1975. Her pretty, white-washed studio, with its workshop and garden, have become a museum of her works, many of which are displayed in the garden. Inevitably, any project of the magnitude of the Tate Gallery's western arm, which cost £3.3 million to build, is bound to arouse controversy. Although a majority of the townspeople welcome the new gallery, feeling it restores well-deserved artistic prestige to St Ives, there have inevitably been critics, who feel that the money could have

19th century poetic eloquence, Hyde Park, London.

been better spent elsewhere.

Historic houses & monuments

England is rich in monuments, churches, galleries, Roman remains, and generally, the country's past has been effectively and efficiently preserved. Some properties are still in private hands, but increasingly, bodies such as the National Trust and English Heritage undertake the running and financing of much of the country's heritage. A major pre-historic site like **Stonehenge**, is currently at the centre of much discussion as to its future, for there are conflicting views on access and on the type of facili-ties deemed necessary for the millions of visitors.

Many of England's stately homes and gardens have gone distinctly commercial and "visitor-friendly". No longer is it enough to offer just a stunning art collection or 18th century landscaped gardens. More and more stately homes are now surrounded by theme parks, mini zoos and amusement rides, a development which leaves purists saddened, but is probably an economic necessity. And if the lure of a safari, or a maze, or an adventure park, attracts families who might not otherwise visit an ancient site, possibly the commercialisation has not all been in vain.

Longleat, the superb Elizabethan family home of the Seventh Marquess of

The Parsonage, Haworth

The Yorkshire Pennines are not a place for the faint-hearted. Their dramatic bleakness can seem daunting at times, but they have a wild beauty that inspired some of the most dramatic prose of the 19th century. Charlotte Brontë's novel *Wuthering Heights* is as much about this Yorkshire landscape, as about the lives of the tormented families who inhabited the moors that surround the village of Haworth. A visit to the Parsonage, which was built in 1779, and where the 3 talented Brontë sisters later lived, explains much about their books. A hike out onto the moors will explain even more.

Haworth is a typical Yorkshire hill village, with a steep, cobbled main street, lined with rows of tiny terrace houses, formerly occupied by textile workers. At the time when the village's most famous family lived there, there were more than 1,200 hand looms in operation. The Reverend Patrick Brontë, his wife, 5 daughters and son came to live at Haworth Parsonage in 1820. It was to be the family's home for the

rest of their lives. Maria and Elizabeth, the eldest girls, died here in childhood, not long after their mother. Charlotte, Branwell, Emily and Anne, all of them creative people of varying degrees of talent, lived in the Parsonage for all their adult lives. Emily died in the Parsonage in 1848, when she was only 30-years-old.

Charlotte's novel *Jane Eyre* and Emily's *Wuthering Heights* were both written in this house. Even in Charlotte Brontë's own lifetime, an ever-increasing stream of visitors came to visit the house hoping to glimpse this extraordinary woman writer. The least known of the trio, Anne, died and was buried in Scarborough, on the Yorkshire coast (see chapter on Yorkshire p.367) but her sisters are buried in Haworth churchyard. The Parsonage rooms have as far as possible been restored to their appearance in the early 1850s. Anne's writing desk lies on the dining-room table, and personal objects are on display, giving a revealing glimpse of their lives of genteel hardship.

Bath, and the first stately home to be opened to the public, was the first to dip a toe in the world of commercialisation. Back in 1966, the **Longleat Safari Park** was opened, famous for its lions, and one of the earliest of the now ubiquitous car stickers used to be, "I've seen the lions of Longleat." The merchandising of Longleat continues, and today's visitors face a bewildering choice: a much enlarged safari park, a butter-

fly garden, a narrow-gauge railway, the world's largest maze (as confirmed by the *Guinness Book of Records*), and "Postman Pat's Village", aimed at younger visitors, who are avid followers of the TV series. There is also, of course, a wonderful Elizabethan house, which is rather over-looked amidst all the amusement fanfare.

Similarly, at one of the country's most prestigious homes, the magnificent 18th century **Blenheim Pal-**

The Beatles

Do you remember *The Beatles* and the "Beatle-mania" they aroused? Screaming fans and sell-out concerts? Their path-breaking long hair, and unconventional clothes? The hippy trail, Ravi Shankar, and Indian sitar music? Royal recognition of success, with the award of an OBE and the scandal of their subsequent, uncer-emonious return to Buckingham Palace? No? Well, you do not have to be a child of the 1960s, to recognize their music, surely? Songs such as *I want to hold your hand, Eleanor Rigby* and *Sgt Pepper's Lonely Hearts Club Band* are now solidly part of musical culture. *The Beatles* have be-come mainstream.

The 4 members of the group, all from a working-class Liverpool background, were Paul McCartney, John Lennon, George Harrison and Ringo Starr. McCartney and Lennon first got together to sing and play in 1956, Harrison joined them a year later, and after the death of an earlier member in 1962, Starr joined them, and the rest, as the cliché goes, was history. Club appearances in their native Liverpool and also in Hamburg preceded their first recording contract in 1962, and their early hits made them the most popular rock group in England.

"Beatlemania" crossed the Atlantic in 1964, when *The Beatles* made their first ever US televi-sion appearance, and their songs were released there. In just 4 years of public performances, virtually all their songs were instant hits, and they also appeared in two well received films, *A Hard Day's Night* (1964) and the following year, *Help!*

Nowadays, when people accept just about anything in the way of dress, hair style and mannerisms; in a world where men wear ear-rings and pony tails, and women have short hair and live in jeans, it is difficult to re-capture the enormous influence that 4 young men could have on society. Yet they did, from their long hair, their avowed "hippy" lifestyle, their ex-periments with hallucinogenic drugs and their flirtation with Indian mysticism. *The Beatles* set trends in what they did, where they went, how they looked, and, overwhelmingly, in what they wrote, sung and played.

In 1971, The Beatles went their separate ways. Paul McCartney founded his own very successful band called *Wings*, and has gone on to produce consistently excellent music, even writing an orchestral symphony, which received good-ish reviews. George Harrison worked a little on his own, and with Lennon and Starr in the 1970s, while Ringo Starr took to films. John Lennon, went his own increasingly controver-sial way with his equally controversial Japanese wife, Yoko Ono, and along with political activ-ism, produced some fine music, before being wantonly murdered in 1980. The music and the fame lives on, of what must have been "pop" music's greatest sensation. It was a revolution that was to change the face of "pop" music forever.

ace (the Oxfordshire birthplace of Sir Winston Churchill), a mere 549 m (600 yard) away from the palace are all the modern trappings of 20th century tour-ism. No longer is it enough to have a tea-room and a shop selling guide-books and postcards, as the **Blenheim Pleas-ure Gardens** complex proves. On offer are a putting green, a childrens' inflat-able castle, a butterfly house, an adven-ture play area, and a maze. This one also has a statistical claim to fame – this time it is the world's largest symbolic hedge maze.

Even one of the most symbolically important places in England, **Land's End**, at the extreme western tip of Corn-wall, has not escaped the current enthu-siasm for leisure complexes. If the sheer, magical beauty of the rugged coast line at Land's End is not enough to enthuse visitors, they can wander round the man-

West End theatre, part of London's cultural scene.

A summer's day at Covent Garden.

made "Land's End", a large complex built a few yards in from the headland, offering everything from a "Smellorium" to what is billed as "the number one multi-sensory experience".

The entertainment business

The English **theatre** scene is a healthy and active one, for there are a wide choice of plays, operas and ballets on offer, the majority of them in London, but not exclusively so. London's West End, the theatre district, has everything from hit musicals, such as *Cats* and *Phantom of the Opera* to the long-running Agatha Christie play, *The Mousetrap,* which has become virtually a permanent fixture on the theatre scene. **Covent Garden** offers excellent opera and ballet performed by their own companies, and many visiting dance troupes come to London.

Outside London, there are theatres in most towns, with excellent regional dance and opera troupes based in the north of England. At Christmas, most towns will have a pantomime, a traditional burlesque, in which the leading male role is always played by a woman, and the leading comic female role, by a man.

Music *fantastico*

The country's leading orchestras, such

as the Royal Philharmonic, and the London Philharmonic, are well known and of a high standard, and music lovers will find many excellent concerts in London, at the **South Bank** complex, or at the **Royal Albert Hall.** For 8 weeks each summer, from mid-July to mid-September, London's Royal Albert Hall is the magnet to which thousands of music lovers are drawn, for it hosts the Promenade Concerts, universally known as "The Proms". This tradition of summer music dates back to 1895, when the conductor Henry Wood inaugurated them. Nearly 100 years later, the orchestral concerts are just as popular, the Royal Albert Hall is usually filled to its capacity of 7,000 people, during the Proms season. The concerts which are sponsored by the British Broadcasting Corporation (BBC) are televised.

The climax of the Proms concerts is the last performance of the season, known, logically, as "the last night of the Proms", which features thousands of vociferous music lovers, and a sense of fun and a noise level not usually seen at classical music performances.

Books & TV

The English literary scene is at an interesting juncture, for many of the country's brightest and most successful writers are not ethnically English. Very often from Commonwealth countries, though fully assimilated into mainstream English life, they write with a

Punk, rock and base.

freshness and a sense of colour that makes their work deservedly popular. Although television has had a negative impact on the reading public, the literary world continues to flourish. Genuine interest is aroused each year at the time of the book awards, especially for the most prestigious of them all, the Booker Prize.

American "soap operas" and game shows are as popular in England as they are across the Atlantic, and the country's broadcasting industry is fully aware of the competition. Accepting that independent television channels are winning increasing numbers of viewers, the hitherto venerable BBC is re-thinking its approach, and aiming to reach out more to the mass market.

London

123

London is the capital city of England and also of the United Kingdom, and unquestionably the most important city in the country. Despite moves to decentralise everything from government to the arts, London still overwhelmingly dominates England. London is home to the monarchy and to the Houses of Parliament, the Bank of England, the Inns of Court, and the country's major theatres and art galleries. It is a large, sprawling city, as noisy and busy as any other world capital, but it is a must for any tourist. The sightseeing, shopping, eating and nightlife opportunities are endless here. There is, let's face it, far too much to see, do, observe and enjoy here, such that one visit can never be enough. Since everything in London just can not be covered, we

London's most famous bridge, Tower Bridge and the Tower of London.

England

Scotland

*North
Sea*

*Northern
Ireland*

Northumberland

Tyne
&-Wear

Cumbria   Durham

*Isle of
Man*   Cleveland

N o r t h

Yorkshire
(North)

Lancashire   Yorkshire   Humberside
              (West)

*I r i s h
S e a*   Manchester   Yorkshire
              (Greater)   (South)

Cheshire   Derbyshire   Lincolnshire

Nottingham

M i d l a n d s   *E a s t*

Staffordshire   Leicestershire   Norfolk

Salop

Midlands
(West)
              Northamptonshire   Cambridgeshire

Hereford &   Warwichshire   Suffolk

W a l e s   Worcester   Bedfordshire

Buckinghamshire

Gloucestershire   Hertfordshire   Essex

Oxfordshire

S o u t h e a s t

*A t l a n t i c
O c e a n*   Avon   London

Wiltshire   Berkshire   *& L o n d o n*

Surrey   Kent

Somerset   Hampshire

S o u t h w e s t   Sussex   Sussex
              (West)   (East)

Devon   Dorset

*Isle of
Wight*

Cornwall

E n g l i s h   C h a n n e l

The distinctive red buses of London, part of the metropolis's extensive transport network.

have highlighted those truly unmissable sights.

Getting around

Transport around London is never a problem whatever the time of day or night. The Underground network is extremely comprehensive even if the interior décor has seen better days. Since the train will drop you right outside the main sites it is extremely popular with tourists, all you have to do is follow the map (see Underground Map p.132) A day ticket will allow you to travel as much as you like at a much cheaper rate than several individual tickets. London buses are a bit more complicated; be sure you know which number bus to take and have a range of coins. London taxis can be hailed anywhere; they can also be booked by telephone to collect you from your home or hotel, but they are not however, particularly cheap.

The City

A logical place to start any visit to London is in the eastern part, called the City. Somewhat confusingly, when Londoners talk about "the City" they are not referring to London in general, but specifically to this one particular district, known as the **City of London.** The City today is the country's financial heart. Within the confines of less than a

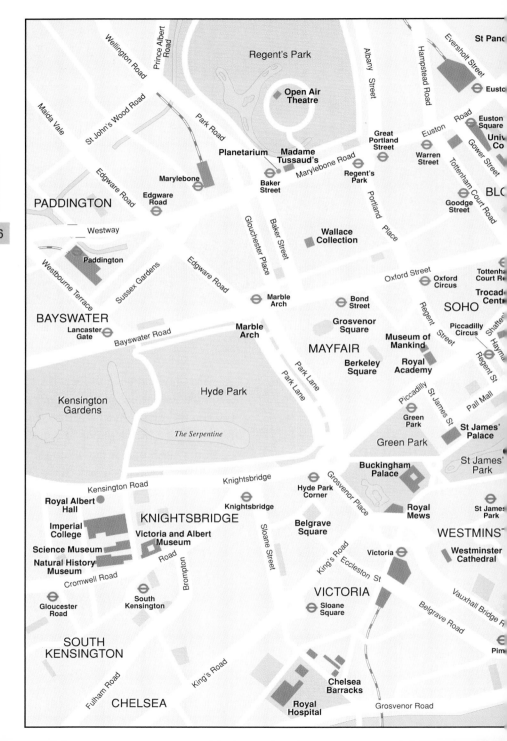

Wellington Road

Prince Albert Road

St Pancr

Everholt Street

Hampstead Road

Albany Street

Regent's Park

Open Air Theatre

Euston

Maida Vale

St John's Wood Road

Park Road

Euston Road

Euston Square

Univ Co

Great Portland Street

Warren Street

Gower Street

Planetarium

Madame Tussaud's

Marylebone Road

Regent's Park

Tottenham Court Road

BLO

Baker Street

Edgware Road

Marylebone

Edgware Road

Goodge Street

PADDINGTON

Westway

Glouchester Place

Baker Street

Portland Place

Wallace Collection

Oxford Street

Oxford Circus

Tottenha Court R

Westbourne Terrace

Paddington

Sussex Gardens

Edgware Road

Marble Arch

Bond Street

Trocad Centr

SOHO

BAYSWATER

Lancaster Gate

Bayswater Road

Marble Arch

Grosvenor Square

Regent Street

Piccadilly Circus

Shaftes

Hayma

Marble Arch

MAYFAIR

Museum of Mankind

Berkeley Square

Royal Academy

Regent St

Kensington Gardens

Hyde Park

Park Lane

Park Lane

Piccadilly

St James St

Pall Mall

The Serpentine

Green Park

St James' Palace

Green Park

St James' Park

Kensington Road

Knightsbridge

Buckingham Palace

Royal Albert Hall

Knightsbridge

Hyde Park Corner

Grosvenor Place

St James Park

Imperial College

KNIGHTSBRIDGE

Royal Mews

WESTMINS

Science Museum

Victoria and Albert Museum

Belgrave Square

Natural History Museum

Road

Brompton

Sloane Street

King's Road

Eccleston St

Victoria

Westminster Cathedral

Cromwell Road

Vauxhall Bridge R

Gloucester Road

South Kensington

VICTORIA

Belgrave Road

Sloane Square

Pim

SOUTH KENSINGTON

Fulham Road

King's Road

Chelsea Barracks

CHELSEA

Royal Hospital

Grosvenor Road

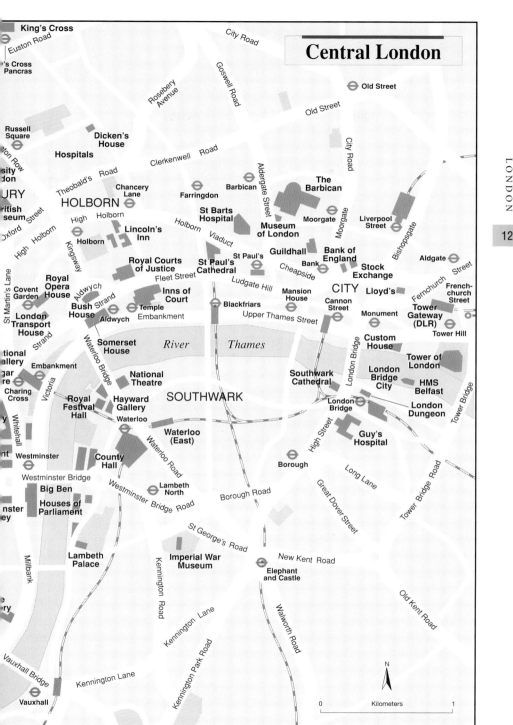

Central London

King's Cross
Euston Road
's Cross
Pancras

City Road

Old Street

Russell
Square

Dicken's
House

Hospitals

Roseberry
Avenue

Goswell Road

Old Street

City Road

ion Row

Clerkenwell Road

sity
lon

Theobald's Road

BURY

Chancery
Lane

Barbican

Farringdon

The
Barbican

ritish
seum

HOLBORN

High Holborn

Holborn

Aldgate Street

Street

Oxford

High Holborn

Chancery
Lane

St Barts
Hospital

Museum
of London

Moorgate

Liverpool
Street

Bishopsgate

Lincoln's
Inn

Holborn

Holborn

Holborn
Viaduct

Guildhall

Bank of
England

Aldgate

Royal Courts
of Justice

St Paul's
Cathedral

St Paul's

Bank

Cheapside

Stock
Exchange

Fenchurch Street

Royal
Opera
House

Aldwych

Fleet Street

Inns of
Court

Ludgate Hill

Mansion
House

CITY

Lloyd's

French-
church
Street

Kingsway

St Martin's Lane

Covent
Garden

Bush
House

Strand

Temple

Blackfriars

Cannon
Street

Monument

Tower
Gateway
(DLR)

London
Transport
House

Aldwych

Embankment

Upper Thames Street

Tower Hill

Custom
House

Tower of
London

Strand

tional
allery

Somerset
House

River
Thames

Embankment

London Bridge

Tower Bridge

gar
re

Victoria

Waterloo Bridge

National
Theatre

Southwark
Cathedral

London
Bridge
City

HMS
Belfast

Charing
Cross

Royal
Festival
Hall

Hayward
Gallery

SOUTHWARK

London
Bridge

London
Dungeon

y

Waterloo

Waterloo
(East)

High Street

Guy's
Hospital

Whitehall

nt

Westminster

County
Hall

Waterloo Road

Borough

Long Lane

Tower Bridge Road

Westminster Bridge

Big Ben

Lambeth
North

Borough Road

Great Dover Street

nster
ey

Houses of
Parliament

Westminster Bridge Road

Millbank

Lambeth
Palace

Imperial War
Museum

St George's Road

New Kent Road

Elephant
and Castle

Old Kent Road

e
ry

Kennington Road

Kennington Lane

Walworth Road

Vauxhall Bridge

Kennington Lane

Kennington Park Road

Vauxhall

N

0   Kilometers   1

St Paul's Cathedral, the architectural triumph of Sir Christopher Wren.

square km (just one square mile) are to be found the headquarters of all the major British banks, as well as the Bank of England, the Stock Exchange, Lloyds Insurance, and offices of most of the world's banks and financial institutions. In a reference to its size, the City is also often called "The Square Mile". The City is home to St Paul's Cathedral, the College of Arms, the Mansion House (residence of the Lord Mayor of London), the Temple, the Law Courts and Fleet Street, the traditional home of the country's press. The City even has its own police force, who have slightly different uniforms, to distinguish them from the rest of their London colleagues.

St Paul's Cathedral dominates the City's skyline, despite all the surrounding tower blocks. The survival of the church, with its distinctive dome, became a potent symbol for Londoners

London is now a truly multi-cultural city, as evidenced by
this supermarket in Chinatown.

during the Blitz (German bombing of London) in World War II. The present day church is the fourth, or possibly the fifth, to stand on the site, and construction began shortly after the Great Fire of London in 1666. St Paul's remains the building with which the architect Sir Christopher Wren is most often associated, and indeed he is buried within its walls, along with a galaxy of the leading figures of the 18th, 19th and 20th centuries.

In the huge crypt of the cathedral there are many tombs and memorials, from Nelson to the soldiers of the Falklands War. If you have the stamina, it is well worth climbing the hundreds of steps that lead up through the cathedral, via the Whispering Gallery to the

Golden Gallery and out on to the roof of the church, from where you literally dominate London.

The City has many other interesting and historic churches, many of them with decidedly intriguing names, such as **St Andrew-by-the-Wardrobe** and **St James Garlickhythe**. Sadly, in the wake of several major terrorist incidents, most of the major financial institutions, including the Bank of England, and the Stock Exchange, can no longer be visited, for security reasons.

Two of London's main markets are in the City, Smithfield and Leadenhall. **Smithfield market** has been on its present site on the western edge of the City since 1868. The market-building houses 65 wholesalers, handling meat

A little urban enclave in Kensington Gardens.

and poultry from both the United Kingdom and from many other countries. **Leadenhall market,** situated near the Lloyds Building in the heart of the city, was at one time a poultry and game market. A fine listed Victorian building, nowadays it provides city workers with excellent retail shopping facilities, pubs and restaurants.

The Tower of London

East of the City and on the north bank of the River Thames, the **Tower of London** is a must for any visitor, but it comes at a price; it costs a cool £6.70 to visit. Nevertheless, in 1991 there were 1,923,520 visitors; so the moral is, take

patience, as well as money, when you set out to visit one of London's most interesting sights. Try to avoid the weekends, and, if possible, the busy summer months, but if you can not, do not worry, the queues do actually move very fast, and the Tower is well worth waiting for.

William the Conqueror built the Tower immediately after his coronation on Christmas Day 1066, as a symbol of his power. Over the ensuing centuries, the central keep, or the **White Tower**, was gradually surrounded by a series of concentric defences. The most famous of the towers is the Bloody Tower, where, according to legend, the little Princes (the sons of King Edward IV) were murdered in 1485. The 13th century **Traitor's Gate**, overlooking the river, used to be the Tower's main gateway when the Thames was the principal means of transport in London. It later acquired its sinister name when the Tower was used as a state prison. The **Crown Jewels** are one of the main attractions of the Tower, including as they do the country's coronation jewellery and state regalia. There are wonderful gem-stones on display, including the 14th century Indian diamond, the *Koh-i-Noor*, as well as the *Star of Africa*, the biggest diamond in the world.

The yeoman warders of the Tower of London are known as "Beefeaters" and they wear a distinctive and colourful Tudor uniform. They are unfailingly polite, and are always ready to be photographed, and equally ready to ex-

Madame Tussauds

If you want to know who is in and who is out of favour in Hollywood, the Royal Family, or in the Houses of Parliament, you could read the gossip columns of the tabloid newpapers, but a visit to Madame Tussauds would probably be more enlightening and definitely more entertaining. Whenever a film star or politician is removed from his or her place in the wax gallery of fame, you can be pretty sure that it is a well-thought out, informed move. Even changes of position can be significant, with estranged couples being moved apart from each other, or warring politicians being separated. All part of the fun, in this wax collection of the famous, the infamous, and the downright notorious.

In real life

Madame Tussaud was born in 1761, and learned her skill early in life, making wax models of the French Royal Family for her uncle Dr Curtius' waxwork museum. She made her first wax model, of Voltaire, when she was 17-years-old, and was subsequently invited to become an art tutor to the French Royal Family at Versailles, where she spent 9 years.

The young woman returned to Paris when the French Revolution broke out in 1789, and quickly put her skills to use, particularly in making death masks of the many people guillotined during the Terror which followed hard on the heels of the Revolution. She made death masks of King Louis XIV and Queen Marie Antoinette, as well as the revolutionaries who themselves later became victims of the guillotine.

Married and the mother of two sons, Madame Tussaud inherited the waxworks on her uncle's death, but France in the aftermath of the Revolution was hard-going economically, so she decided to leave the country. Leaving her husband and her baby son in France, she moved to England in 1802 with her exhibition and her eldest son.

For the next 33 years, she travelled the country with her exhibition, until, in 1835, aged 74, she settled down in London, in Marylebone. She modelled her own self-portrait when she was 81 years old, and it still stands today at the

entrance, welcoming visitors. Madame Tussaud died in 1850, at the age of 89.

Encounters with the rich & famous

Today, $2\frac{1}{2}$ million visitors come each year to the best-known waxwork museum in the world to see the amazingly life-like models of the rich and famous, the footballers and the murderers, the Royals and the politicians. Many of the models are dressed in actual clothes belonging to their original, human versions. The wax Pavarotti wears the real Pavarotti's evening dress and shoes. The wax model of the actor Bob Hoskins shows him in his role as Eddie Valiant, in the film *Who Framed Roger Rabbit*, and he wears the clothes used in the film. The late Henry Moore, the British sculptor, gave his own clothes for his model, forgot that he had so done, and thought he had lost them, until he came face to face with himself in the museum.

Popular, long-standing personalities even have their models updated, to take into account extra grey hairs or paunch, more wrinkles, or a face lift! Many of the personalities give several sittings during the modelling, hundreds of photographs are consulted, and films are often made to capture facial expressions. Visitors can see a video of the model Jerry Hall during the sculpting sessions to make her model, and to confuse reality and artifice even more, the artist who made the wax Jerry Hall is also there himself - in wax.

Meetings with murderers

There are many different sections to the waxworks - the Grand Hall portrays major historical personalities and current politicians, but one of the most popular displays is the Chamber of Horrors. From the 19th century enigmatic murderer, Jack the Ripper, to the electric chair, visitors can be thoroughly frightened - and to add to all the horror, the original death masks of Louis XIV and his Queen are there, lying next to the very guillotine blade that beheaded them.

The London Underg

UNDERGROUND

Travel Information 071-222-1234
Travelcheck 071-222-1200

und

Epping †Ongar

Theydon Bois

Debden

North
Weald †

Loughton

Buckhurst Hill

Roding
Valley Chigwell †

No service after 20.00

Grange Hill†

Tottenham
Hale

Walthamstow
Central ≋

eaven Blackhorse
isters Road

South Woodford

Peak hours
only

Hainault

Fairlop

Barkingside

ry Park

Snaresbrook

Redbridge

Newbury Park

Wanstead Gants
Hill ≋ Upminster

Leytonstone

Upminster Bridge

& Islington

Leyton

Hornchurch

Elm Park

Hackney Hackney
onbury Central Wick

Dagenham East
Dagenham
Heathway

Dalston
Kingsland

Homerton

Stratford

Becontree
Upney

Barking ≋

Bethnal Mile
Green End

East Ham

Upton Park

Plaistow

West Ham

Bromley-
by-Bow

oreditch †

Stepney Bow
Green Road

Bow
Church

dgate Devons
East Road

Whitechapel

All Saints

Brunswick
Wharf

Limehouse Poplar

Canning Town

Shadwell Westferry

Blackwall

Royal Victoria

Tower
Gateway

West India
Quay

Wapping

Canary Custom
Wharf House

Prince Regent

Royal Albert

Beckton Park

Under construction

Cyprus

Heron Quays

Gallions
Reach

South Quay

herhithe

Crossharbour

y Quays

Mudchute

Silvertown
& London
City Airport

Beckton

Island
Gardens

North Woolwich

ate

New Cross ≋

Greenwich via
Foot Tunnel

KEY TO LINES

Bakerloo	○ Interchange stations
Central	≋ Connections with British Rail
Circle	🅿 Connections within distance
District	★ Closed Sundays
East London	⭐ Closed Saturdays and Sundays
Hammersmith & City	
Jubilee	▲ Served by Piccadilly line early mornings and late evening Monday to Saturday and all day Sundays
Metropolitan	
Northern	
Piccadilly	† For opening times see poster journey planners
Victoria	
Docklands Light Railway†	Certain stations are closed during holidays
Network SouthEast ≋	

*Beefeaters keep watch over the
Tower of London.*

plain to visitors the history and traditions of the Tower.

The Docklands

East of the Tower, is the former dock area of London, long neglected, but now a busy, though controversial, growth area. The on-going regeneration of London's **Docklands**, started in 1981, when it quickly became a symbol of the booming Thatcherite 1980s. The massive rejuvenation plan was one of the largest of such programmes to have been undertaken in Europe. By the year 2001, this 3 km (8 $1/_2$ square mile) urban development area will be home to 110,000 people, the equivalent of a city

Buckingham Palace

Buckingham Palace, the official residence of the Queen.

One of the main talking points in London during the spring of 1993, was the totally unexpected news that **Buckingham Palace** was to be opened to the general public. Interpreted by many as a public relations gesture by an increasingly beleaguered Royal Family, it was announced, officially, that the principal reason for opening the Palace to visitors, was to off-set the enormous repair bill for Windsor Castle, which had been severely damaged by fire in November 1992. Parts of Buckingham Palace were therefore to be opened, for an entrance fee.

Immediately after the announcement, speculation was rife that the public would be able to bump into the Royal Family in the corridors of Buckingham Palace, known familiarly as "Buck House" but a Palace follow-up statement quickly put paid to that particular fantasy: Buck House would only be open to the public for the months of August and September each year,

when, not surprisingly, the Royals are not in residence.

Although it will take years to raise enough from the £8.00 entrance fee, to foot the Windsor Castle repair bill, mathematical considerations did nothing to dampen the enthusiasm of tour operators, and within a few days of the announcement, all group bookings for the year had already been filled. From 7 August 1993, Buckingham Palace was officially on the tourist map. Within a couple of days of the opening, the Palace announced that it was opening a second souvenir shop, to handle the huge demand for royal souvenirs.

Palace history

What lies in store for visitors to the early 18th century former town house of the Duke of Buckingham? Firstly, an architectural hotchpotch, for the brick town house has undergone modifications and additions over the years, as it progressed from a house to a palace. In 1825, King George IV and the architect John Nash planned a major over-haul of the building, with a palace of Bath stone being built around the core of the original brick house. All of this cost a great deal of money, and the King died 5 years later in 1830, leaving Nash to shoulder much of the blame for the cost of the Palace. He retired, in some discredit; another architect called Edward Blore took over and the next monarch King William IV also died before Buckingham Palace was finally completed in 1837. Queen Victoria finally took up residence in the Palace, 3 weeks after her accession to the throne, even though construction was still not finished.

The inside story

Buckingham Place is situated in the heart of London, but is protected from the noise of the traffic hurtling round the nearby Hyde Park Corner, by 40 acres of gardens, including a huge lake.

The Royal apartments are in the North wing of the Palace, and will remain resolutely closed to the public. Until the opening, the only parts of the Palace familiar to the public from TV pictures, were the Ball Room, with its canopied royal dais, where investitures and large state banquets take place, and the Bow Room, which gives access to the thousands of people invited each summer to the Queen's garden parties. The opening gives access to a number of state rooms.

When the Queen is in residence, the Royal Standard flies over the Palace, and each morning, at 1130, the popular ceremony of the Changing of the Guard takes place. The distinctive uniform of the Guards – scarlet tunic, and huge bear-skin helmets – and the pageantry involved, makes the Changing of the Guard one of London's favourite events for visitors. There are such large crowds every day, that there is a campaign to make the area in front of the Victoria Memorial, into a pedestrian precinct, to protect onlookers from the London traffic.

the size of Oxford. It is an exciting project, transforming warehouses into smart apartments, and former industrial moorings into luxury marinas, like **St Katharine's Dock**. The multi-million pound development of **Canary Wharf** has seen its fair share of controversy, but as more companies move east out of the confines of the City, to larger and less expensive property, the area is bound to prosper. Another shot in the arm for the area was the decision by some of the country's major newspaper groups, to leave their traditional area, **Fleet Street**, and move instead to **Wapping**, the town which provided the setting for many of the novels of Charles Dickens, itself the subject of urban renewal.

Billingsgate Market is the oldest of the markets owned, controlled and operated by the Corporation of the City of London. London's principal fish-market was formerly located in the City, where it developed over some 800 years: in 1982, it moved to West India Dock, becoming the first major development in Docklands.

Transport options in and out of the busy City and Docklands areas are many: the traditional red, double-decker London bus; the underground train; the Docklands Light Railway; and "The Drain", a direct underground train running from Waterloo to Bank station, in the heart of the City of London. From May 1993, the Limehouse Link has connected London City airport to the City of London. Perhaps the most charming way of commuting to work in London is the RiverBus, a boat service operating from Chelsea Harbour via the West End, the City, and on to Canary Wharf.

The River Thames

Moving from the East End westwards take the RiverBus for a journey along London's river, the **Thames.** Leaving behind the Tower and the picturesque, gothic **Tower Bridge**, you will sail under the modern **London Bridge** – the original 19th century bridge was sold for £1 million, and now sits in the Arizona Desert. The boat travels on past various historic ships moored on the river banks, including HMS *Wellington* and HMS *Chrysanthemum*, then the mass of **Waterloo Station** appears and the **South Bank Arts Centre** where if you alight there is a pleasant riverside walk in front of the **Royal Festival Hall**. Again if you are on your feet you might stop for an intermission at the **Museum of the Moving Image**, which traces the history of film. The river continues due west, past the Houses of Parliament, through Chelsea, Hammersmith and Putney, the setting for the annual Oxford and Cambridge Boat Race, before arriving at Chiswick and Kew. After that, the Thames flows on towards Hampton Court and on into the Thames Valley.

One last word on the Thames. It may well be the historic lifeline of the city, but it is also a potential danger to London. As the city slowly sinks on its bed of clay, the tide level rises, and in the

last 100 years, tide levels have risen by 0.6 m (2 feet) at London Bridge. In order to protect the city, the **Thames Barrier** was constructed between 1972-82. It is the world's largest flood barrier, spanning 502 metres across the Thames. The barrier is raised monthly for a two-and-a half hour test period on weekdays and annually for a full day, and it makes for

View of the National Gallery from Trafalgar Square, the latter a regular haunt of pigeons and people.

an intriguing, and decidedly off-beat visit.

Trafalgar Square

Disembarking the Riverbus opposite the South Bank Arts Centre, walk the short distance on the north bank to the **Strand** and into **Trafalgar Square**. The famous square dating from the early 19th century is dominated by a 60 m (185 feet) column topped by Lord Nelson, built to commemorate his victory over Napo-

Waxwork models of the Royal Family in Madame Tussaud's.

leon at the Battle of Trafalgar in 1805. The massive Landseer lions stand guard, whilst pigeons hop around near the fountains, over-fed by hundreds of well-intentioned visitors each day. Every Christmas, the people of Norway send a Christmas tree to the British people, which is erected in Trafalgar Square. On New Year's Eve, at midnight, the square is packed with thousands of people who come to see in the new year to the chimes of Big Ben, the clock of the Houses of Parliament. Numerous political demonstrations have also been held here.

The National Galleries

Overlooking Trafalgar Square is the

National Gallery, one of the world's major art collections, with a display of over 2,000 paintings. The recently opened Sainsbury Wing, slightly to the west of the main 19th century building, houses the Early Renaissance Collection. The National Gallery's collection ranges from 13th and 14th century Early Italian paintings through to the 19th century French Impressionists. Some of the best works of the 17th and 18th century English painters are exhibited, amongst them Gainsborough, Hogarth, Turner, Reynolds and, of course, Constable's quintessential English landscapes.

Just behind the National Gallery, is the **National Portrait Gallery**, one of London's most interesting and impres-

Free theatre at Covent Garden.

sive collections. If you want a historical run-down on "who was who" in England, visit this Victorian interpretation of an Italian Renaissance building. Head for the top floor, where the Tudors are on display, and work your way slowly downstairs, seeing as you go, the portraits of all the country's major literary figures, members of the royalty, politicians and Victorian explorers.

Covent Garden

A few minutes walk northeast of Trafalgar Square is **Covent Garden**, one of the most colourful and entertaining places in London. The white opera-house, famed for its opera and ballet perform-

ances, sits in suitably elegant grandeur, surrounded by a former fruit and vegetable market area, which has been converted into a shopping and arts centre. Covent Garden is one of the few places in London where you can eat out-of-doors continental pavement-style, in terrace cafés and restaurants, while at the same time being entertained by musicians, jugglers, and mime-artists.

When it comes to street-theatre, Covent Garden has all types, from the weird and wonderful, to the talented and the hopeless beginner. There are serious-faced student string quartets, playing quietly next to café tables, and punk rockers sporting virulently dyed mohican style haircuts, who spend ages tuning their electric guitars, before un-

Soho

Chinatown, Soho, will satisfy all your cravings for things Oriental.

and Italian eating places in London used to be in Soho. They still are, though these days you go to Soho less for European food, and increasingly for Chinese food, since the area has undergone a change in the last 20 years or so.

Hong Kong Chinese have moved to the area, opening Chinese restaurants and shops galore. Some street signs are written in Chinese, especially in the vicinity of the heart of Chinatown, **Gerrard Street** where there is a ceremonial Chinese archway, and the place is bursting at the seams during the Chinese New Year.

Soho is the name of a small area south of Oxford Street and north of Piccadilly which is not favoured with any noteworthy monuments, but which has an atmosphere all of its own and it is a distinctively un-English one.

Refugees & restaurants

Soho has been a place of political and economic refuge to foreigners for centuries, and successive communities have come, settled there, and given some of their character to it. The French were the first to arrive, fleeing the 16th century Wars of Religion. In 1677, Greeks, fleeing the Ottoman Turks arrived, and a few years later, after the 1685 Revocation of the Edict of Nantes, more French Huguenots arrived, fleeing religious persecution. Many more Frenchmen came after the French Revolution, and during the 19th century, Italians arrived.

These waves of refugees often set up restaurants and cafés, and some of the best French

Soho sleaze

Soho has another side, traditionally a sleazy one. Despite the fact that in recent years the area has been significantly cleaned up – nothing on the scale or crudity of Paris' Pigalle – sexshops and peep-shows are numerous and part of the tradition of what Soho is. At night the area is aglow with red and neon lights.

For most tourists however Soho remains the place to head for if you crave a *dim sum* (Chinese snacks) lunch, or want to buy a Greek newspaper, some exotic cooking ingredients or Chinese New Year cards. Perhaps you are looking for a home-from-home experience in this unEnglish side of London and maybe a glimpse at the sleaze.

The British Museum resides in the intellectual district of Bloomsbury.

expectedly erupting into a wild rock number. If you are fortunate enough to be in Covent Garden on a sunny English summer day, just follow the crowd to the loudest music, or the funniest juggler, get a cold drink, find yourself an empty patch of cobble-stone, and sit back and watch the free show.

Bloomsbury & the British Museum

North of Covent Garden is **Bloomsbury**, a quiet area dominated by London University and the **British Museum**. The British Museum owes its current status to Sir Hans Sloane, an 18th century naturalist and traveller, who left his collection to the nation, a decision which forced Parliament into founding a museum to house it. The Sloane collection, along with other bequests scattered throughout London, was brought together, forming the nucleus of today's stunning collection. There are some particularly excellent displays, such as the now controversial *Elgin Marbles*, which the Greek government wants back. The Egyptian Sculpture Gallery includes the *Rosetta Stone*, which was the key to deciphering ancient hieroglyphics. The *Magna Carta* and the *Lindisfarne Gospels* are also housed here as is the pre-historic treasure of Sutton Hoo. Like many of the world's great collections, you need more than one visit to the British Museum, to really appreciate

Piccadilly Circus, the hub of the West End.

the extent of its exhibits in any detail.

The West End

For a complete change of scene and rhythm, you can walk the short distance from literary Bloomsbury, to **Oxford Street**, the mecca of shoppers. Oxford Street and the adjoining **Tottenham Court Road** are always busy, always full of life, and have shops galore to tempt you. (see Shopping chapter p.409). From Oxford Street, head south through **Soho** (see box story p.140) towards Piccadilly Circus.

   Piccadilly Circus is one of the timeless images of London, with the little *statue of Eros*, against a back-drop of

neon signs. Eros was returned to his perch in May 1993 after 5 months of repair, just in time to celebrate his 100th birthday in June of the same year. This is the heart of London's theatre and entertainment district, the place to catch up on the latest Andrew-Lloyd-Webber musical, a newly released film, or to go night-clubbing in style at the Hippodrome nightlife.

Whitehall & Horse Guards Parade

From Piccadilly Circus, there are several options. One option is to head back to Trafalgar Square, cut across it, and walk down **Whitehall**, where many of the

Kew Gardens

The 54 metre high, Chinese Pagoda, is the landmark of Kew Gardens.

The 300 acre expanse of Kew Gardens is situated on the site of a former royal estate, to the west of London, in the borough of Richmond-upon-Thames. Kew is known for its botanical collection, and the gardens also contain the biggest herbarium in the world, an important botanical library, and a wood museum. Kew also offers a three year training course for student gardeners.

Garden roots

There used to be a deer park on the site, with a small keeper's lodge, until King George II and Queen Caroline bought the land in 1721, along with Richmond Lodge. Frederick, Prince of Wales, built a house nearby, and King George III, Queen Charlotte and their 15 children later lived at Kew. Sadly, most of the buildings from that period no longer exist. Only **Kew Palace**, also known as the Dutch House, survives and can be visited. In 1761, Sir William Chambers designed the pretty Georgian Orangery, and the most famous landmark in the Gardens, the 10 storeyed Chinese pagoda, which stands 54 m (163 ft) high.

The actual origins of the botanical collection date back to a Lord Capel, who lived in the late 17th century, but most of the impetus came from Princess Augusta, wife of Frederick. She was personally responsible for the foundation of a botanical garden, as well as their enlargement.

Over the years, the collection grew, and in 1841, the gardens were given to the nation. They quickly became an important botanical institution, with more than 40,000 different kinds of plants, and a staggering 6,500,000 dried specimens.

Showpieces

Kew originated the plantation industry of rubber, and even today plays an important role in plant introduction and plant quarantine.

There are wonderful flower displays, superb trees, some of which are over 200 years old, and plant houses. Some of these houses are "climatic" houses, such as the pretty, 19th century iron and glass Palm House, the Temperate House, the Alpine House, and the Princess of Wales Tropical Conservatory. Others are devoted to one particular plant variety, such as the Fern House, the Tropical Waterlily House and the Australian House. Visitors can enter these houses and one can gain a wonderfully educational and aesthetic insight into flora and plant life from all over the world.

Outside Buckingham Palace where the guards go off duty with the ceremony of trooping the colour.

government ministries are located. As you walk down Whitehall, past the solid Victorian façades of the Ministry offices, you will pass **Horse Guards Parade**, where there is a changing of the guard every day at 1100 hours (1000 on Sundays). The mounted guards, and their superb horses, stand virtually motionless, despite the futile attempts of visitors to try and make them smile. Opposite Horse Guards Parade is the **Banqueting House**, built in 1619, and famous for one sad event in history: on 30 January 1649, King Charles I stepped

The chimes of Big Ben have become synonymous with London.

from a window of the Banqueting House out onto the scaffold.

the home of the Chancellor of the Exchequer.

At the southern end of Whitehall is The Palace of Westminster, better known as the **Houses of Parliament**. After a disastrous fire destroyed the original Palace of Westminster, a competition was held in 1836, to choose the architect for a new building for the country's Parliament. The result was the current Houses of Parliament, which quickly became a symbol of the country's authority and solidity, especially **Big Ben**, the 103 m (316 ft) high clock tower. The chimes of Big Ben's clock are probably the best known in the world, introducing as they do, many of the British Broadcasting Corporation's programmes.

Downing Street & the Houses of Parliament

Continuing south down Whitehall, just after Horse Guards Parade, a small street leads off to the right, and as the barriers and the policemen indicate, this is **Downing Street**. Number 10 has been the residence of the Prime Minister since 1731, and its black front door, guarded by a policeman, is without doubt the most famous one in the country. Innumerable pictures have been taken of politicians in front of the door of Number 10. The house next door, Number 11, is

Westminster Abbey

Next to Parliament is **Westminster Abbey**, built by Edward the Confessor, and the site of the Christmas Day Coronation of William the Conqueror in 1066. Most of the country's sovereigns have been crowned in the Abbey and many of them are buried there. In the 13th century, it was rebuilt by King Henry III; Henry VII added to it, and further additions were made in the 18th century. The beautiful medieval chapter house was built by the royal masons in 1250 and contains some of the finest medieval sculpture in England. The floor of this high-ceilinged octagonal building still has its original glazed tiles. Amongst

Westminster Abbey has witnessed the coronations, weddings and funerals of many of England's Kings and Queens.

a wealth of treasure in the Abbey, you can see the oak Coronation Chair, the gorgeous Henry VII Chapel, with its delicate fan-vaulted roof, and Poets' Corner, where there are memorials to some of the country's most distinguished writers.

The Tate Gallery

Further south of the Abbey is the **Tate Gallery**, which houses a substantial national collection of British and modern art. The works of the major English painters from the 16th century onwards are on display, and there is a wonderful collection of the Pre-Raphaelites and Victorians.

Royal walks

From the Tate, it is a fairly long, but pleasant walk northwest, past the Roman Catholic **Westminster Cathedral**, an example of pure 19th century Byzantine architecture, and on towards **Buckingham Palace**, the Queen's London residence (see box story p134). From the Queen Victoria Memorial opposite the Palace, you can walk through pictureque **St James's Park** – the oldest royal park in London, and the most sedate – or along the tree lined path of **The Mall** and rejoin Trafalgar Square. Or, you can head west to the infernal traffic of **Hyde Park Corner**, and from there either walk back along **Piccadilly**

A liveried porter awaits you and your shopping, outside Harrods department store.

to Piccadilly Circus, or walk north along the highly expensive **Park Lane**, to **Marble Arch**, which marks the western end of Oxford Street. As you walk along Piccadilly, you pass Burlington House, home to the **Royal Academy**. In addition to its permanent collection, the Royal Academy often holds important art exhibitions. Every summer, it holds its own very popular Summer Exhibition, where little known artists get the chance to exhibit their works. In 1993 1,798 works of art went on display.

Knightsbridge & the museum district

West of Piccadilly and south of Hyde Park is **Knightsbridge**, an up-market district most famous for the **Harrods** department store (see Shopping chapter p409).

Continuing west on the Kensington Road you will reach the **Royal Albert Hall**. This most striking oval arena, was built in 1871 in memory of Prince Albert. The interior is ornately decorated and tiered with boxes and galleries. The hall is most famous for its annual classical Promenade Concerts, known affectionately as "The Proms".

Turning south out of the Royal Albert along Exhibition Road, is the museum district. The **Natural History Museum** is perhaps Londons' most popular museum and well worth a visit. Among the famous attractions are the

Dinosaur Diplodoctus, the Natural History Museum.

dinosaur skeletons; that of *Diplodoctus* can be found in the spectacular central hall.

Adjacent to the Natural History Museum is the **Science Museum**, the museum has a number of "hands-on" sections to keep the children entertained. Among the most popular exhibits are those of locomotives, aeroplanes and the gallery of the Exploration of Space.

Oppposite the Natural History Mu-

seum, the huge **Victoria and Albert Museum** ("The V&A") is an entirely different proposition. The museum is highly specialized in various decorative aspects of art. The Chippendale furniture and the Dress Collection are favourites; there are hundreds of other numerous pottery, music and art exhibits, from all over the world and from many historical eras. You have to be selective or you will be totally confused.

the two men and a dog who may or may not be listening, can stand on a soapbox and hold forth, about anything and everything.

London's parks are really great places to let yourself go; although often crowded, there is a pleasant relaxed feel about them, business men come for a lunch-time breather, children play ballgames, people fish, jog, read or boat on the lake. The London parks have the delightful feeling of a city at rest and play, despite the hum and sirens of traffic beyond.

Parks are not however, all that London has to offer in the way of greenery, some more residential areas are surrounded by open stretches of ground called heaths. One of the largest heaths is **Hampstead Heath**, a general name for several hills and heaths. It is situated just 4 miles from the centre of London, and covers 791 acres. Throughout the year, there are musical events on the Heath, which offer a wonderful alternative to an indoor concert. On Saturdays during the summer, there are the Kenwood Lakeside concerts, and on Sunday evenings, there are indoor recitals at the Kenwood Orangery.

Parkland

One of the joys of London are the **parks**, which, for such a huge city, are numerous. Among the well-known central parks, are **St James Park**, **Green Park** and **Hyde Park** on the northeast corner of which – near Marble Arch – is **Speakers' Corner**, where, on Sunday mornings, you can go and hear public oratory at its unfettered best. Anyone who wishes to address the nation, or at least

London Zoo

Last but not least, for animal lovers, there is one major sight still to be seen. **London Zoo** is in Regent's Park, has a comprehensive collection, and is especially noted for its rare species.

A short drive Southwest of London is **Hampton Court Palace**, which, despite its modern urban setting, is still as impressive today as its builder, Cardinal Wolsey, intended it to be. The powerful Cardinal started building his palace in 1515, and in keeping with his rumoured enormous wealth, Hampton Court soon outshone the royal palaces in splendour. Wolsey fell out of favour with his king, the quixotic Henry VIII, who seized Hampton Court on Wolsey's death in 1530. Generations of successive monarchs lived there, decorating, re-furnishing, and adding to it. A fire in 1986 damaged some of the magnificent State Apartments, but most of the damage has now been repaired, and visitors can once again see the apart-

The changing of Her Majesty's guard, Windsor Castle.

151

Windsor, Oxford & The Thames Valley

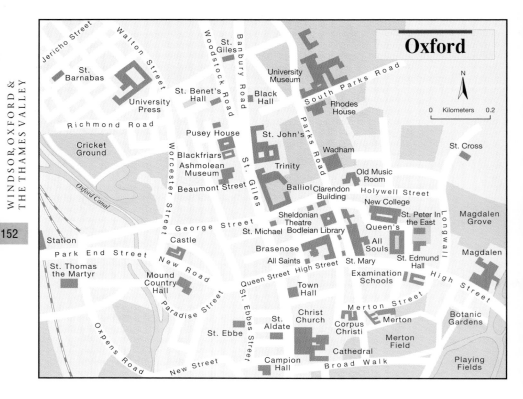

Oxford

ments, which illustrate the evolution of architectural and decorative styles from the Tudor age onwards.

Royal Windsor

Take the A308 west from Hampton Court, leaving behind the Outer London suburbs, to **Windsor**, a royal town by the River Thames. Both the historical destiny and the contemporary face of Windsor are dominated by **Windsor Castle**, one of the Queen's favourite residences. It is the largest castle in England, as well as the largest inhabited stronghold in the world. Parts of the castle were badly damaged by fire in late 1992, and although it is once again open to the public, the repairs and restoration work will take many more years. (see box story p158).

Windsor town and the castle are surrounded by **Windsor Great Park**, the remnant of what was once a huge royal hunting forest which originally covered much of southern Berkshire. Today "only" 4,800 acres survive, but they offer marvellous walking and hiking opportunities. **The Long Walk**, is a 3 mile-long avenue which leads from a statue of George III on horseback to the walls of the castle.

Two miles Southwest of Windsor, is

Eton College, Windsor, one of England's top public schools.

Windsor Safari Park, one of the country's leading wildlife sanctuaries. Visitors can drive through the Park, seeing lions, tigers and elephants from the safety of their car. A word of warning; though you may be perfectly safe, your car may not be.

Woe betide any driver who spends a long time in the baboon reserve, with his radio aerial up, or with a loose petrol cap: baboons are extremely inquisitive, and will take great pleasure in "playing" with your car. You can walk though the deer park, there is a childrens' zoo, a recently opened chimpanzee enclosure and an impressive open-air Seaworld complex.

The Etonian elite

Across the Thames, opposite Windsor, is

Etonians heading for class.

a school. Nothing unusual in that, except that this is not any school, but **Eton**, the best known of all the English public schools. According to the Duke of Wellington, "The Battle of Waterloo was won on the playing fields of Eton", which says a lot for the spirit and ethos of the school, but not much for the French army.

Possibly Wellington was indulging in nostalgic hindsight, since he was unhappy at Eton, and left when he was only 15. The school, which is actually called a college, was founded in 1440 by Henry VI, and has produced the Eton jacket and the Eton Collar, as well as 20 English Prime Ministers.

From Eton, you can drive north on the A355 for a short while, through the suburban sprawl of Slough, join the M40 motorway, and be in Oxford in no time at all. A far more pleasant route, however, is to join the A4 in Slough in the direction of Maidenhead, but turn off onto the A4094 before you reach the town. From here you can follow the meandering course of the **Thames Valley** to Oxford, stopping by *en route* at some of the prettiest villages in the south of England.

Along the Thames Valley

Following the A4094 road, you arrive at **Cookham**, a charming village, immortalised in many of the paintings of the local artist Sir Stanley Spencer (1891-

The vast expanse of Windrush Valley, near Burford, Oxfordshire.

1959). North of Cookham the road becomes the A4155; continue on beyond Marlow to the pretty village of **Cliveden**, where you can see a 19th century manor house, the former home of the Astor family. The house is now a hotel, but the superb gardens are run by the National Trust, and are open to the public. There are breathtaking views from Cliveden over the surrounding countryside.

Back on the A4155, you arrive at **Henley-on-Thames**, an attractive town with a late 13th century church and elegant Georgian town houses. In July, during the Henley Royal Regatta, the world's best oarsmen compete here in England's leading amateur regatta.

Out of Henley, take the A4155 south to **Reading**, the county town of Berk-shire. Leaving Reading, on A329 westwards, you will reach the red-brick Elizabethan manor house of **Mapledurham**, which has a magnificent oak staircase, and fine Jacobean plaster work.

The early 18th poet Alexander Pope was a frequent visitor here, dedicating some of his poems to the ladies of the house. The owners of Mapledurham, the Roman Catholic Blount family, used to hide and protect persecuted fellow Catholics. They installed a sign one little window gable, high up at the back of the house, studded with oyster shells, which was once a sign of safe refuge for Catholics.

The road meanders westwards alongside the Thames, crossing it at the village of **Pangbourne**, where Kenneth

Grahame lived from 1922-32, and where he wrote the childrens' story *The Wind in the Willows*. A mile or so north of Pangbourne (on the A329) and set in 400 acres of wooded park land, is the Palladian mansion, **Basildon Park**, which has had a chequered history. It was built in 1776, and in the early 20th century, there was a plan to ship it to the USA. In the event, only a few fittings were sold, which now grace New York's Waldorf Astoria Hotel. The house was then narrowly saved from demolition in 1952, and is now run by the National Trust.

The picturesque villages of **Streatley**, on the west bank of the Thames and **Goring**, exactly opposite on the east bank, are made even prettier by Goring Lock and the weir. Taking the A329 north through Wallingford and joining the A423 towards Oxford, you will reach the village of **Dorchester**. The village dates back to the Bronze Age, and has a beautiful Norman Abbey, with a superb 14th century east window, the Jesse window, depicting the family tree of Christ.

From Dorchester take the A415 to the town of **Abingdon**, which has some fine 15th century buildings and a ruined Abbey – founded in 675 but demol-ished during the dissolution of the monasteries in 1538. Beyond Abingdon it is only a few miles north along the A4183 to Oxford.

The dreaming spires of Oxford

Oxford, the "city of dreaming spires" is the home of England's oldest university. Like its counterpart and long-time rival, Cambridge, Oxford is a federation of autonomous colleges. There is no building to which you can point, and say "That is Oxford University"; the university consists of colleges, libraries and various administrative buildings, scattered throughout the city. The town was founded back in Saxon times, whilst the university dates from the early 13th century.

Like any old, rather elitist institution, which is what Oxford is, it has its own language. Oxford does not have students, but undergraduates, whose traditional outfit for examinations and official ceremonies is a dark outfit, always known by its Latin name of *sub fusc*.

Nearly everyone is fiercely loyal to, and proud of, their college, which is

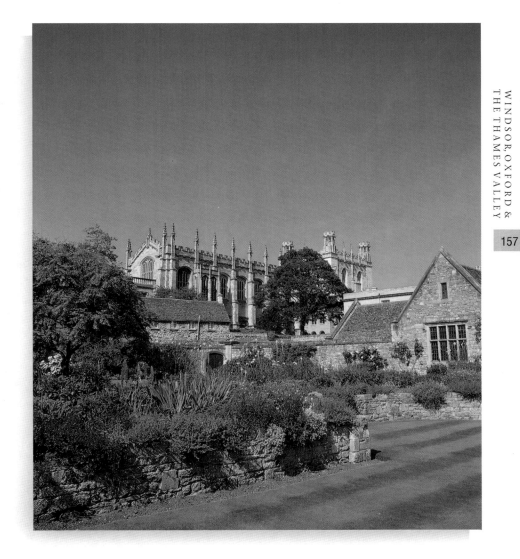

Christchurch Cathedral and College Gardens, Oxford.

both a home and educational institution – there are rooms for students in the college and some dons (university lectureres and fellows) even "live in". Today, the majority of colleges are co-educational, although a few still offer single-sex education.

Outstanding colleges

One of the most beautiful colleges in Oxford is **Christchurch**, known to all Oxford undergraduates and graduates alike as "The House". It was founded in

Windsor Castle

Windsor Castle seen from its secluded gardens.

national heritage, it was in some ways the catalyst for a re-appraisal of the relevance of the monarchy in Britain today.

Palace treasures

Windsor is the only royal residence to have been in continuous use since the Norman Conquest. In 1070, William the Conqueror chose a hillside overlooking the Thames to fortify the western approach to London, and the current outer walls of the castle actually occupy the lines of William's original defences. Attracted by the excellent hunting in the surrounding forests, successive monarchs added to the fortress. Henry I built a chapel and better accommodation. Henry II built the **Round Tower**. Edward III built **St George's Hall**, a meeting place for the knights of the Order of the Garter, which he had founded. Over the centuries, the castle grew and 14 monarchs were buried there. Windsor was not however to everyone's taste; Queen Elizabeth I and Queen Anne both disliked it, but Queen Victoria loved it, as does the present Queen.

When fire ravaged parts of Windsor Castle in late November 1993, another chapter was written in the long history of England's largest castle and one of the favourite homes of Her Majesty Queen Elizabeth II. The fire came at the end of a particularly bad year for the Royal Family, whose marital squabbles and quarrels had dominated most of the worlds' press for much of 1992. Even while the fire was still raging, watched by the horrified Queen, it was announced that the country would foot the not inconsiderable bill for the repairs.

For once, the normally restrained English were outraged. The country was in the middle of the worst economic recession of the century, the Royal family had staggered from one scandal to the other, and now, to cap it all, they were expected to find millions of pounds to repair the royal weekend home. There was such a protest that the Queen decided to find another solution to her problems. She subsequently decided to open her London home, **Buckingham Palace**, to visitors to raise money to pay for the repairs. The fire had not only damaged part of the

Although any degree of damage to such a unique place is a tragedy, luckily one of the glories of Windsor was undamaged, **St George's Chapel**. This gorgeous chapel was begun by King Edward IV, and took over a century to build. It was completed after the comparably beautiful rivals of the chapels of Eton and King's College, Cambridge. The chapel is justly celebrated for its fan-vaulted ceiling, its 16th century stained glass, and its highly ornate three-tiered choir stalls.

Most of the damage was done to the structure of the Private Apartments, which were virtually empty of furnishings at the time. The State Apartments escaped unharmed, so visitors can still see this section of the castle, which is largely 19th century.

Christchurch College, a view from the meadow.

1525 by Cardinal Wolsey, and is Oxford's biggest college, with the country's smallest cathedral (the college chapel) and the university's largest quadrangle, **Tom Quad**. A quadrangle is a feature of most Oxford colleges, a square, often with a small garden or fountain in the centre, and surrounded on all four sides by the college buildings, which are often residential "staircases".

You can enjoy a pleasant walk in **Christchuch Meadow**, which leads to the River Isis where the various college boathouses are situated – at most times of the day you will see a keen 8 putting in some arduous training for one of the numerous university regattas, the most famous being "Eights Week", held in the summer term. Those who excel in

sport at the university are awarded a "blue"; an Oxford or Cambridge blue is considered almost – or perhaps as – prestigious as a degree. Punting on the **River Cherwell** is for the less energetic and more romantically inclined, punts can be hired by the hour – ask at the **Tourist Information Office** on St Aldates Street (opposite Christchurch) for details.

Magdalen College, pronounced "maudlen", was founded in the mid-15th century, and has a magnificent location by the River Cherwell, with its own deer park, and 492 m (150 ft) high bell tower, which is the setting, at dawn on May Day, for what must be the most beautiful choral recital in the country. Many of the colleges own important

Entrance to Magdalen College, Oxford.

works of art; **Keble College**, for example, has a Pre-Raphaelite painting hanging in its chapel, while the altar-piece of **Corpus Christi College** chapel, is thought to be by Rubens.

Libraries and museums

Oxford is home to one of the world's great libraries, the **Bodleian Library**. In 1598, Sir Thomas Bodley offered to help the university to restore its 15th century library, using his many contacts to secure donations – an early example of academic net-working. The result was the Bodleian Library, which opened in 1602, the first major public library in the country, and today one of the world's most important libraries. Since the Bodleian has a legal right to receive a copy of every published work in Britain,

The dome of learning, the Radcliffe Camera, Oxford.

it has an unparalleled collection, which is accessible to the university's undergraduates, as well as selected non-University members. Perhaps the most famous architectural feature of the library is the round building of the **Radcliffe Camera**. The camera was built in 1737-48 in memory of the well-known physician John Radcliffe. The upper and lower rooms of the library are linked by a tunnel and a conveyor belt on which books are transported.

In front of the Bodleian Library on Broad Street (opposite the famous Blackwells book shop) is the **Sheldonian Theatre**, built from 1664-69 by Sir Christopher Wren. The building was designed for university ceremonies and every student comes here at least twice, for his/her matriculation to the university and for the degree ceremony itself.

The **Ashmolean Museum**, on St

Giles has an important archaeological collection, and a large prints and drawing collection; it is especially known for its Pre-Raphaelites.

Woodstock & Blenheim

Within a small radius of Oxford, there are a number of important places to visit, which makes the city an ideal base for visitors. **Woodstock**, 8 miles north of Oxford on the A44, is a charming and prosperous country town, on the edge of the Cotswolds Hills. The town is renowned for its unspoiled 18th century buildings and for **Blenheim Palace**. The main streets present dignified Georgian facades whilst the narrow lanes behind are lined with old cottages, many the former houses of glove-makers.

Home of the 11th Duke of Marlborough, birthplace of Sir Winston Churchill, Blenheim Palace was built for John Churchill, the first Duke of Marlborough, in recognition of his great victory over the French at the battle of Blenheim in 1704. The palace, designed by Sir John Vanbrugh, is set in 2,100 acres of parkland landscaped by Capability Brown, and is one of the finest examples of English baroque architecture.

The magnificent state rooms contain tapestries, paintings, sculptures and fine furniture. The long library, 600 m (183 feet) in length, is one of the longest rooms in an English private house. It contains some 10,000 volumes.

Blenheim Lake, created by Capability Brown when he landscaped the park in the late 18th century, is home to many varieties of waterfowl, and is spanned by Vanburgh's Grand Bridge which divides Queen Pool from the lake. Sir Winston Churchill was born in Blenheim on 30 November 1874 and there are a number of mementos of his

Blenheim Palace, Woodstock, birthplace of Sir Winston Churchill.

life and his distinguished political career, on view.

Attractive towns

Further north from Oxford off the M40,

is **Banbury**, known to many children from the nursery rhyme *Ride a cock horse to Banbury Cross...*, the eponymous cross was destroyed by the Puritans who found it offensive, but a hexagonal neo-Gothic cross (1860) stands in its place.

Another attraction is the **Edgehill**

Battle Museum. On 23 October 1642, the Army of Parliament clashed at Edgehill with the Royalist Army, commanded by King Charles I. The museum commemorates the events of that day and of the period, when 30,000 Englishmen fought this first major battle of the English Civil War. For those who enjoy dressing up, here is your chance, since people in 17th century style costume are admitted free to the museum.

Six km (10 miles) south of Oxford on the A34, **Didcot**, is home to the **Didcot Railway Centre**, which cheerfully describes itself as recreating the golden age of the Great Western Railway, for children of all ages from 4 to 104.

Isambard Kingdom Brunel designed the Great Western Railway to be the finest in the world, with the so-called "broad gauge" track, and it retained its independence until nationalization in 1948. Now, visitors can see a large collection of steam locomotives, many lovingly restored, whilst others are in various stages of repair and restoration.

The pretty market town of **Witney**, west of Oxford (off the A40) in the Oxfordshire Cotswolds owes many of its fine buildings and monuments to the blanket trade of the 17th century. Like many of the delightful Oxfordshire villages, it is a delightful place to stop to wander the quaint streets and perhaps take a cup of tea in one of the homely teashops. Keen walkers, might like to wander beyond Witney, into the delightful surrounding countryside.

The River Thames at Henley.

Kent & Surrey

Kent, the closest place in England to continental Europe, has always had to defend itself and the rest of the country against sea-borne invasions. Kent's great coastal castles were built to guard the invaders' traditional gateway into England. In 53 BC Julius Caesar landed near Dover and with his army built a lighthouse on Dover's cliffs, and forts along the coast. St Augustine landed in Kent in AD597, bringing with him not aggression, but Christianity. The two oldest cathedrals in England, Canterbury, the "Mother Church of England", and Rochester, are both in Kent.

The medieval cathedral of Canterbury, has been a place of pilgrimage for centuries.

Famous holidaymakers

Kent is often called the "garden of Eng-

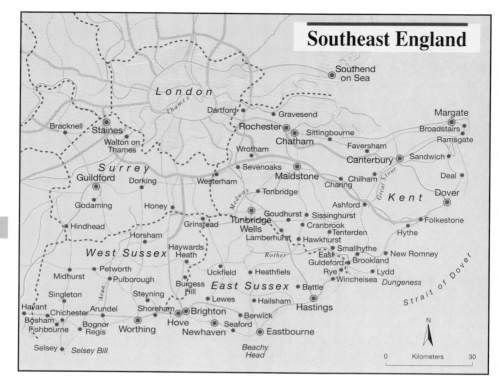

Southeast England

land", a county of fruit orchards and hop farms. Its proximity to London has given it a wealth of historic and beautiful country homes. Henry VIII was frequently drawn to Kent, mainly because of Anne Boleyn, whose childhood home was Hever Castle. Both Leeds and Lullingstone Castles were much loved by Henry and Anne during the early days of their marriage.

Broadstairs and Rochester have close links with Charles Dickens, who based many of his novels in the area. Dickens rented Bleak House in Broadstairs, for his summer home, and eventually retired to Gadshill near Rochester. Chartwell, was the country home of Sir Winston Churchill, and

General Wolfe spent most of his life at Quebec House, a 17th century gabled red-brick building.

Forts & castles

Most of Kent's castles and fortresses were built to defend England from foreign invaders. The ruins of Roman forts may be seen at **Richborough** (a few miles north of Sandwich) and **Reculver** (to the East of Herne Bay). The remains of **Port Lemanis** and **Lympne Castle**, on the site of a Roman watch tower, offers superb views across **Romney Marsh**.

Two points on Kent's coast have always been particularly vulnerable, the

Hands together, English children provide a welcome to Kent and Surrey.

Medway Estuary in the north of the county and the coastline of "White Cliff Country" on the east coast.

Both areas are therefore protected by numerous forts; the Medway primarily by Rochester castle; the east coast by forts at Romney, Hythe, Sandwich and **Dover** – 4 of the 5 founder members of the Confederation of Cinque Forts, formed by Edward I (the fifth was Hastings).

Little remains of these fortifications today except for the imposing **Dover Castle**, standing on a hill it overlooks the England Channel, at the point where England and France are the shortest distance apart. In its heyday Dover castle was called the "Key of England", and once welcomed Henry VIII, *en route* to the Field of the Cloth of Gold. Meanwhile the impressive castles at **Deal**, **Walmer**, and **Sandgate**, are evidence of Henry VIII's work on coastal fortification. Deal was however altered during the 18th century. Walmer castle remains the Lord Warden of the Cinque ports official residence.

Dover today is an important ferry port with regular ferries to Calais, Boulogne and Oostende. A few miles further south, the pretty town of **Folke stone** also sees ferries set sail daily for Boulogne. Folkestone is in itself a popular resort.

Between Dover and Folkestone the **Channel Tunnel** breaks through the Dover-Folkestone Heritage Coast to its opening north of Folkestone.

Hampton Court Palace and its glorious array of formal gardens.

Dover Castle was seen in medieval times as the strategic "Key to all England."

White cliffs

In this eastern area of Kent, Dover, Deal and Sandwich form the area known as **"White Cliffs Country"** and on a clear day, France is visible from the cliff tops. From the days of Julius Caesar in 53 BC to the present day, this part of England, the closest to continental Europe, has been the cornerstone of Britain's defence.

The Romans set up one of their strongest military bases in Richborough, near Sandwich. **Richborough castle** stands on the site where the Romans are thought to have first landed, there is a very impressive collection of Roman finds on view.

Today, most visitors go to **Sandwich** for golf, for there are three famous golf courses nearby, but for hundreds of

Dover

Fishing boats on the beach at Dover, the gateway to the English Channel.

There is a nostalgic war-time song which has the refrain, "There'll be blue birds over, the white cliffs of Dover..."

The threat of invasion, which has always hung over this corner of the country, was rendered all the more poignant through the image of the famous white cliffs, which had been, for generations of British travellers, their first (or last) sight of England.

Despite war damage, Dover has an elegance which belies its image as a busy Channel port. In medieval times, the pilgrimage to Canterbury was among the most famous routes in the Christian world, and the 14th century **Maison Dieu** in Dover was built to provide shelter to pilgrims along the way. It still stands today.

"Hellfire" in Dover Castle

Dover Castle is over 800 years old, and towers massively above the town. Recently, the castle has opened "Hellfire Corner", an underground network of secret tunnels which played a vital role in Britain's defence during World War II. The tunnels, which honeycomb Dover Castle Hill, were the operations rooms used by defence commanders during the War. During the critical years of the conflict, this area was known as hell-fire corner, because of the constant bombing and shelling.

An interesting and unusual exhibition has been opened in Dover Castle, called *Live and Let's Spy*. "Q" is well known as the inventor of ingenious gadgets in the James Bond books and films. What is less well known is that Ian Fleming based the character on a real person, and in this exhibition, visitors can see for the first time some of the original gadgets Q devised for putting his theories into practice.

Some of the tricks of the trade on show are Q's specially made shaving brushes, in which agents smuggled film back to London, and ordinary-looking buttons, which were, in fact, directional compasses, hidden deep inside the flying jackets of thousands of airmen. It is indeed, a most fascinating exhibition.

years it was a busy harbour, sheltered from the Channel gales. In the 15th century, the bay silted up, and today, the River Stour winds its way for several miles before emerging into the sea.

Paradoxically, the failure of Sandwich as a port saved the place as a unique example of a medieval town, and, with more timbered buildings in Sandwich than anywhere else in Kent, the entire centre of the town is now a conservation area.

Resorts of the Isle of Thanet

In northern Kent, the resorts of Ramsgate, Broadstairs and Margate have over 20 miles of magnificent coastline with excellent sandy beaches all very popular with Londoners. The resorts are in an area known as the **Isle of Thanet**, although it is not an island anymore. The sea channel which once isolated Thanet has silted into little more than a drainage ditch.

The Romans, the Christians and the Saxons used Thanet as a stepping-stone to the mainland. Julius Caesar met a little local resistance but St Augustine was welcomed and a cross marks the spot where he landed near **Pegwell Bay** (south Ramsgate). A short walk up the road from Pegwell lies the replica of a Viking ship *Hugin*.

Ramsgate was painted by Turner, and Oscar Wilde confused it with Margate. Queen Victoria visited it as a child and Vincent Van Gogh spent part of his troubled life teaching art there.

Built in 1749, the harbour was a haven for vessels fleeing the treacherous sand banks of the Goodwin Sands and in the 19th century the town had the largest fleet of fishing smacks on the south coast.

So impressed was King George IV with the welcome he received when passing through Ramsgate, that he bestowed the "Royal" title on its harbour, and it remains to this day the only Royal harbour in the country.

During World War II, the little ships that aided in the evacuation of troops from Dunkirk in France returned more than 42,000 men to the safety of Ramsgate Harbour.

Today, in more peaceful times, you can take a day trip from Ramsgate to Dunkirk, shop, have lunch, and return to England for tea, and all for £12.50, or £13.50 in July and August.

Margate can genuinely claim to have been Britain's first seaside resort. In 1753, a local Quaker called Benjamin Beale, invented a covered bathing machine which enabled people to take to the water without being seen undressed. Things have changed greatly now, but it is still worth taking a dip.

The historic city of Canterbury, Christchurch Gate.

Castles of the heartland

In the heart of Kent, you will be closer to more castles than anywhere else in England. The most famous is probably **Leeds Castle** (just off the M20, east of Maidstone) built upon two small islands in a lake, and surrounded by acres of beautiful parkland. Leeds was originally a Norman castle, rebuilt and modified over the centuries, and still stunning in its dramatic lake setting. The castle was one of Henry VIII's favourite residences, and it was he who transformed it from a fortress into palatial living quarters.

Another well known castle with beautiful gardens is **Hever Castle** (west of Tunbridge Wells), which dates back to 1270 when the massive gate-house, the outer walls and the moat were first constructed. Two hundred years later,

Tales of times gone by in a Canterbury Cathedral window.

the Bullen or Boleyn family constructed a comfortable Tudor dwelling house inside the walls. Hever Castle was the childhood home of Anne Boleyn, the second wife of Henry VIII and mother of Elizabeth I, and the castle contains many memories of her.

In 1903, William Waldorf Astor, acquired the estate and invested time, money and imagination in restoring the castle. From 1904 to 1908 he recreated the gardens, in Italian style, decorating them with statues and sculptures from Roman to Renaissance eras, collected in Italy, by the first Viscount. He also added a 35 acre lake, a walled grove garden, some fine topiary work and a maze, measuring 80 foot square. You can walk along its pathways for one

quarter of a mile. The Astors left a superb collection of furniture and paintings in the house.

Other notable castles in the area are ruined **Scotney Castle**, 17th century **Chiddingstone Castle**, Tudor **Lullingstone Castle** and **Tunbridge Castle**. **Chartwell Manor** situated near Hever Castle (south of the M25 motorway, west of Sevenoaks) was the country home of Sir Winston Churchill and remains almost exactly as he and Lady Churchill left it. One of England's great houses, **Knole** (approximately one mile east of Sevenoaks) has been the home of the Sackville family since 1566, though it dates back to the mid-15th century. This rambling house – one of the largest private houses in England – has 7 courtyards, 12 entrances, 52 staircases and 365 rooms.

Maritime Kent

In maritime Kent the most important reminder of England's sea-going heritage is the former naval base in **Chatham** which was in use for more than 400 years. Since its closure in 1984 it has been re-named the **Historic Dockyard** and is a living museum to a working dockyard. Admiral Lord Nelson started his service in Chatham at the age of 12 and his most famous ship, HMS *Victory*, was launched at the dockyard in 1765. At **Faversham**, the **Chart Gunpowder Mills** produced gunpowder for the battles of Trafalgar and Waterloo, and in **Dartford**, in Powder Mill Lane, there are the remains of an 18th century gunpowder factory.

Rochester & Canterbury

Soon after the Battle of Hastings, the Normans built a castle at **Rochester** to guard the point where the Roman London to Dover road, known as Watling Street (the present A2), crossed the river Medway. Today the massive stone walls of Rochester's 12th century castle keep one of the largest and best preserved towers in England which rises to a height of over 33m (100 feet) with walls 4 m (12 feet) thick.

One of the towns lying on Watling

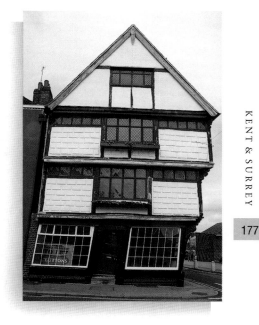

The nursery-rhyme charm of a crooked house.

Street was the walled town of **Durovernum**, better known today as **Canterbury**. Medieval **Canterbury Cathedral** is the country's leading Anglican cathedral, a place of major religious and historical significance. The cathedral was originally on the site of a church given to Saint Augustine in AD 602, but was substantially rebuilt following a fire in 1174. Of special interest are the numerous examples of medieval stained-glass and the impressive Norman crypt.

There are also many fine modern works of art, but the cathedral is best known as the site of the martyrdom in 1170 of Saint Thomas à Becket. In Trinity Chapel a series of 13th-century stained-glass windows depict the mira-

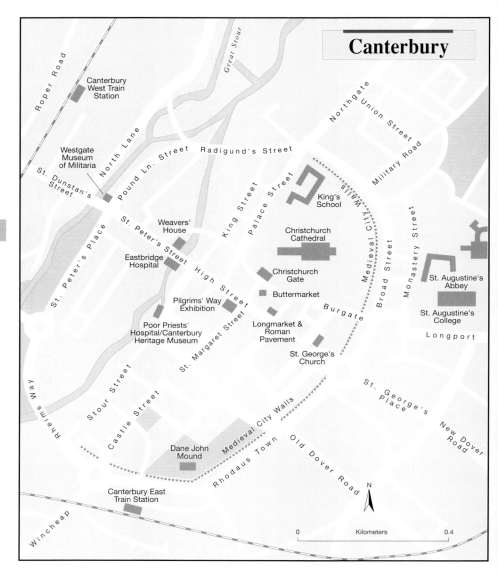

Canterbury

Canterbury West Train Station

Westgate Museum of Militaria

Roper Road

North Lane

St. Dunstan's Street

Pound Ln. Street

Radigund's Street

Great Stour

Northgate

Union Street

Military Road

King Street

Palace Street

King's School

Christchurch Cathedral

Weavers' House

St. Peter's Street

St. Peter's Place

Eastbridge Hospital

High Street

Christchurch Gate

Buttermarket

Medieval City Walls

Broad Street

Monastery Street

St. Augustine's Abbey

St. Augustine's College

Longport

Pilgrims' Way Exhibition

Burgate

Poor Priests' Hospital/Canterbury Heritage Museum

St. Margaret Street

Longmarket & Roman Pavement

St. George's Church

St. George's Place

Rheims Way

Stour Street

Castle Street

Dane John Mound

Medieval City Walls

Rhodaus Town

Old Dover Road

New Dover Road

Canterbury East Train Station

Wincheap

N

0   Kilometers   0.4

cles performed by Thomas, which were to earn him his sainthood. An altar commemorates the great and humble man.

Canterbury is a fascinating historic town, which largely developed because of the cathedral's importance as a pilgrimage site, pilgrims came to pay hom-age to Thomas à Beckett. The stories of such pilgrims are found in Chaucer's *Canterbury Tales.*

A true taste of England

Despite its proximity to London, and

Rochester Castle, Kent.

the steady flow of traffic heading for the Channel ports, and, soon, to the Channel Tunnel, Kent is still dotted with quiet little towns and picturesque villages where ferries to France seem as remote as, well, France itself. **Meopham**, on the A227, has its windmill, cricket on the village green and a number of delightful pubs.

A few miles south (still on the A227) of the picturesque village of **Ightham** (pronounced "item") there is **Ightham Mote**, the most perfect surviving moated manor house in England. Kent's oldest

Oast houses in the "garden of England".

building, a pre-historic tomb, is to be found at **Kits Coty** near Maidstone. **Royal Tunbridge Wells** maintains the grace and style of a Georgian spa town, with its elegant colonnaded shopping area, the **Pantiles**.

Bountiful land

Since the time of Henry VIII, orchards have been associated with Kent and the county is still a rich fruit growing area, with apple, pear, plum, damson, cherry and quince trees. The National Fruit Collections at Brogdale Trust near Faversham, contain over 2,300 apple and 550 pear varieties.

Kent still has a number of tradi-

tional orchards, with many of the trees supporting hives of honey-producing bees. There are also a number of nut orchards. An increasingly rare sight is the cobnut plantation, but 150 acres of Kent cob still exist, many in the Plaxtol and Iththan areas.

Although Kent is traditionally renowned for its beers, it is also a flourishing wine producing area. Most Kentish wines are white, and include prize winners from the Penshurst, Lamberhurst, Biddenden, Tenterden and St Nicholas vineyards.

Aristocratic Surrey

The small county of Surrey, immediately to the south of London, was a commuter belt long before commuting was even thought of. Aristocrats built homes in Surrey as they do today, to take advantage of its proximity to London whilst still allowing them a country lifestyle. The splendid Tudor **Loseley House** and the elegant 18th century **Clandon Park** and **Hatchlands**, all in the vicinity of Guildford, were the forerunners of today's open-plan housing estates, many of which are constructed in a late 20th century amalgam style jokingly called "Tudorbethan".

Guildford is the county town of Surrey. The town has a striking modern **cathedral** consecrated in 1961. In nearby **Wisley**, the Royal Horticultural Society has a leading experimental garden established in 1904, with 250 acres devoted to flowers, fruit and vegetables.

Farnham Castle serves as a reminder of the power of the Bishops of Winchester and is remarkable for having been continuously occupied from the 12th to the 20th century. Built as a fortified manor house by Bishop Henry of Blois, grandson of William the Conqueror, it was used by his successors as Bishop of Winchester until 1927. Charles I stayed the night here on his way to trial.

Gillingham

One of **Gillingham's** most famous sons is William Adams. Born in 1564, he was in charge of Sir Francis Drake's supply

The Guildford Guildhall, Surrey.

vessels during the Spanish Armada. Later, he became the Pilot Major for a fleet of Dutch ships searching for new trading routes to the Far East. On one such voyage his ship, the *Deeliefde* landed in Japan in 1600, and Adams became the first Englishman to set foot on Japanese soil. He became a trusted advisor to the Japanese Shogun, and achieved the honoured rank of *samurai*. Adams remained in Japan for the rest of his life and helped to establish the first trading links between Britain and Japan.

Today Adams is commemorated by memorials in the Japanese cities of Yokosuka and Ito, where he lived and worked and back in Gillingham, he is commemorated by the **Clock Tower Memorial**.

Sussex

There are two counties called Sussex, East Sussex, which stretches along the coast from Kent to Brighton, and West Sussex, which continues along the coast to Chichester, and the Hampshire border. The Sussex coast is backed by the grassy slopes of the **South Downs**, and energetic visitors can follow the **South Downs Way**, 80 miles of good riding and walking countryside. In places, the South Downs make an abrupt sheer-drop into the sea, forming cliffs just as white as those of Dover to the east. In other places the flat land between the Downs and the coast has resulted in popular holiday resorts such as Hastings, Eastbourne and Brighton.

Chichester Cathedral, the centre-piece of a delightful medieval town.

183

Norman Sussex

Although **Hastings** has given its name to the most

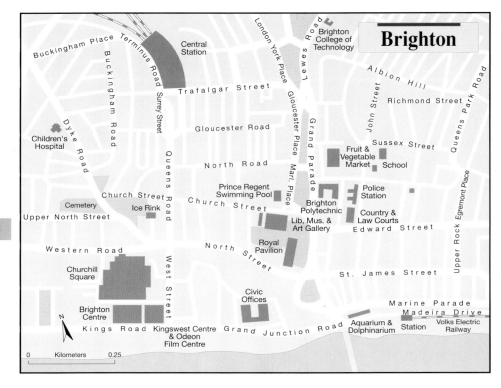

Brighton

SUSSEX

184

famous battle in English history, the actual clash between William the Conqueror and the English, took place 7 miles inland, at the spot now marked by **Battle Abbey**. Here the crucial engagement between the English Army led by King Harold, and the invading troops of William Duke of Normandy, took place on 14 October 1066. William had earlier landed at **Pevensey** a little further west down the coast, where he immediately ordered the first Norman castle to be put up on English soil, within the encircling walls of the existing Roman fortress. This was soon followed by a second castle at Hastings, in preparation for the great confrontation.

On 14 October, William's well trained army met the defending English forces at **Senlac Hill**, in what became known as the Battle of Hastings. The battle ended with Harold's death from an arrow shot into his eye, and the subsequent defeat of the English. In just one day the invasion of England had succeeded and the Crown was secured for the Normans.

Today, the battlefield looks much as it did in 1066, with the exception of Battle Abbey, founded by William four years later, in penance for the bloodshed he had caused. The high altar stood on the very spot where Harold fell, mortally wounded. A memorial stone marks the place today. Although much of William's original Abbey has disap-

The magnificent castle of Bodiam, set in its defensive moat.

peared, the 13th century dormitory remains, along with the graceful vaulting of the monks common room. A mile-long **Battlefield Walk** takes you around the perimeter of the battlefield, with relief models to help recreate what happened.

In the centuries after William the Conqueror built the first Norman castle at Pevensey, the castle was attacked and besieged many times. But to this day, its massive walls have never been breached under attack. In 1940, it was fortified again, when the medieval towers were made habitable, and gun emplacements and pill-boxes were constructed on the keep.

St Mary's Church in Rye (northeast of Hastings, on the Kent border)

had its bells stolen by the French in 1377, only to have them retrieved by men from Rye and nearby Winchelsea, on their own subsequent, vengeful mission to France.

The village of **Bodiam** (follow the A268 inland from Rye) which is mentioned in the *Domesday Book*, has a picture-book **Castle**, complete with moat and the original walls and battlements. Although Bodiam is inland, on the Kent border, the castle was built in 1385 to protect the Rother river valley from raiding French parties.

Brighton

Brighton owes its existence to the sea,

The exotic Royal Brighton Pavilion.

first as a small fishing and smuggling town, then as a fashionable watering hole of the rich and famous. The magnificent Regency squares and terraces in Brighton's **Kemp Town**, form a spectacular backdrop to the sea front. The **Lanes area** still resembles the higgledy-piggledy layout of ancient *Brighthelmstone*, as Brighton was known until the middle of the 18th century. The **Volk's Railway**, Britain's first electric railway, built in 1883, still runs between the Marina and the Palace Pier, passing *en route* a carefully marked 400 metre

Fun for the children along the Bluebell
Railway, West Sussex.

section of nudist beach.

Though not to everyone's taste, the **Royal Pavilion**, the seaside palace of King George IV, is one of the most exotic buildings in the country. First built as a simple classical villa by Henry Holland in 1787, the Pavilion was rebuilt by John Nash from 1815-22 in an Indian style, with Chinese style interiors. The enthusiasm of George IV for Brighton ensured that it became a leading resort, nick-named "London by the sea", but nevertheless, George's Royal Pavilion was still mocked by contemporaries. The writer William Cobbett said that it resembled a combination of "a square box, a large Norfolk turnip and four onions", whilst another Regency wit, Sydney Smith, suggested that the dome of St. Paul's Cathedral in London had gone to Brighton and had pups.

The Hampshire border

As East Sussex becomes West Sussex, there is a little more coastal development, and inland, to the north of the

The beach and pier at Brighton, a traditional British holiday resort.

county are the commuter towns of **Horsham**, **Crawley** and **Hayward's** Heath. Towards the western boundary with Hampshire, is the 17th century mansion house, **Petworth House** (take the A285 north out of Chichester) built by the sixth Duke of Somerset, nick-

named the Proud Duke, from his habit of expecting to be served on bended knee. In the 18th century, the wood-carver Grinling Gibbons was commissioned to create the **Carved Room**, which displays his stunning lime wood-carvings. The landscape painter Turner was

housed in a complex of converted 17th century and 19th century farm buildings.

Virtually on the Hampshire border, just south of Haslemere is the **Hollycombe Steam Collection**, where adults can happily become children again for the day, re-living the age of steam. Among the exhibits is a steam railway, a traction engine, steam-operated fairground rides, and a magnificent steam organ.

Littlehampton cosmetics

Down on the coast at **Littlehampton** is the headquarters of the highly successful cosmetics company, The Body Shop, which proudly describes itself as "being a loudmouth present on the High Street". The Body Shop is vocally concerned about the environment and animal testing, and has carried its principles to the logical conclusion of inviting the public in to see how their factory is run. In what must be instant history being made, you can also visit a replica of the very first branch of The Body Shop , dating, as they enthusiastically put it, "way back to 1976".

Arundel Castle

Arundel Castle is situated in magnificent grounds overlooking the river Arun, a couple of miles inland from Littlehampton. It was built at the end of

a frequent visitor to Petworth in the 1830s, and one room of the house is devoted entirely to his works.

From Petworth follow the A283 for about 4 miles and turn off to **Blackdown Hill**, the highest point in the county, where Alfred Lord Tennyson once had his home, **Aldworth**. Nestling beneath the hill, is the **Lurgashall Winery**,

Arundel Castle.

the 11th Century by Roger de Montgomery, Earl of Arundel. It has been the seat of the dukes of Norfolk, the foremost Catholic layman in the country, for over 700 years. In 1643, during the Civil War, the original castle was very badly damaged, and it was later restored in the 18th and 19th centuries. Amongst its treasures are a fine collection of furniture dating from the 16th century, tapestries and many famous paintings, including works by Gainsborough, Reynolds and Van Dyck. There is also the prayer-book and golden

demonstration of Christian unity, the two denominations today, worship under the same roof.

If you are a bird lover, Arundel has a **Wildlife, Wild fowl and Wetland Centre** and is one of 8 such centres throughout the UK, all part of The Wild Fowl & Wetlands Trust.

Chichester, city of the arts

Chichester is situated on the small area of flat land between the downs and the sea, and was once a Roman town, the original street plan still surviving today. Construction began on the **Cathedral** in 1091, and most of the building was completed by 1123. In the south aisle are two of the most important Norman sculptures surviving in Britain, carved in 1125 out of Purbeck stone, they represent the biblical story of the raising of Lazarus.

The composer Gustav Holst is buried in the cathedral. Another arts contribution came in 1955-77, when the Dean of the cathedral, who happened to be a keen lover of modern art, established an excellent collection of modern painting, sculpture and stained glass, including a window by the French artist Chagall, an extremely rare sight for a 900-year old cathedral. Chichester is host each summer to an important theatre festival, and in 1962, the hexagonal **Chichester Festival Theatre** was constructed, a sign of the festivals much increased popularity.

rosary of Mary Queen of Scots, carried by her at her execution, and bequeathed by her to the family. The mahogany wood library, built in 1800, is designed to resemble a church. Arundel parish church, the **Church of St Nicholas** on the boundary of the castle grounds is Protestant, whilst the attached family chapel is Catholic, and so, in a nice

Rudyard Kipling

Say "Rudyard Kipling" to most people, and they instantly think of India. Kipling's name is synonymous with *Kim* and *The Jungle Book, Gunga Din,* and *The Great Game, Mandalay,* and his famous statement on the British imperial destiny, "The White Man's Burden". But what few people know about is Rudyard Kipling's link with Sussex.

In 1634, a wealthy local ironmaster built himself a stone house just south of the picture-postcard village of Burwash, east of Heathfield, close to the river Dudwell. In 1902, Rudyard Kipling bought the house, Bateman's, minus electricity, but surrounded by 300 acres.

When Kipling bought his country home, he was already well known, for *Kim* had been published the previous year, and *The Jungle Book* in 1894. Kipling seems to have been happy at Bateman's and was to produce yet more books during his many years here; many of them are still being read. He lived in the house until his death in 1936. His widow, Caroline, left the house to the National Trust on her own death, 3 years later.

Bateman's house

In 1906, he wrote *Puck of Pook's Hill,* which features Bateman's. He solved the problem of electricity by converting an existing 18th century water-mill to provide power. In the 1970s, it was re-converted back to its original role, and now produces stone-ground flour for sale. When he was not writing or fixing the electricity, Kipling drove around the pretty surrounding countryside, in a 1928 Rolls Royce, which is on display in its original garage.

Today **Bateman's House**, which is run by the National Trust, has been restored as much as possible to the way it would have been in Kipling's day. His study appears ready for a day's work, with his pen and inkwell laid out. His chair is there, raised 5 cm (2 inches), to enable him to write and still look out of the window at the view. All around the house are mementos of Kipling's beloved India, there are family pictures taken in Lahore and Bombay, sculptures, bronzes, and statues of Indian gods.

Chichester environs

At **Fishbourne Roman Palace**, just outside Chichester, are the remains of the largest Roman residence yet to be found in Britain. The Palace was probably the palace of a local king, Tiberius Claudius Cogidubnus, and it is claimed, was perhaps the most splendid Roman building north of the Alps. The interior of Fishbourne was sumptuous, with gorgeous mosaics, which can still be seen, despite the destruction of the palace by fire in about AD 280.

Three miles to the north of Chichester lies **Goodwood House**, the ancestral seat of the Dukes of Richmond and Gordon. The magnificent state apartments of Goodwood House are filled with many treasures, including paintings by Canaletto, Stubbs, and Reynolds. **Goodwood Racecourse** is widely acclaimed for its top-class horse racing, and its winning post is 230 m (700 feet) above sea level. In 1948, the ninth Duke founded Goodwood's **Motor Circuit**, and the track is still in regular use throughout the year.

Innovative museums

Amongst all the historical and architec-

The seven limestone sisters at Beachy Head.

tural treasures of Sussex, there are two very different, but highly innovative museums.

In the centre of Chichester, there is a gracious house, built in 1712, called **Pallant House**. It was built for a wealthy wine merchant and was decorated with some of the finest craftsmanship then available. The house was turned into a local government office in 1919, but 60 years later was restored and converted into an art gallery.

The "authentic" restoration is complemented and off-set by the modern art on display, much of it collected by the Dean of Chichester, the man responsible for much of the modern art in the cathedral. Pallant House is a very happy fusion of old and new in a traditional urban setting.

The **Weald** and **Downland Open Air Museum,** situated a few miles inland from Chichester along the A286, is a very different museum. The aim of this museum is to "rescue" local buildings and artefacts of historic interest that are in danger of demolition or collapse and re-erect them in this pretty 40 acre site.

Nothing is too humble or simple for this fascinating museum – there is a wind pump, scarred wooden school benches, a set of Victorian carpenter's tools and the reconstructed 15th century Bayleaf Farm. Visiting this museum, which is just west of the village of Singleton, is a one-stop history lesson, minus the text books.

Hampshire & Dorset

195

The county of **Hampshire**, home to thousands of London commuters, has a varied and historic past, much of which has been dominated by Hampshire's excellent coastline. The major naval towns of Southampton and Portsmouth have both played an important role in English history and they remain key military and civil ports. Meanwhile the area also has a tradition for watersports, **Hayling island**, being the largest of many centres in the area. Southampton and Portsmouth both suffered much bomb damage during World War II, but happily their historic quarters were preserved. Many of **Southampton's** medieval buildings are still standing, and in the **Maritime Museum**, you can learn about the sad fate of the *Titanic*, which sunk on its maiden voyage from Southampton to New York.

Nelson's flagship HMS Victory, Portsmouth.

Maritime Portsmouth

Portsmouth is the country's most important naval base, and has a history dating back to the 15th century, when Henry VII fortified the sea walls, and the world's first ever dry dock was constructed there in 1495. Henry VIII expanded it and made it the first royal dockyard. The naval base and the harbour grew progressively in size and importance during the 17th and 18th centuries and it was from Portsmouth that the fleet set sail for the Battle of Trafalgar, in 1805.

Three of the greatest ships that ever sailed from Portsmouth harbour are now on display there; Nelson's flagship HMS *Victory*, Henry VIII's favourite war-ship the *Mary Rose,* and the pride of Queen Victoria's fleet HMS *Warrior*.

On 19 July 1545, the **Mary Rose**, Henry VIII's favourite war-ship was sailing from Portsmouth to go to battle with the French invasion fleet, when she keeled over, and sank quickly, taking with her 700 men and all the equipment of war. The horrified Henry could hear the cries of the drowning men from the shore. Lost for over 4 centuries, in 1965 British divers began searching for the remains and discovered that a large part of the ship and her contents had been preserved in the sediment. The raising of the *Mary Rose* in October 1982 was the culmination of the world's largest underwater archaeological operation. A special charity the *Mary Rose*

Trust which has HRH Prince Charles as its President, pays for the maintenance of the ship and the cost of research.

The task of maintenance is really phenomenal, visitors can see the 500-year-old hull of the *Mary Rose*, kept cool and damp with water jets. A personal stereo guide points out the various parts of the ship. In the **Mary Rose Exhibition** over 1,000 objects from the ship are on display, including cannon, long-bows, gold coins, pewter plates and navigation instruments, as well as the personal possessions of many sailors – clothing and games, and even the medical chest belonging to the barber surgeon. The museum also has a presentation on the history of the ship and on the splendid recovery operation which led to the salvage of the ship. The *Mary Rose* is situated in the **Historic Ships district** next to the railway station. You can also tour HMS **Victory** and HMS **Warrior** 's engine room can also be seen here. Seeing all 3 may however prove a bit expensive as you have to pay for each ship.

Portsmouth has many interesting museums, including the **Royal Naval Museum** in Portsmouth's Historic Naval Base, and the **Royal Marines Museum**. The centrepiece of the **D-Day Museum** is the **Overlord Embroidery**, measuring 80 metres (272 ft) in length. Inspired by the Bayeux tapestry, and 5 years in the making, the Overlord Embroidery is a colourful and moving testimony to the endeavours that led to the Allied victory in World War II. Catamarans make the short journey across the

Scuba-diving off the Dorset Coast at Lulworth.

Solent to the Isle of Wight, from Portsmouth regularly – several times an hour in the summer – it takes 15 minutes to reach Ryde.

Watersports centres

Close to Portsmouth, **Hayling Island**, **Emsworth** and **Langstone**, are leading centres for watersport activities. Hayling Island is the place where board sailing was invented, for, in 1958, a 12-year-old local boy, Peter Chilvers, invented the sail board, using a sheet of plywood, a tent fly sheet, a pole and some curtain rings, to sail up the island creek. Technology has come a long way since then, but Hayling Island still provides some of the most challenging waters for windsurfers, whilst in the quieter waters of Langstone and Chichester harbours,

Romsey Abbey, Hampshire.

conditions are ideal for beginners. One of the major events is the Round the Island wind-surfing marathon, one of the largest in the world.

Portsmouth environs

Havant, which connects Hayling Island to the mainland by a road bridge, was formerly well-known for its parchment-making. It is claimed that the *Magna Carta* was written on Havant parchment, while the 1919. Treaty of Versailles certainly used Havant parchment.

Three miles to the south of Portsmouth, in the middle of the Solent, is one of the most unusual properties in England. The doughnut-shaped three-quarter acre **Spit Bank Fort** was completed in 1880 to defend the harbour.

Bought over in 1986, it was converted into living accommodation. It has its own lighthouse and 3 helicopter landing pads and in 1993, was on sale for a cool £2.5 million.

Famous people & houses

Hampshire is the home county of two remarkable English writers, Charles Dickens, who was born in Portsmouth, and Jane Austen, who was born in the village of Steventon. Ten miles away is **Chawton** (just south of Alton) and you can visit the 17th century house, where the novelist lived from 1809 until 1817.

At **Romsey**, just north of Southampton, you can visit **Broadlands**, home of Lord Mountbatten. It is an elegant Palladian house with landscaped gardens by Capability Brown, and a Mountbatten exhibition and audio-visual.

In the north of the county is **Highclere Castle**, the family home of the seventh Earl of Carnarvon. It was transformed from a Georgian country house and completed in 1842 and is one of the finest creations of Sir Charles Barry, architect of the Houses of the Parliament. Some of the surrounding parkland was designed by Capability Brown. The fifth Earl of Carnarvon, along with Howard Carter, discovered King Tutankhamen's tomb, and Highclere has an Egyptian exhibition, which features some of the Egyptian collection of the fifth Earl. The collection

The round table of the legendary King Arthur, Winchester.

was re-discovered in 1987, hidden behind secret panelling between the drawing and the smoking rooms.

Winchester

North of Southampton on the A33, is the historic town of Winchester. **Winchester Cathedral** was first built by the Saxons in AD 648 to be replaced by a Norman cathedral in 1079. The present cathedral, is an assortment of styles, that is, Norman, Early English, Decorated, Perpendicular and Late Gothic, reflecting the cathedral's many layers of history. A monument to St Swithan stands on the site of an old shrine which was demolished during the dissolution

A Winchester street scene.

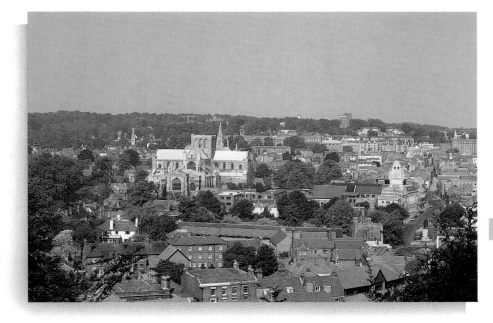

Aerial view of the medieval city of Winchester.

of the monasteries in 1538. Pilgrims came to the old shrine, in search of Bishop Swithan's renowned posthumous power to heal the sick. In the cathedral library lies the beautiful 12th century illuminated *Winchester Bible*, a paragon of its kind.

Castle Hall, built in 1235, is another of the cities "unmissables". The Hall is one of the finest medieval halls in England and contains the legendary **Round Table of King Arthur** and his knights – though historically it post-dates the king.

Winchester college is one of the oldest and most prestigious public schools in England, its quadrangles having something of an Oxbridge ambience.

Steam trains & silk mills

For steam train fans, Hampshire has the **Watercress Line** which runs for ten miles between the market towns of Alton and Alresford. Watercress is still grown in large commercial beds around Alresford, fed by the pure chalk-spring waters of the river Arle, and this local produce has given the mid-Hampshire railway its name. Freshly gathered watercress was bundled, packed into large wicker hampers and carried by rail to be sold in London the same day. This regular traffic flourished for almost 100 years, until it succumbed to the fall of Dr Beeching's infamous "axe" in the 1960s.

Close to Andover, situated on Frog

The Isle of Wight

Nature exposed, the beautiful coast of the Isle of Wight.

Off the coast of Hampshire and facing the New Forest is the **Isle of Wight**, an island of only 147 square miles. It has a sunny climate, good sandy beaches, a rather pretty countryside, and a beautiful 65 mile-long coastal path all around the island.

The Isle of Wight has been firmly on the holiday map ever since Queen Victoria started spending holidays there. John Keats, Charles Dickens and Lewis Carroll were also frequent visitors and from his house in Farrington, Lord Tennyson wrote much of his poetry.

Osbourne House

In 1845, Queen Victoria and Prince Albert had a holiday villa built for themselves, overlooking the Solent; its name was **Osborne House**. After Albert's death in 1861, Victoria spent much of her 40 years of widowhood there, insisting that everything be left as it was during Albert's life. Today, this enables visitors to have a unique glimpse into mid-19th century royal life. Osborne House was given to the nation by Victoria's son, Edward VII. In the grounds is a real Swiss Cottage, imported from Switzerland in 1853, and used as the royal childrens' playhouse.

Carisbrooke Castle

Carisbrooke Castle is one of the finest moated Norman castles in the south of England. King Charles I was imprisoned there, and his daring escape plan was foiled when he got stuck climbing out of a window. It has always been the most important castle on the Isle of Wight and the Lordship of the island went with it.

At the centre of the castle are the Great Hall and chamber. It was in the **Great Hall** that the

Island in the River Test, is **Whitchurch Silk Mill**, the last working silk mill in the south of England. The water-wheel installed in 1890 has been completely restored and once again provides power for weaving silk. Incidentally, the River Test has excellent trout fishing.

The New Forest

In the southwestern corner of Hampshire, close to its border with Dorset, is one of the glories of this part of the country, the **New Forest**. The forest was

Royal prisoner whiled away the dreary hours, writing a justification for his actions, and where Princess Beatrice, daughter of Queen Victoria ruled as the last resident governor of the castle and the island. At the **Well House**, you can still see a donkey working a 16th century wheel, to draw water from a 53 m (161 ft) deep well. Decorative today, the well was once an essential part of Carisbrooke's defences since without a reliable water supply, no castle could withstand a siege.

The Needles

At **Alum Bay**, the westernmost bay on the island, the biggest attraction is the famous chalk stacks called **The Needles** which jut out from the bay. The view from the cliffs across to the Needles is wonderful, especially when the sun is out and the sun glistens on the gleaming white cliffs. There are about 20 different mineral hues in the sands at Alum Bay, and it is fun to make your own souvenir. In the Sand Shop, you can fill your choice of glass shape with layers of different coloured sands.

Cowes

Cowes, at the north of the island, is the undisputed yachting centre of the Isle of Wight, and, during the annual **Cowes Week**, it becomes the undisputed yachting centre of the entire country. Cowes Week, which usually takes place in the beginning of August is an international yachting festival, attracting top level sailors and competitors.

set aside as a special place more than 9 centuries ago by William the Conqueror, who called it his new hunting forest. Synonymous with the New Forest are its famous ponies, which roam the forest freely. Each animal is owned by a commoner and must be branded before be-

ing allowed to wander. Anyone can become a commoner; the term simply refers to a person who owns a plot of land to which privileges are attached, known as rights of common.

Four official Agisters – a name unique to the New Forest – deal with the daily management of over 5,000 ponies and cattle which roam wild over 45,000 acres of open forest. Each autumn, the Agisters organize the annual round-ups known locally as "Drifts", to check the condition of animals and to ensure the annual marking fees have been paid.

Historic figures

Dorset is so often referred to as "Thomas Hardy country" that people tend to forget that the county has a history dating back to the Iron Age, well before Hardy's "Wessex" – the name of a Saxon Kingdom, which included Doset, but is now geographically extinct. Hardy was born in 1840 near **Dorchester**, and the little thatched cottage where he was born and lived until his marriage, can be visited.

Travel north of Dorchester on the A352 to see one of the oldest sites in the county, the **Cerne Abbas Giant**. This huge figure has been cut into the hill, to expose the natural chalk rock below, and has been lovingly maintained over hundreds of years. The giant is 59 m (180 ft) long, and in his right hand he brandishes a club, 39 m (120 ft) long. The semi-naturalistic style in which he

The Cerne Abbas giant, Dorset, a
very ancient piece of artwork.

is portrayed suggests a Romano-British
origin.

Sherbourne & Poole

From Cerne Abbas continue north for 9
km (10 miles) on the A352 to the pretty
town of **Sherborne**, famed for its **castle**,
its stunning abbey, and its public school.
The Abbey was built between the 12th
and the 15th centuries from a warm,
honey-coloured sandstone. "A malicious
and mischievous castle, like its owner",
declared Cromwell, when he laid siege
to Sherborne Old Castle in 1645. It was
16 days before the castle surrendered,
whereupon its defences were dismantled. The castle's most illustrious inhabitant was Sir Walter Raleigh, who leased
it from Queen Elizabeth. The surrounding landscape, created by Capability
Brown, makes a peaceful and pleasing
setting for the castle.

Poole has a good sandy beach, and,
along with nearby Bournemouth, is a
popular holiday area. There is an interesting **Old Quarter**, with many well
preserved 18th century buildings. **Poole
Pottery** has been making ceramics on
the quay since 1873.

In Poole Harbour, there is a little
island called **Brownsea Island**, one of
the few places in the country where the
red squirrel still thrives. The island covers 500 acres, has good beaches, nature
trails, peacocks, a colony of tiny Japanese Sika deer, and, of course, red squir-
rels galore. There is a 200 acre nature
reserve, containing a marsh, a saltwa-
ter lagoon and two lakes.

The Purbeck Coast

Coming from the quiet environs of Chesil
Bank on the West Dorset Heritage Coast,
you will be quite surprised to arrive at
the large resort of **Weymouth**. The resort has numerous hotels and other
accomodation, the prime position being the elegant Georgian buildings along
the seafront.

There are indeed a great number of
resorts along the Dorset coast, **Bournemouth** is the largest and despite its size
still has an aura of elegance, with its
majestic hotels and pier. The town has a

Boats at Lyme Regis, Dorset.

considerable population of students, with its university and many language schools. East of Bounemouth is the pleasant yachting harbour at **Christchurch**, while west of Weymouth is the pretty resort of **Lyme Regis**, immortalised in Jane Austen's novel *Persuasion*. This extremely pretty town is built on a hill which descends to a pleasant harbour and beach. Beauty has however, been somewhat exploited by tourism and in the summer months you will find the town extremely crowded.

Leaving Lyme Regis, travelling in the direction of Bridport, stop by at the village of **Chideock**, where nearly every cottage is thatched. If you have time, leave the main road and explore more of these charming Dorset villages; there

are a number of "B&B" in the region.

To enjoy the Purbeck limestone cliffs at their best, travel to the village of **West Lulworth**, about 15 miles east of Weymouth; the limestone here has been eroded into the **Durdle Door** arch and the tranquil **Lulworth Cove**. There is a pleasant walk along the coast starting from the village.

Abbotsbury Swannery

Travelling from Bridport to Weymouth on the B3175, which runs parallel to the West Dorset Heritage Coast, you will come to the charming village of **Abbotsbury**. The main street of the village is lined with stone cottages, many

Eroded by weather and time, Durdle Door in Dorset is an interesting geographical feature.

of them thatched with reeds from the nearby Fleet lagoon. Before the Dissolution of the monasteries, the great Benedictine Abbey of St Peter's which stood here was an important religious site, but very little survives today, other than the superb tithe barn. This **Great Abbey Barn** was built around 1400, to store the grain generated by the ecclesiastical estates.

Three years ago, the barn was made into a **Museum of Old Agricultural Equipment**. Most people however, come to Abbotsbury visit it. The **Swannery** is

On the beach at Abbotsbury
Swannery.

Peter's and in 1393, there is the first authenticated record of a managed herd. In 1543, the Fox Strangways family bought the manor of Abbotsbury and were granted the right to keep the Abbotsbury herd by Henry VIII. The family still owns it today. In 1591, the first swan census during the reign of Queen Elizabeth I recorded 410 swans and 90 cygnets.

Today, although the herd of mute swans fluctuates in number, it is usually 400 to 500 in summer and up to 900 in winter. The birds are free to come and go at will and are not pinioned. Nest-making occurs from April to May, and Abbotsbury is the only swannery in the world which can be visited during this fascinating time.

a unique swan nesting colony. Abbotsbury stands near the The Fleet lagoon, an area of water which separates Chesil Bank and the mainland, a wetland area of international importance and home to the largest colony of mute swans in the country.

Originally, the swannery was owned by the monks of the Abbey of St

Devon is a large, beautiful county, with strong maritime links, renowned for its natural beauty, and its superb cream teas. Within its 772 sq km (2,000 sq miles) are two national parks, and two very different coastlines. In the north, the expanse of Exmoor looks on to the Bristol Channel, whilst in the south, Dartmoor faces the more sheltered English Channel.

209

The pretty village of Clovelly, has been preserved from the modern world.

The English Riviera

The two largest and busiest towns in Devon are both to the south, the coastal town of Plymouth, virtually on the Cornish border and the cathedral town of Exeter, situated a little inland on the River Exe. Bideford and Barnstaple are

Clovelly – A Unique Village

On Devon's Atlantic coast, there is a tiny village, called **Clovelly**, with a resident population of about 200. Nothing new in that, you might say, Devon is full of little villages, each one prettier than the next.

True, but Clovelly is totally different. For one thing, there are no cars in Clovelly. And for another thing, it is a privately owned village, owned by the same family for generations, and run by an estate company.

Clovelly, founded in the Iron Age, was already a thousand years old, when it was recorded in the 11th century Domesday Book. In about 1370, the Caireys, one of the great families of Clovelly became lords of the manor. For 11 generations they looked after Clovelly, and it was during this time that the village began to prosper.

The Queen of Clovelly

Frequently, the Manor of Clovelly passed through the female line, and in 1884, Christine Hamlin inherited it from her brother. Christine Hamlin, the "Queen of Clovelly", loved the village, devoting her life to it, and she believed that everyone should know of its beauty. Clovelly by now was already a major tourist attraction, with thousands of visitors. But Christine ensured that the village remained unspoiled and

kept the coaches and cars out of sight, as they still are today.

In addition to keeping her own personal diary, Christine also complied *The Clovelly Chronicles*, nine volumes of press-cuttings and pictures of people and events connected with Clovelly, as well as writing *The Annals of Clovelly*, a complete record of all the improvements she carried out on the estate. High taxation and impending death duties would have crippled the estate, so in 1928, at the age of 72, she formed the Clovelly Estate Company.

Christine Hamlin died in 1936 and is buried in **All Saints Church** above the village. It is because of her foresight in forming the Clovelly Estate Company that her direct descendants today are still able to manage the estate.

The 19th century writer, Charles Kingsley spent his youth in Clovelly, as his father was the rector and part of the *Water Babies* is set there. You will also find many more Clovelly characters and places appearing in his famous novel, **Westward Ho**.

Clovelly traditions

Despite the crowds, time has definitely managed to stand still in Clovelly. The only method of transport along the steeply cobbled streets is still sledge and donkey. Many of the houses

busy market towns in the north, and between Plymouth and Exeter are the popular holiday resort towns of Torquay, Paignton and Brixham. This 14 km (22 mile) stretch of coastline is known as the **English Riviera**, with its 18 beaches, and its sheltered, sunny weather. The sun shone every single day during the summer of 1990, breaking a 40-year-old temperature record, whilst June 1992 was the sunniest ever on record, very good indeed, by English standards.

Plymouth & environs

Plymouth is synonymous with some of the country's greatest sailors: Sir Francis Drake, Sir Walter Raleigh, Hawkins, Captain Cook and of course, the Pilgrim Fathers. Francis Drake sailed from Plymouth in the *Golden Hinde* on 13 December 1577 to circumnavigate the world and returned there on 26 September 1580. He sailed again from Plymouth

were built over 400 years ago, of stone and boulder, many have ships' timbers hidden inside, and some have unique decorations, including one, whose façade was brought back from Oberammergau in Germany.

The High Street is called "Upalong" or "Downalong", by local people, depending on which way you are going! Half-way down to the harbour is a lookout, where the wives of sailors and fishermen used to keep watch for returning boats. As you walk down to the harbour, you pass under **Templebar**, one of the oldest houses in the village, built on 4 different levels. Continuing down, you pass the old lime kiln, once an essential part of the economy of the village, and now a resting place for unused boats.

Clovelly Harbour is a working harbour but full of charm, and in a county full of beautiful little harbours, one of the most picturesque. On the quay, is the **Red Lion Inn**, dating from the 18th century and one of the oldest buildings in Clovelly.

Tradition is still strong in Clovelly. At the beginning of Lent, children race up and down the street in a centuries old festival, dragging tins to drive out the devil. To ensure the fishermens' safe return and a bountiful catch, a sea blessing service is carried out every July. And whenever there is a wedding in the village, the traditional donkeys accompany the bride up the hill.

in 1588, to defeat the Spanish Armada. In 1620 the *Mayflower* sailed out of Plymouth, carrying the Pilgrim Fathers to the New World and in 1768 Captain Cook sailed from the harbour in search of a southern continent.

Plymouth Hoe is the place to head for, to try and recapture the spirit of Plymouth's history. As every English school-child knows, it was here on Plymouth Hoe that Sir Francis Drake calmly finished his game of bowls, whilst wait-

Beautiful detail on Exeter Cathedral, one of England's finest buildings.

ing for the tide to turn, so he could set sail against the approaching Spanish Armada. Drake's statue is one of several naval memorials on the Hoe, along with a bright red and white lighthouse, **Smeaton's Tower**, designed in 1755, which used to stand on the Eddystone Rocks, 14 miles out to sea.

At one end of the Hoe is the massive 17th century **Royal Citadel** and round the other side of the headland, the **Mayflower steps**. These simple steps are decorated with many plaques commemorating famous departures from the West Pier.

Just north of Plymouth off the A386 is **Buckland Abbey**, a 13th century Cistercian monastery, bought by Sir Francis Drake in 1581. The Abbey be-

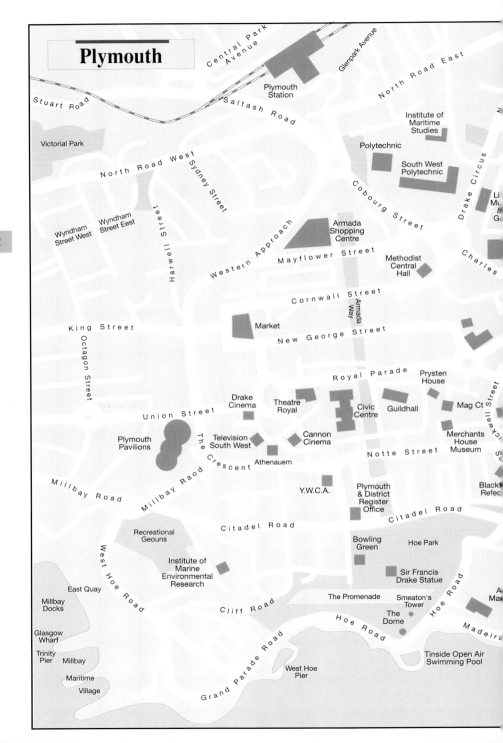

Plymouth

Central Park Avenue

Glenpark Avenue

North Road East

Plymouth Station

Saltash Road

Stuart Road

Victorial Park

Institute of Maritime Studies

Polytechnic

South West Polytechnic

North Road West

Sydney Street

Cobourg Street

Drake Circus

Li Mu & G

Wyndham Street West

Wyndham Street Eest

Harwell Street

Western Approach

Mayflower Street

Armada Shopping Centre

Methodist Central Hall

Charles

Cornwall Street

Armada Way

King Street

Octagon Street

Market

New George Street

Royal Parade

Prysten House

Drake Cinema

Theatre Royal

Civic Centre

Guildhall

Mag Ct

Union Street

Plymouth Pavilions

The Crescent

Television South West

Cannon Cinema

Merchants House Museum

Notte Street

ckwell

Athenauem

Millbay Road

Millbay Raod

Y.W.C.A.

Plymouth & District Register Office

Black Refec

Citadel Road

Citadel Road

Recreational Geouns

West Hoe Road

Institute of Marine Environmental Research

Bowling Green

Hoe Park

Sir Francis Drake Statue

East Quay

Cliff Road

The Promenade

Smeaton's Tower

Hoe Road

A Ma

Millbay Docks

Glasgow Wharf

The Dome

Madeira

Trinity Pier

Millbay

Hoe Road

Tinside Open Air Swimming Pool

Maritime

Village

Grand Parade Road

West Hoe Pier

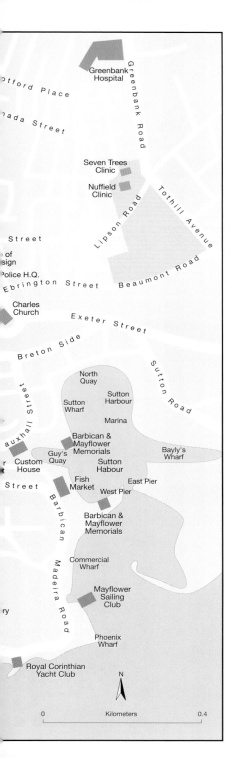

came Drake's home until his death and contains many mementos of Drake, including his will and the drum which was with him when he died at sea in 1596.

Exeter

One of the glories of English medieval architecture is the great west front of **Exeter Cathedral**, with its superb image screen; the 238 kings, knights, prophets, apostles and angels, many now eroded beyond identification, probably representing the Tree of Jesse, Christ's family. The image screen is a near miraculous survivor of the Reformation, as well as 500 years of salt-laden west country gales and the depredations of misguided restorers.

The modern appearance of Exeter and indeed many other cathedrals, is dramatically different from that intended by their makers. This is largely the result of a Victorian aesthetic which emphasised unadorned purity, removing anything that interfered with it. What is missing from Exeter's west front is paint. It has been known since the 1950s that medieval cathedrals were extensively decorated with vivid colours and that painting formed an integral part of the architects' scheme. Recent research at Exeter has revealed microscopic pigment samples, which would indicate that the present, plain stone façade was once a riot of colour.

The **Guildhall** is one of the oldest municipal buildings in the United King-

Dartmouth

Following the indented coastline east from Plymouth, you arrive in **Dartmouth**, home to the **Britannia Royal Naval College**. Jutting out into the narrow entrance to the Dart Estuary, with tidal waters in front, and steep wooded slopes rising behind, **Dartmouth Castle** was well-placed to guard what was once one of England's most important ports. Dartmouth was the first castle in the country to be built specifically with artillery in mind, and many new fortifications have been added to it over the past 450 years. You can see the restored Victorian coastal defence battery, with fully

dom, still regularly used for council meetings and civic functions: the earliest reference to it is in a deed of 1160. In a busy canal basin, on the River Exe, is the interesting **Exeter Maritime Museum**, many of the museum's boats moored on the quayside, whilst across the river, the remainder are housed in 19th century warehouses.

A short distance form the Cathedral is The **Ship Inn**, which comes with excellent references, for on display is a 1587 quotation from Sir Francis Drake: "Next to mine own shippe I do most love that old ship in Exon, a tavern in Sir Martin's Lane".

Action on the quay
outside Exeter's
Maritime Museum.

The Ship Inn, a public house in Exeter, evidence of this region's maritime links.

equipped guns. The upper gun emplacement was in use as late as World War II.

Dartmoor National Park

Behind the south Devon coast, with its deep water harbours and busy ports, lies **Dartmoor**, 141 sq km (365 square miles) of open, dramatic moorland. Dartmoor is a National Park, with herds of ponies, sheep and cattle roaming freely. Only two roads cross Dartmoor, both following the route of ancient tracks, and they meet in a tiny hamlet called **Two Bridges**. There are no towns on the moor,

only villages and hamlets, volcanic hills and pre-historic stone circles, 2 abbeys and a castle. The latter, **Castle Drogo**, is a turn-of-the-century melodramatic piece of architecture, designed by the eminent architect Edward Lutyens, for a retired grocer.

Buckfast Abbey was founded in Saxon times and grew in size and influence during the Middle Ages, until the Dissolution of the monasteries in 1539 when it was closed and fell into ruin. Three hundred and fifty years later, Benedictine monks settled again at Buckfast, and set about re-raising the Abbey on its original foundation. Shortly after arriving at Buckfast, the monks discovered

The wild landscape of Dartmoor.

The pretty town of Dartmouth nestles beside the sea.

the foundations of the medieval Abbey beneath their vegetable garden.

Between 1906 and 1938, the whole church was rebuilt by just 6 monks, only one of whom had previously worked as a mason, an undertaking financed entirely from donations. Much of the art on display in the church is also the work of the monks. At the Abbey, you can buy the Buckfast honey and the monks' special tonic wine.

North Devon

The northern **Atlantic coastline** is spectacularly beautiful, especially around **Woolacombe**, **Mortehoe**, and **Croyde**. The three villages are located beside beautiful sandy beaches and flanked by the two dramatic headlands of **Morte Point** and **Baggy Point**. Opportunities for bathing, surfing and wind-surfing are excellent on the clean, spacious beaches of Woolacombe, Saunton and Croyde.

It may come as a surprise to learn that this idyllic part of the country played an important part in World War II; from the autumn of 1943 to the spring of 1944, the **Woolacombe Bay Hotel** was the headquarters of the US Assault Training Centre. Here on Woolacombe and on Saunton sands, the thousands of American troops who would spearhead the landing assaults on the Normandy beaches, underwent rigorous and specialized training which led to victory on

Ilfracombe harbour.

6 June 1944, D-Day.

Further to the east along the coast, close to the Somerset border, are two villages, **Lynton** and **Lynmouth**. Lynmouth is on the shore, while Lynton is 164 m (500 ft) above on the cliff, and they both have superb views across the Bristol Channel to Wales. The combination of waterfalls, cliffs and valleys prompted the Victorians to call this area, "the little Switzerland of England". Victorian ingenuity came to the fore in 1890, when the two villages were linked by a unique water-operated cliff railway, still in service today. The two cars operate by water ballast, the top car taking on water to hoist the lower one, and emptying it as it reaches the bottom.

The seas along the Atlantic coast can be treacherous and there is one particularly dramatic story, which illustrates the courage of the local sailors. On a stormy night in January 1899, a large ship was seen sending distress signals off Porlock, in Somerset. Launching the lifeboat from Lynmouth was impossible because of the violent weather conditions, so the local people decided to carry the lifeboat 13 miles overland to Porlock Weir. The boat had to be hauled up Countisbury Hill and down Porlock Hill, both with gradients of one-in-four 25%. Other hazards included narrow roads that had to be widened, walls and gateposts to be removed and trees felled. The lifeboat reached Porlock 10 hours later and was

Saint George, the patron saint of England, at Exeter Cathedral.

was founded soon after 1157. It was dissolved in 1539, surviving longer than any other monastery in the country. Henry VIII made a gift of the abbey to the sergeant of his wine cellar, William Abbott. The house, which is still a lived-in family home, descended to the present owners through a series of marriages and has never been sold.

Further west, just off the A39 and right on the coast is the beautiful village of **Clovelly**, a virtually unspoiled time-capsule, where cars are banned. (see box story p210).

launched, reaching the distressed ship at 7.30 the following morning.

From Lynmouth, journey south along the A39 to Barnstaple and westwards along the coast to **Westward Ho!** with its sheltered bay and vast expanses of sand - and yes, the name does have an exclamation mark. Back on to the A39 and you will arrive at the town of **Bideford** which has been a crossing place on the River Torridge for centuries. The original wooden bridge was replaced by a stone one in the 15th century, and each of its 24 arches is different. Bideford **Pannier Market** takes place on Tuesday and Saturday mornings all year round: the market charter was first granted by Henry III in 1272.

Hartland Abbey, near Bideford,

Ilfracombe

Ilfracombe is the resort capital of north

A quaint thatched cottage in this most homely part of the world.

Pony rides for the children.

Devon and has been a popular seaside centre since the 1830s. Today it still has a charming Victorian atmosphere, the town clustering around the harbour, still an active fishing port. On the summit of Langton Hill above the harbour, is the tiny **Chapel of St Nicholas**, originally built in the early 14th century. Since that time, a light has shone continuously to aid mariners seeking the haven of Ilfracombe harbour.

The **Tunnel Beaches** are a good example of Victorian ingenuity, for they were quarried beneath the cliffs to create a safe and sheltered bathing area among the tidal rock pools. Until 1905, a strict segregation of male and female bathers was imposed, but today a more relaxed attitude prevails.

Do not be fooled by the prevailing holiday atmosphere, into thinking that the tide of history passed by Ilfracombe. Not at all, as the story of the Red Petticoats proves. After the French Revolution, the French were preparing to invade England, and in order to create a diversion, they organized a force of 15,000 men with orders to land in Ireland, which was already in revolt against England. Violent storms, however, broke up the formation, and on 22 February 1797, the people of Ilfracombe were astonished to see four French ships sailing towards Ilfracombe harbour. Since most of the Ilfracombe men were absent, the women, led by Old Betsy Gammon, put on red petticoats and lined Capstone and Langton Hills, fooling the

Fields of mustard brighten the Devon landscape.

French into believing they were soldiers. The French were scared off, but scuttled several vessels before departing.

In the footsteps of an otter

Henry Williamson's novel, *Tarka the Otter*, written in the 1920s is a superb evocation of the wildlife and country-side of north Devon. It tells of the "joyful water-life and death in the country of the two rivers" of an otter born beside the River Torridge. Williamson's inspi-ration was his own love for the country-side around his home in Georgeham and the rivers Taw and Torridge, as well as his own experience of caring for an orphaned otter cub.

Tarka's wanderings reveal some of the prettiest landscapes in north Devon from rolling hills to coastal shores, and a Tarka Project has recently been estab-lished to protect this area of north Devon. The **Tarka Trail**, a long-distance foot-path, follows the journeys of Tarka and also incorporates one of the loveliest train journeys in Britain, the **Tarka Line**, which links Barnstaple and Exeter along the banks of the river Tor.

The Lundy Islands

Islands always seem to exert a special fascination, and **Lundy** is no exception. Seven km (11 miles) away in the Bristol channel and a two and a quarter hour

Lush green fields lie in the heart of the beautiful countryside of Devon.

sail from the north Devon coast, is a tiny island, only nearly 2 km (3 miles long) and less than 1 km (half a mile) wide, but with a delightful mixture of ingredients: the 13th century **Marisco castle**; a church; a lighthouse; a windmill to generate electricity and hundreds of puffins and seals.

Despite a population of only 17 people, the island produces its own stamps and its own beer and has one shop-cum-pub. To add to the atmosphere, 137 ships have been mysteriously wrecked off the Lundy coast.

Cornwall

Cornwall is one of England's most beautiful and mysterious counties, a land of rocky cliffs and jagged headlands, of pretty villages, ruined castles and the enduring legends of King Arthur and his Knights of the Round Table. It is an area beloved of holiday makers, sportsmen, artists and painters, inspiring among many, Barbara Hepworth and Daphne de Maurier.

Spectacular cliffs and blue seas characterize the Cornish coast.

Cornwall's mild climate, which enjoys the warmth of the Gulf Stream, has made it home to some of the country's most spectacular gardens, with many rare and beautiful plants. These gardens include Trewithen and Trelissick, near Truro; Pentewan at St Austell, and the "Lost Gardens of Heligan", forgotten for more than 70 years, and now the scene of the largest garden restoration project in Europe.

223

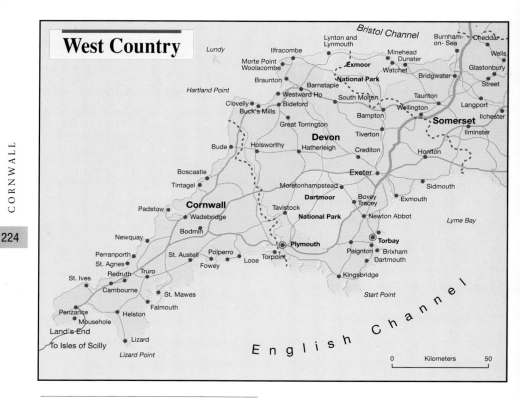

West Country

Bristol Channel

Lundy

Lynton and Lynmouth

Ilfracombe
Morte Point
Woolacombe
Braunton

Exmoor
National Park

Minehead
Dunster
Watchet

Burnham-on-Sea
Wells

Cheddar

Glastonbury

Bridgwater

Street

Hartland Point

Westward Ho
Barnstaple

South Molton

Taunton

Wellington

Langport

Ilchester

Clovelly
Buck's Mills

Bideford

Bampton

Somerset

Great Torrington

Tiverton

Ilminster

Devon

Bude

Holsworthy

Hatherleigh

Crediton

Honiton

Boscastle

Tintagel

Moretonhampstead

Exeter

Sidmouth

Cornwall

Dartmoor

Bovey
Tracey

Exmouth

Padstow
Wadebridge

Tavistock

National Park

Newton Abbot

Lyme Bay

Bodmin

Newquay

Perranporth
St. Agnes
Redruth
St. Ives
Cambourne
Penzance
Mousehole
Land's End
To Isles of Scilly

St. Austell
Fowey

Polperro
Looe

Torpoint

Plymouth

Paignton

Torbay

Brixham

Dartmouth

Kingsbridge

Truro
Helston

St. Mawes
Falmouth

Start Point

Lizard
Lizard Point

English Channel

0   Kilometers   50

King Arthur's country

Cornwall's Atlantic coastline is a great place to go if you are a watersports enthusiast for its magnificent breakers are ideal for surfing and body-boarding. The area also enjoys a close romantic association with the legendary King Arthur, a 5th century figure, whose victories over the Saxons formed an idealized and enduring image of chivalry, in the English psyche.

Tintagel Castle, where King Arthur is alleged to have been born, is truly the stuff of legend, the stunning remains of the medieval castle, perched perilously close to the tip of a rugged cliff, the

waves of the Atlantic Ocean crashing below. Over the centuries, the medieval castle has split in two, and one part stands on a cliff on the mainland, and the other on an island, linked to the mainland by a narrow neck of land. Each year, more and more of the neck disappears, as the cliffs slowly subside into the sea. The sea has already carved a huge sea cave below the island, eventually, the roof of this cave will collapse, taking with it what remains of the castle above.

One thousand five hundred years ago, when Britain was part of the Roman empire, there was a settlement at Tintagel, which may well have been the enigmatic place the Romans called

The coast at Tintagel.

Durocornovium, whereabouts of which have never been traced. When the Roman Empire fell, and much of England was overrun by pagan Saxons, Tintagel may have become the Christian stronghold of a Cornish King.

From about AD 600 to 1200, Tintagel seems to have been abandoned, with only St Juliette's Chapel standing on the deserted island. The medieval castle was probably added about AD 1233-1236 by Earl Richard of Cornwall, brother of King Henry III.

The connection of King Arthur with Tintagel goes back in legend and literature for more than 850 years. If indeed King Arthur ever existed, it was in the late 5th century, and realistically speaking, he was unlikely ever to have come to Tintagel. Yet, by the 12th century, stories about Arthur were becoming fashionable at the English court, and the chronicler Geoffrey of Monmouth wrote a fanciful account of Arthur's birth, which he set in Tintagel, and so the legend took root.

Close by Tintagel, and belonging to a completely different era, **Delabole Wind Farm** is Britain's first commercial wind farm, located in one of the windiest regions of the UK. The 10 wind turbines can produce enough electricity for 3,000 homes.

The far west

Cornwall's far west coast, was histori-

The medieval fortress of Tintagel Castle where the legendary King Arthur, is alleged to have been born.

cally the most remote part of the county, indeed country, and it still retains a very special atmosphere. The fishing port of **St Ives** is a classic image of Cornwall; an endearing medley of golden beaches and picturesque cottages, of fishing boats and artists hunched over their easels. The town is a magnet for artists of all kinds, from enthusiastic amateurs, hoping to paint the definitive view of the harbour, to a host of well-known profes-

sional painters and sculptors who have made St Ives their home. Turner started the trend in 1811, Dame Barbara Hepworth continued it, and the town's destiny as an artistic magnet has been recently confirmed by the opening of an outpost of the Tate Gallery there in 1993.

Take the B3306 road out of St Ives for approximately 3 miles and you will reach the village of **Zennor**, which has

A touch of the Mediterranean at St Ives beach.

St Michael's Mount has been a place of pilgrimage since the Middle Ages.

The quaint old back lanes of St Jves.

an interesting "plague stone". The village had two major outbreaks of cholera, in 1832 and 1849, and the stone was used by the villagers to disinfect money. In a hollow on the surface of the stone, they poured vinegar, and left their money there. Delivery men would take the disinfected coins out, in payment for food left for the villagers.

Penzance, on the south coast of the far west is a large, busy port, famous for its stunning views across to the off-shore islet of **St Michael's Mount**. Access to the Mount at low tide is across a cobbled

The first and last house in England at Land's End at dusk.

causeway, and at high tide you take a launch from the harbour at Marazion. St Michael's Mount has been a place of pilgrimage since the Middle Ages, a hermitage, a priory, a fortress, and for the last 300 years, a private home. In the Iron Age, the Mount may well have been "Ictis", to which the Mediterranean fleet came for tin. The monks of Mont St Michel in Normandy – of which St Michael's Mount is a replica – built the monastery, which was later annexed by Henry IV. During the Civil War, it was a fiercely Royalist strong-hold.

Less than 1 km (1 mile) east of Penzance, in the village of Gulval, is **Chysauster Ancient Village**, the remains of an ancient Romano-Cornish village with the oldest identifiable street in England. The ruins of the 8 surviving houses with their terraced gardens give an impression of life here 2,000 years ago.

The Cornish far west, is the symbolic end of England, with **Land's End** the most westerly part of the country, and the **Lizard Peninsula** the most southerly point. The Romans called Land's End *Belerion* (Seat of Storms), but on a clear day, the outline of the Isles of Scilly, and the profiles of the Wolf and Longships lighthouses are clearly visible. The Lizard peninsula, part of the "toe" of Cornwall, so named for its recognizable resemblance to a foot, boasts two coves of stunning beauty, **Kynance Cove** and **Mullion Cove**.

Kynance Cove has been one of the

This quaint old pub offers a varied fare of shellfish, the local speciality.

great traditional sights of Cornwall since Victorian days, when "Excursionists" would journey here, often by donkey. Kynance's unique combination of a mild maritime climate, and a lack of agricultural disturbance, has created an extraordinary botanical community, and plants found nowhere else in Britain grow here in profusion. All over the hillsides and moors of this westerly part of Cornwall, you can see the remains of tin mines, their chimneys pointing up to the deep blue sky, like thin fingers.

South coast resorts

The south coast of Cornwall, facing the English channel, is altogether warmer and sunnier than its Atlantic counterpart and is popularly known as the English Riviera. The Riviera coast is famous for its thickly wooded river valleys, its sub-tropical gardens, and its pretty, pastel-coloured fishing villages that remain so much a part of the image of Cornwall. A succession of delightful villages and little towns line the coast, including Falmouth, Fowey, Looe, Mevagissey and Polperro.

Falmouth is the largest of the riviera resorts its exceptional natural deepwater harbour being the third largest in the world. **Pendennis Castle** on the outskirts of the city, was built by Henry VIII, to guard the mile-wide entrance to the Carrick Roads, the most westerly safe anchorage in the channel.

Perfect tranquillity at Porthleven harbour.

Ironically, when attack came, it was from the land. Pendennis was attacked by Parliamentary forces during the Civil War, surrendering after 6 gruelling months. The castle itself remained virtually intact and was again re-armed during the Napoleonic wars, and was manned during both World Wars. Look across the Carrick Roads and directly opposite you will see **St Mawes Castle**, another of Henry VIII's forts.

Fowey

The delightful little village of **Fowey** nearly 6 km (10 miles) east of St Austell, has a tiny square and a tortuous main street, which seems to cling for dear life to the busy water-side. Yet history has not passed Fowey by, for in 1346, 147 ships set sail to join the siege of Calais. Ships and men of Fowey later sailed

The Scilly Isles

About 25-36 miles off Land's End are a cluster of tiny islands, the Isles of Scilly, which, according to legend, may or may not be part of the lost city of Atlantis, or alternatively, the Islands of the Blessed, where dead heroes were buried.

Geologically they are a continuation of the granite masses of the Cornish headland but they have a micro-climate of their own. The temperature is considerably milder than on the mainland, so the range of flora and fauna is quite different. On the islands, you can see many sub-tropical plants and a wide variety of sea birds. One of the main "industries" of the islands is flower growing and over a 1,000 tons of cut flowers are produced each year.

There are 5 inhabited islands, 40 uninhabited islands, and 150 named rocks. The sea around them is clean, but icy cold, and there are many rocky, dangerous headlands, reefs galore and long, white, sandy beaches. These islands have been inhabited by Bronze and Iron Age settlers, by the Romans, the Vikings, and from AD 400-1,000, there were Christian hermits on the islands. Perhaps inevitably, given their location and distance from the mainland, the islands were a focal point for pirates and smugglers. In 1834, Augustus Smith succeeded the Godolphin family as lessee and a century later in 1933, the main islands were handed over to the British crown.

St Mary's

The largest of the islands, yet still only 2 $1/2$ by one and three quarters, St Mary's is the hub of social and commercial life in Scilly. It has a small town, **Hugh Town**, which sits on a narrow sand-bar and is in reality no bigger than a village, with its hotels, houses and shops all built close together. A ferry to the mainland and pleasure boats operate from the Old Quay. There are many ancient monuments to be discovered on the island, from a megalithic village and tombs, to civil war fortifications.

Tresco

The second largest island is **Tresco**, which has an amazing variety of scenery, basically of 3 kinds: in the north the landscape is wild and barren, with wind-blasted heathland and granite outcrops. The central section of the island is made up of green fields, cottages and farmland, including the Abbey Garden, with a collection

with John Rashleigh in his ship *Frances of Fowey* on many voyages with Sir Francis Drake and Sir Walter Raleigh. In 1578, the same ship sailed with Admiral Frobisher, on his voyage of discovery to Baffin's Land. Later, under the command of his son John, and with 70 men of Fowey, the ship fought with Drake against the Spanish Armada.

A young naval Lieutenant, later to become Captain James Cook, surveyed the harbour in 1750. By the time Queen Victoria and her husband Prince Albert, after whom Albert Quay is named, vis-ited the town in 1846, the previously thriving smuggling trade had all but ceased. The docks proved valuable during World War II, as Fowey was the base of the air-sea rescue service and a departure point for American forces on D-Day.

The **Ship Inn** on the quay was built in 1570 by John Rashleigh and is named after his famous ship *Frances of Fowey*. Although greatly altered over the centuries, one room remains much as it was originally, with its ornamental ceiling and oak panelled walls. Carved over the

of sub-tropical and exotic plants growing with a luxuriance unknown elsewhere in the United Kingdom. In the 1830s, when the first trees were planted as windbreaks, the garden began to take shape. Apart from plants obtained from Kew gardens, ships captains and master mariners from the islands would bring back seedlings from distant lands. Along the southwards and eastern shoreline are some of the island's magnificent beaches and it is here that you can find countless shells. Tresco is a private island and a landing fee is charged for day visitors. It is served by a daily year-round helicopter link with Penzance.

The smaller Scillies

St Martins is the most northeasterly island, and has cliff scenery on the north side and many magnificent beaches. It is a narrow ridge of land about 1 km (2 miles) long with small enclosed flower fields which lead down to white, sandy, sheltered beaches. The eastern isles are close by with their large seal and bird colonies. On Chapel Down is the **Daymark**, which was originally built as a daylight navigational aid in 1683.

St Agnes is the most southwesterly community in the British Isles. Surrounded by deep water and with countless rocks and reefs to the southwest, this tiny island has produced some of the finest sea pilots in the world.

Nowadays, the charm of St Agnes lies in its remoteness and rugged nature where a friendly-looking disused coal-burning lighthouse overlooks an island of cottages, bulb-fields and tamarisk hedges. St Agnes is linked to the islet of **Gugh** by a sandbar at low water. Gugh has many megalithic remains and outstanding views from the summit.

Bryher is the smallest of the inhabited islands. The western side looks down across the well-named **Hell Bay**, which even on a day of moderate swell can display some staggering effects, as the tumultuous waves break on the granite.

The unmistakable twin-hills of **Samson** lie northwest of St Mary's. Until the 1850s, the population of Samson was as many as 50. Worn down by hard living, lack of water, poor shelter, and eventually by enforced removal by Augustus Smith, the proprietor of the island, the people moved away, and Samson was finished as a home. The people have long since gone, but the ruins of their cottages and their ghosts remain.

fireplace is the inscription "John & Alice Rashleigh, 1570".

Lanhydrock House

Inland from Fowey on the B3269 road towards Bodmin, is **Lanhydrock House.** The present building is Victorian, but has a much earlier history. After the Dissolution of the monasteries in the 1530s, the estate passed through several hands until 1620, when it was sold to Sir Richard Robartes, a powerful local merchant. Robartes began building a new house at Lanhydrock in 1630. In 1881, the house suffered a disastrous fire which destroyed all but the north wing, where fortunately, the long gallery with its superb plasterwork ceiling survived. The first Lord and Lady Robartes never recovered from the shock, and both died shortly afterwards. It was left to their son, the second Lord Robartes, to rebuild the house, with every Victorian convenience to meet the needs of his large family. The splendid Victorian kitchens are the highlight of the house.

Wiltshire & Avon

The small county of Avon, facing Wales across the Bristol Channel, is dominated by 2 towns of very different character. Bath is an elegant Regency spa town, whose origins predate the Romans, whilst Bristol a busy, outward looking city, has been at the crossroads of trade and exploration, ever since John Cabot sailed from its quay for the New World in 1496. **Bath** (see box story p.244) was established as a spa town by the Romans, who named the settlement *Aqua Sul* (Waters of Sul – a Roman deity) and built a complex of baths, the remains of which can still be seen. Bath was revived as a spa town in the 18th century and many of the Georgian buildings date from this period. **Bath Abbey**, which stands next to the **Roman baths**, was built in the 10th century. The Abbey's vault, is particularly striking.

The verdant landscape of Coombe Down Avon.

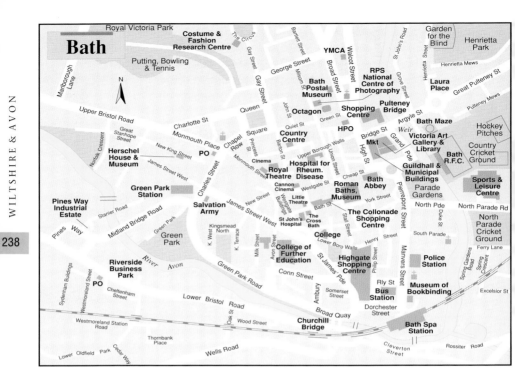

Bath

Royal Victoria Park
Costume & Fashion Research Centre
Putting, Bowling & Tennis
Marlborough Lane
Upper Bristol Road
Great Stanhope Street
Norfolk Crescent
Herschel House & Museum
James Street West
Green Park Station
Pines Way Industrial Estate
Stanier Road
Midland Bridge Road
Green Park Road
Green Park
Pines Way
Riverside Business Park
Sydenham Buildings
Westmoreland Street
PO
Cheltenham Street
Lower Bristol Road
Westmoreland Station Road
Thornbank Place
Lower Oldfield Park
Cedar Way
Wells Road
Charlotte St
Monmouth Place
Chapel Row
New King Street
Charles Street
Gay Street
Queen Square
Princess St
James Street West
New Street
Salvation Army
Kingsmead North
K. West
K. Terrace
Milk Street
Avon Street
River Avon
Green Park Road
Conn Street
Ambury
Oak St
Wood Street
Churchill Bridge
The Circus
Gay Street
George Street
Barton St
Monmouth Street
Cinema
Royal Theatre
Cannon Cinema
Little Theatre
St John's Hospital
The Cross Bath
College of Further Education
Lower Boro Walls
St James' Pde
Somerset Street
Broad Quay
Barrett Street
Milsom St
John St
Octagon
Quiet St
Country Centre
Green St
Upper Borough Walls
Union Street
Westgate St
Bath St
College
Henry Street
Philip Street
Conn Street
Rly St
Bus Station
Dorchester Street
Broad Street
Bath Postal Museum
Shopping Centre
HPO
Cheap St
Roman Baths, Museum
York Street
The Colonnade Shopping Centre
Stall Street
Highgate Shopping Centre
Walcot Street
YMCA
RPS National Centre of Photography
Pulteney Bridge
Bridge St
Weir
Mkt
High St
Bath Abbey
Parade Gardens
North Pde
South Parade
Grand Pde
Pierrepont Street
Manvers Street
St John's Road
Grove Street
Henrietta Street
Argyle St
Bath Maze
Victoria Art Gallery & Library
Guildhall & Municipal Buildings
Bath St
Police Station
Museum of Bookbinding
Cleverton Street
Bath Spa Station
Garden for the Blind
Henrietta Park
Henrietta Mews
Laura Place
Great Pulteney St
Pulteney Mews
Hockey Pitches
Country Cricket Ground
Bath R.F.C.
Sports & Leisure Centre
North Parade Rd
North Parade Cricket Ground
Ferry Lane
Duke St
Spring Gardens Road
Spring Crescent
Excelsior St
Rossiter Road
Hospital for Rheum. Disease

Bristol

Bristol is a friendly, thriving place where history co-exists quite happily with the demands of a modern, busy town. The fascinating **Floating Harbour** is home not only to historic old ships and warehouses but more recently, to corporations who are re-locating there.

The area is acquiring a new lease of life, as commuters hop onto boats to travel down the river to work, rubbing shoulders with visitors to the harbour and the ships moored there. Brunel's magnificent ship, the SS *Great Britain*, is the centrepiece of the Floating Harbour, and renovation work on the area con-

tinues.

The names of Harvey's and Bristol are synonymous with Spanish sherry, for Bristol is home to one of the oldest wine firms in the world, Harvey's, founded in 1796 by a local merchant. The medieval cellars beneath Harvey's head office in Denmark Street, which were the centre of the company's bottling and storage operation until 1960, now house **Harvey's Wine Museum** and **Harvey's Restaurant**.

Bristol's **Theatre Royal** is the oldest working theatre in Britain. It opened in 1766 after 49 Bristol merchants contributed £50 each towards the building costs. Their reward was a silver token, entitling them and their heirs to a seat at

Brunel's Clifton Suspension Bridge, spans the Avon Gorge.

every performance. A few tokens survive to this day and still guarantee the holder a place in the audience.

A little outside central Bristol is the suburb of Clifton, where the 214 metre (702 ft) long **Clifton Suspension Bridge**, designed by Brunel, spans the Avon Gorge 75 metres (245 ft) high above the water.

Prehistoric Wiltshire

Some of the richest prehistoric landscapes in Europe can be found in **Wiltshire**, a county whose character has been profoundly marked by the vast, bare expanse of **Salisbury Plain**, an area dotted with numerous prehistoric sites. The area of Wiltshire around Marlborough and Devizes is known as **Kennet**, home to Neolithic tribes, who left behind ceremonial monuments comparable to the Egyptian pyramids, and often at least as old.

Oldest of all is **Avebury**, certainly older than its better-known neighbour, Stonehenge, which lies to the south. The small, picturesque village of Avebury lies at the centre of a large circle of earthworks and 200 standing stones. The stone circle is the largest in the world, consisting of 3 phases of stone circles, of which the outer ring still survives. It is arguably the most impressive Neolithic ceremonial site in Europe, and was probably built around 2500 BC.

Close by is **Silbury Hill**, 43 metres

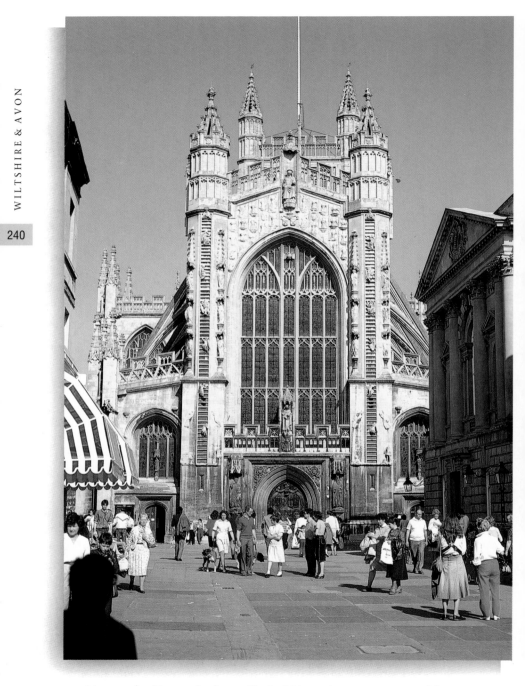

Next to the Roman baths, is Bath Abbey, the centre-point of the city.

(130 ft) high and with a 33 metres (100 ft) wide flat top, it is the largest man-made mound in Europe, equal in size to some of the pyramids of Egypt. Despite excavations the reasons for its construction still remain a mystery. The **West Kennet Long Barrow** is the largest chambered burial ground in England. It was built around 2500 BC and is believed to have been used as a burial chamber for more than 1,000 years.

Stonehenge was started 5,000 years ago, and represents one of the most remarkable achievements of prehistoric engineering, yet why it was built remains a mystery. As its major axis is aligned with the rising of the midsummer sun, the stone circle has long been thought to be a temple.

To the south, the massive earthworks of **Old Sarum** once boasted a walled city. Originally a huge Iron Age hill fort, Old Sarum was later occupied by the Romans and Saxons and finally by the Normans who built the castle, cathedral and Bishop's Palace. Only in the 13th century was the cathedral moved to New Sarum (modern day Salisbury), while the old city became deserted.

Salisbury & environs

Salisbury is dominated by its Cathedral, which epitomises the Early English style at its best, medieval Gothic in its purest form. It has slim Purbeck marble columns and a single, elegant spire, at

Georgian elegance pervades Bath.

123 meters (404 ft) the tallest in England.

The 13th century **Red Lion Inn**, known in 1756 as the Red Lion and Cross Keys, was famous for its regular daily stagecoach service to London, the "Salisbury Flying Machine". It is a fine example of an 18th century coaching inn, with a high arch and a pretty, ivy-clad galleried courtyard. The southern medieval wing was built between 1280-1320 as a hostel for draftsmen constructing the cathedral.

Famous houses

Just outside Salisbury in the western outskirts, is **Wilton House**, considered

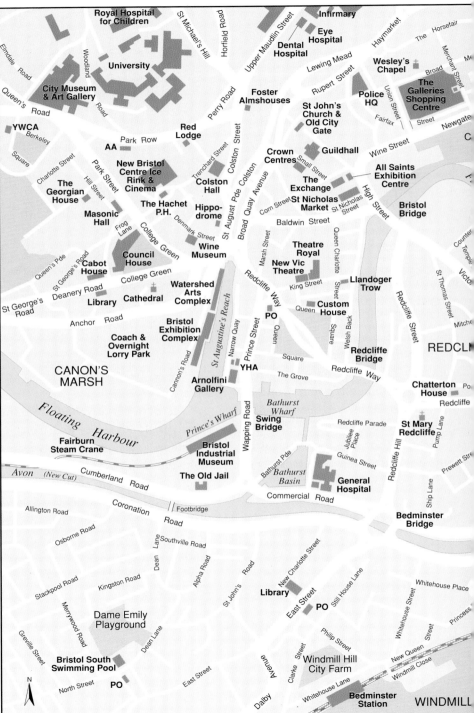

Royal Hospital for Children
St Michael's Hill
Horfield Road
Upper Maudlin Street
Infirmary
Eye Hospital
Dental Hospital
Haymarket
The Horsefair
University
Woodland
Lewing Mead
Wesley's Chapel
Broad
Merchant Street
City Museum & Art Gallery
Elmdale Road
Queen's Road
Rupert Street
Police HQ
Union Street
The Galleries Shopping Centre
Foster Almshouses
St John's Church & Old City Gate
Fairfax
Street
Newgate
YWCA
Berkeley Square
Park Row
Red Lodge
Perry Road
Crown Centres
Guildhall
Wine Street
AA
Charlotte Street
Hill Street
Park Street
Trenchard Street
Colston Street
Small Street
All Saints Exhibition Centre
New Bristol Centre Ice Rink & Cinema
Colston Hall
Colston
St Augustine Pde
Broad Quay Avenue
The Exchange
St Nicholas Market
St Nicholas Street
High Street
The Georgian House
The Hachet P.H.
Hippo-drome
Corn Street
Bristol Bridge
Masonic Hall
Frog Lane
Denmark Street
Baldwin Street
Counter
Temple
Council House
College Green
Wine Museum
Marsh Street
Theatre Royal
Queen Charlotte Street
St Thomas Street
Victo
Mitch
Cabot House
Queen's Pde
St George's Road
College Green
New Vic Theatre
King Street
Redcliffe Way
Llandoger Trow
Redcliffe Street
REDCL
Deanery Road
Library
Cathedral
Watershed Arts Complex
PO
Queen Square
Custom House
Welsh Back
St George's Road
Anchor Road
Bristol Exhibition Complex
Narrow Quay
Prince Street
Square
Redcliffe Bridge
Chatterton House
Po
Redcliffe
Coach & Overnight Lorry Park
St Augustine's Reach
YHA
The Grove
Redcliffe Way
CANON'S MARSH
Cannon's Road
Arnolfini Gallery
Bathurst Wharf
Wapping Road
Swing Bridge
Redcliffe Parade
St Mary Redcliffe
Pump Lane
Prewett Str
Floating
Harbour
Prince's Wharf
Jubilee Place
Redcliffe Hill
Fairburn Steam Crane
Bristol Industrial Museum
Guinea Street
Ship Lane
Avon (New Cut)
Cumberland Road
The Old Jail
Bathurst Pde
Bathurst Basin
General Hospital
Coronation Road
Footbridge
Commercial Road
Bedminster Bridge
Allington Road
Osborne Road
Southville Road
Dean Lane
Alpha Road
New Charlotte Street
Whitehouse Place
Stackpool Road
Kingston Road
St John's Road
Library
East Street
Still House Lane
Whitehouse Street
Princess
Merrywood Road
Dame Emily Playground
Dean Lane
PO
Philip Street
New Queen Street
Whitehouse Lane
Greville Street
Bristol South Swimming Pool
North Street
PO
East Street
Avenue
Clarke Street
Windmill Hill City Farm
Dalby
Windmill Close
N
Bedminster Station
WINDMILL

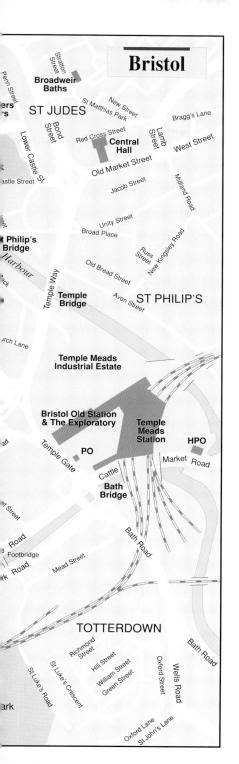

Bristol

by King James I to be the "finest house in the land". Wilton House has been the home of the Earls of Pembroke since 1544, when King Henry VIII gave the Abbey and lands of Wilton to Sir William Herbert, who had married the sister of the Queen, Catherine Parr. The house contains superb 17th century state rooms by Inigo Jones, including the magnificent **Double Cube room**, and a superb private art collection.

Malmesbury House, in north Wiltshire (west of Swindon), was originally a 13th century cannonry but was refurbished in the 17th and 18th centuries. King Charles II sheltered there in 1651 on his way to exile and revisited the house after his restoration in 1665. The young composer George Frederick Handel stayed at Malmesbury, using **St Anne's Chapel** above the gate for his recitals.

Close to the Somerset border in the southwest of the county, are two of Wiltshire's important stately homes, Stourhead and Longleat. **Stourhead** has one of the finest landscape gardens in the world, designed by the owner of the 18th century Palladian-style house, Henry Hoare. Hoare dammed springs to create a lake, around which he designed classical temples and bridges, in an attempt to recreate a formal geometrical design, in the manner of the French. His dream was, and still is, a success.

The gardens of Stourhead are beautiful at any time of the year, but especially so in May and June, when they are ablaze with riotously coloured rhodo-

Elegant Bath

The Roman Baths, Bath.

The city of **Bath** is a beautiful, elegant and historic town, situated in the Avon valley, in the Downs between the Cotswolds and Mendip Hills. Bath owes much of its prosperity to the hot springs which pour forth a quarter of a million gallons of rich mineral water a day, at a constant temperature of 46.5°C. It was these hot springs, the only ones in Britain, that brought the Celts here to worship, and inspired the Romans to build their magnificent temples and baths.

Bath finds

If legend is to be believed, the hot springs were discovered in 500 BC, by Prince Bladud, the father of King Lear, who was cured of leprosy by the mineral waters. True or not, Bath was known for its springs long before the Romans arrived in the 1st century AD. They made the town into a spa resort, building a temple and a gymnasium, and, most importantly, a reservoir around the hot spring, to feed an elaborate complex of baths. Now known as the King's Bath, and overlooked by the Georgian **Pump Room**, the spring, known as *Aquae Sulis* to the Romans, was sacred, and in the excellent museum which has been built on the site, are displayed some of the objects dropped into the sacred waters by pious Romans. These include almost 13,000 Roman coins, as well as a few local pre-Roman coins, indicating native activity at the sacred spring at the time of the invasion. Some of the coins were clipped, marking them as the property of the Goddess of the spring, and no longer legal tender. More fascinating than the coins, however, are over 100 curses which have been recovered from the spring. Curses were written on lead or pewter, and some of them contain the names of suspected criminals. These curses have been translated, and give an intriguing glimpse into everyday Roman life: Docimedis, for example, "has lost two gloves. He asks that the person who has stolen them should lose his minds and his eyes".

A Gentleman's city

Modern Bath owes much of its character to the Georgians, and, in little under 100 years from the beginning of the 18th century, the small, medieval west country resort was transformed into one of the most famous cities in Europe. Architects and designers descended upon Bath to build the neo-classical parades, squares and crescents, out of the characteristic ochre stone quarried from the surrounding hills.

One of the dominant figures in the town's 18th century history is Beau Nash, a dandy and

dendrons.

Longleat is the Elizabethan home of the Seventh Marquess of Bath. It is also home to some exotic wildlife: lions, white tigers and the only white lion in Europe. In 1949, Lord Bath became the

leading society figure, who became the un-crowned king of Georgian Bath. Nash organized the city, opened the **Pump Room**, and popularized the taking of the waters, which gradually evolved into a ritualistic part of society. This is the Bath of Jane Austen's novels, where young ladies in search of a wealthy husband take the waters in the morning, and attend evening concerts in the **Assembly Rooms**.

Bath has superb architecture, much of it in stone from Combe Down, now known as Bath stone. The **Royal Crescent**, an elegant arc of 30 terrace houses, was built between 1767-74, and is a harmony of horizontal lines and counterbalancing Ionic columns. **The Circus** is a perfect circle of identical houses, pierced by three equidistant roads. The Assembly Rooms were built at the same time, between 1769-71, and a little later **Pulteney Bridge** was built in Florentine style, lined with small shops.

The **Shire's Yard**, now a covered shopping area, has an interesting history. In the 1740s, Walter Wiltshire, Alderman, Justice of the Peace and Mayor of Bath, built the stables that accommodated his carting and carrying business. Every Wednesday and Sunday evening, Wiltshire's "Flying Wagons" would set off from here, at the start of their two and a half day journey to Holborn Bridge in London. One of Wiltshire's clients was the artist Thomas Gainsborough, who lived and painted in Bath between 1760-74. Although Wiltshire regularly transported Gainsborough's paintings, he never accepted payment, saying he loved the works too well to charge for carriage. The two men became friends, and Gainsborough, having asked his friend to lend him a favourite Shire horse and wagon, as a subject for a painting, received the horse as a present. Gainsborough reciprocated by producing his famous painting *The Harvest Wagon* and giving it to Wiltshire. The painting has since become a national treasure.

first peer of the realm to open his home to the public on a commercial basis, and in 1966 a drive-through safari was suc-cessfully opened.

Glastonbury & the Holy Grail

From the summit of **Glastonbury Tor**, you can see more than half of the small county of **Somerset**, its plains, known as the Somerset Levels, broken by the spires of Wells Cathedral. Hills can be seen on both sides; the Quantocks to the west, and to the east, the Mendips, marked by massive gorges such as Cheddar, and caves at Wookey Hole.

Glastonbury, at the centre of the county, is a suitable place to begin to explore Somerset, a place where history and legend run seamlessly into each other. This small market town on the hills that rise abruptly out of the Somerset Levels is said to be the place where Joseph of Arimathea came after the Crucifixion of Jesus Christ, to establish the first Christian church in England.

In 1191 a log coffin was found buried between 2 stone crosses in the burial ground beside **St Mary's Chapel**. In it, the monks claimed, were the bones of a tall man and a delicate woman, and a leaden cross beneath the lid told them who lay buried there, "Here lies buried the famous King Arthur in the Isle of Avalon". The bones were re-buried in the presence of King Edward I in 1278 in the new choir.

In the town, there is a small well, the **Chalice Well**, fed by a spring which rises on the slope of Chalice Hill. The

The prehistoric circle of Avebury.

spring has never been known to fail and in the dry years of 1921 and 1922, was the sole means of saving the whole town from drought. According to tradition, Joseph of Arimathea settled near the Chalice Well, having bought the chalice of the Last Supper to Glastonbury in AD 37, although this has never been accepted as history by the Christian Church. The pre-Christian story of the Grail, a pagan cup of plenty, was gradually "christianized", becoming, over the centuries, the chalice containing the Holy Blood of Christ.

Joseph is said to have put his staff into the ground on **Wearyall Hill**, where it took root, and grew into a thorn tree, which blossomed at the unseasonal time of Christmas. Two descendants of the thorn bush still flower in Glastonbury, one tree in the Abbey grounds, and the other in the grounds of **St John the Baptist Church**. It is this bush that blossoms every December and a sprig is sent to the Queen.

The Lady Chapel of **Glastonbury Abbey** is an interesting specimen of late Norman architecture.

Wells

A short drive north of Glastonbury along the A39, is **Wells**, the smallest cathedral city in England, with its vast 800-year-old **Cathedral of St Andrew**. Building work began around 1175, but it took over 3 centuries to complete. The spectacular **West Front** would once have been a blaze of colour, the statues in its 400 niches painted and gilded, but the soft stone colour visible today is gorgeous enough.

Many of the figures in the niches are larger than life-size, and despite much destruction by the Puritans, under Oliver Cromwell, it remains England's richest display of 13th century sculpture.

The interior of the cathedral is every bit as impressive as the exterior, exhibiting a succession of soaring scissor-arches and a lofty 12th century nave.

The popularity of the Grail romance reached its height in the late 12th and early 13th centuries. By that time the Grail had become the Holy Grail, and the Arthurian legend and the Joseph tradition were inextricably entwined. The legend of Avalon had taken root, just as firmly as the mysterious Glastonbury thorn bushes.

A thatched cottage at Castle Combe.

The little **Chapter House**, completed in 1306, is charming and airy; the original windows were smashed by Cromwell's soldiers, to be replaced by plain glass. It is said that the little carved heads over each stall represent characters alive at the time of the building, though whether there were ever 6 popes and 10 bishops at one time, is dubious! The beautiful roof of the Chapter House has 32 ribs springing from the central shaft, a precursor of fan vaulting.

Close by the cathedral is the **Bishop's Palace**, one of the oldest inhabited houses in England, it dates back to 1206. Nearby, the delightful **Vicars Close**, a row of little terraced cottages, is to this day occupied by employees of the cathedral and is believed to be the oldest

intact 14th century street in Europe.

Hills & caverns

Somerset's limestone **Mendip Hills** stretch for about 31 km (50 miles) from the coast at Weston-Super-Mare, east to Frome. Underground, the Mendips are honeycombed with caverns, carved by the erosive power of water over millions of years. Some like **Wookey Hole Cave**, just over 1 km (2 miles) north of Wells, have long been well-known visitor attractions, but many more are known only to experienced cavers. A little further north, in a plunging two mile cleft in the Mendip Hills, with 131 m (400 ft) cliffs hemming in a narrow road, is the

Cheddar Gorge. Since the 12th century, when the historian Henry of Huntingdon included "Chedar Hole" in his list of the 4 wonders of England, visitors have marvelled at these sheer limestone cliffs towering above the road.

Streams riddle the hills and there are more than 400 caves and holes in the area, some of which can be visited. The caves are at the lower end of the Gorge, where one of the largest underground rivers in Britain, the Cheddar Yeo, resurges into daylight through 18 separate springs. The **Cheddar Man skeleton** is one of the few remains of the Mesolithic Age (about 9,000 years ago), to be found at Cheddar.

The first stalactite cavern at Cheddar was discovered in 1837 by accident, as George Cox was removing limestone. His show-cave was such a success that several adventurers, in particular Richard Gough, spent years searching for similar attractions, and Gough, in the 1890s, dug open the finest cave of all, which bears his name.

In contrast to the Mendips, are the broad, flat landscapes of the **Somerset Levels**, mainly to the south and west of Wells and Glastonbury. These are characterized by low-lying meadows, and drainage ditches, called rhynes, but pronounced "reens". It was only from the late Middle Ages onwards that the marshy sea covering this area was artificially drained. Significant archaeological finds have been made in the area, due to the excellent preservation properties of the peaty soils. Finds include

Wiltshire's white horses

Hill figures cutting into chalk escarpments are a feature of the Wiltshire countryside, though they are not exclusive to the region, and can also be found in Sussex, Dorset and Oxfordshire. Some of the figures are prehistoric, whilst others date from the 20th century. One of the oldest, the **Uffington White Horse**, is technically across the Berkshire border, but the best place to view it is from roads leading out of Swindon. The date of this horse is unknown, but has been put at anything between 100 BC to AD100.

The 6 visible white horses in Wiltshire are more recent in origin. The **Westbury Bratton White Horse**, cut in 1778, measures 54 m (166 ft) by 53 m (163 ft), while the **Cherhill White Horse** dates from 1780. The 15 m (47 ft) high **Marlborough White Horse** was cut in 1804 by local school boys. The **Alton Barnes White Horse**, cut in 1812, measures a massive 54 m (166 ft) by 52 m (160 ft), and his eye alone is 3.6 m (11 ft) long.

The **Hackpen White Horse** is thought to have been cut to celebrate Queen Victoria's coronation in 1838, and a century later, in 1937, the **Pewsey White Horse** was commissioned by the town council, to celebrate the coronation of George VI.

Outside the little village of Fovant, a few miles west of Salisbury, a series of regimental badges, dating back to 1916, have been cut into the hills.

Just remember one thing: because of their size, the figures are best viewed from a distance, so ask in the neighbouring villages for the best vantage points.

the Iron Age, **Lake Village** discovered near Glastonbury and a wooden causeway thought to be around 4,000 years-old.

Somerset specials

Somerset is synonymous with the drink,

The gardens at Stourhead are some of the finest landscaped
gardens in the country.

Take the Severn Bridge to cross from Bristol into Wales.

cider, made from locally grown apples, which are collected and pressed in the autumn. After fermentation the cider is matured in barrels. Farmhouse cider is medium sweet, medium dry or dry. The strong dry "scrumpy" cider is the previous year's pressing. Vintage cider is either sweet, medium dry or dry, and is made from selected varieties of apples.

In the south of Somerset, close to the Dorset border, is the Elizabethan **Montacute House.** Sir Edward Phelips began work on the H-shaped house in 1588, and Montacute remained in his family until 1931, when the National Trust took it over. Elizabethan and Jacobean portraits from the National Portrait Gallery are displayed in the **Long Gallery**.

On the eastern edge of Exmoor, the remains of **Cleeve Abbey** are remarkably well preserved. After the Dissolu-

Beautiful English gardens are open to tourists at Dunster Priory, Somerset.

tion of the Monasteries, Cleeve's cloister buildings were put to domestic use soon afterwards, and are now among the most complete in England. Features to note are the medieval tiled floor in the original dining room, a magnificent 15th century timber roof carved with crowned angels and beautiful detailed wall paintings, so detailed that you can pick out the difference.

Exmoor National Park, one of the smallest of Britain's national parks, covers 102 sq km (265 miles), and was formerly a royal deer forest. Besides deer, there are also Exmoor ponies, badgers, foxes, and otters, and over 240 different species of birds. Ancient stone circles are a reminder of the early inhabitants of Exmoor, but the most notorious of all the people to roam the moors were the Doone family of RD Blackmore's novel, *Lorna Doone*.

The Cotswolds

Think for a moment how you would imagine a "typical English village" to look; pretty stone cottages, a village church, the village green, a busy weekly market, a low stone bridge over a clear stream, and over the horizon peaceful, green, gently rolling countryside. This imaginary description could, in fact, be of any one of the beautiful villages that are dotted throughout the Cotswolds, which, to many visitors, represent the essence of picturesque rural England.

The quaint streets of Castle Combe.

The Cotswolds are a range of limestone hills, which extend for about 31 km (50 miles) across the western Midlands, from Chipping Campden in the north, through the heart of Gloucestershire, before levelling out to the south. On their way, they take in portions of Warwickshire, Worcestershire, Oxfordshire, Wiltshire and Avon. This range of hills is 175 million years old, and the limestone provides good quality building stone. Through-

Cottages by the river, Castle Combe.

out, the Cotswolds are characterized by honey-coloured stone villages, as well as a gently rolling landscape, and a peaceful quality of life. Cotswold wool was amongst the finest in Europe during the 11th and 12th centuries, and it has been estimated that there were 10 million sheep at that time in England. All the great Abbeys, including Cirencester, had their own flocks, the wool from which was often sold months before shearing, to buyers from Flanders and Florence. Many fine cathedrals and churches, usually referred to as "wool churches", were built with the money earned. Wool sales declined in the 14th century because of the heavy taxes imposed under state control. Cotswold sheep are descended from the "long wool" breed, introduced to Britain by the Romans. By selective breeding, large sheep were produced for their heavy

Girls enjoying the lush landscape and lovely daffodils.

fleeces, earning themselves the name "Cotswold Lions". Sadly, very few of this distinctive breed survive today.

The Northern Cotswolds

The Vale of Evesham lies to the north of the Cotswolds, an area of outstanding natural beauty, and probably the most prolific fruit and vegetable growing region in the country. In the spring, you can follow the spring blossom trail. The first kind of blossom to be seen is plum, then, 10 to 14 days later, depending on the weather, apple blossom follows, and a little later, cherry blossom, though very little cherry is now grown in the vale because of the damage caused to the fruit by bird attacks. Blossom time is a short season, usually between late March and early May, depending on the climate.

In the North Cotswolds are many of the Cotswolds' best known villages, including Bourton-on-the-Water, Upper and Lower Slaughter, and Broadway, and some of the great wool and market towns such as Chipping Campden, Moreton-in-Marsh and Stow-on-the-Wold.

Founded by the Saxons, **Chipping Campden** is the perfect example of a prosperous north Cotswolds wool town. Individual buildings are impressive, but the distinctive "feel" of Chipping Campden is one of overall harmony and elegance. The town, with its long,

Chipping Camden high street.

curving High Street, has resisted many of the intrusive trappings of 20th century commercialization, adding to its charm.

It has a magnificent 15th century church, and beautiful stone houses, many built by wealthy wool merchants. **St James' church**, which was rebuilt in the 15th century, occupies the site of earlier churches. At the entrance to the church are two pavilions, "pepper-pot" lodges and a gateway, all that remains of the former mansion of Sir Baptist Hicks, which was destroyed during the Civil War.

Opposite the church is a row of almshouses built by Sir Baptist in 1617. In the south chapel of the church, there are memorials to the Hicks and the Noel families. One of them is a small mural monument of their daughter, Penelope Noel, who died from blood poisoning through pricking her finger when working with coloured silks.

Moreton-in-Marsh, about 4 km (7 miles) to the south, is a thriving little market town, whose main street is formed by the former Roman Fosse Way. There are many attractive Cotswold stone inns here, a reminder of the town's days as a major coaching stop. Three kilometers (5 miles) further south, **Stow-on-the-Wold**, standing at 262 metres (800 ft), is the highest town in the Cotswolds, built around its market square, which was once the scene of sheep trading.

The town was important during the

Cotswold architecture at Stow-on-the-Wold.

Middle Ages, since it stood at the junction of several main roads. The local saying "Stow-on-the-Wold, where the wind blows cold" probably explains why the buildings are seemingly bunched together. The town is now known for its tea shops, its inns and its high quality antique business. **Stow Fair**, held every year in May and October, used to be one of the biggest livestock markets in the country.

Today the fair is mainly an agricultural show, although some livestock trading still takes place.

Travelling south on the A429 from Stow-on-the-Wold, **Bourton-on-the-Water** is almost too pretty to be true; a beautiful village with the River Windrush flowing down its main street, under a

succession of low stone bridges. "The Slaughters" is a slightly alarming, general name for the two delightful villages of **Lower Slaughter** and **Upper Slaughter**, which represent for many people the quintessential Cotswolds. Although popular, they are completely unspoilt and are characterised by pretty cottages along the side of the little River Eye.

The Oxfordshire Cotswolds

Towards their eastern edge, the Cotswolds slope gently into Oxfordshire, where they meet the water meadows of the rivers Windrush, Glyme and Evenlode.

The Oxfordshire region of the Cots-

Historical residences of Arlington Row epitomize
the ambiance of the Cotswolds.

wolds is one of the less explored regions, yet there are fine historic houses, and small busy market towns like Burford, Chipping Norton, Banbury and Woodstock. A fragment of the former royal hunting **Forest of Wychwood** overlooks the Evenlode valley, all that remains of a forest that was once as large as Hampshire's New Forest, in the Middle Ages.

The forest is still remembered, in the names of villages such as Shipton-under-Wychwood, Milton-under-Wychwood, and Ascott-under-Wychwood.

From the superbly situated hill top town of **Chipping Norton**, standing at 230 metres (700 ft), there are spectacular views across the surrounding coun-

tryside. Many elegant merchants houses reflect the town's former importance in the wool trade. The town was mentioned in the *Domesday Book*, but only as Norton. Chipping, which means "market" was added to the name in the 13th century.

The Southern Cotswolds

Cirencester, the capital of the Cotswolds, is by far the best known town of the South Cotswolds. In the excellent **Corinium Museum**, there is a full scale reconstruction of life in *Corinium* (modern Cirencester), the second largest town of Roman Britain during the 2nd century AD.

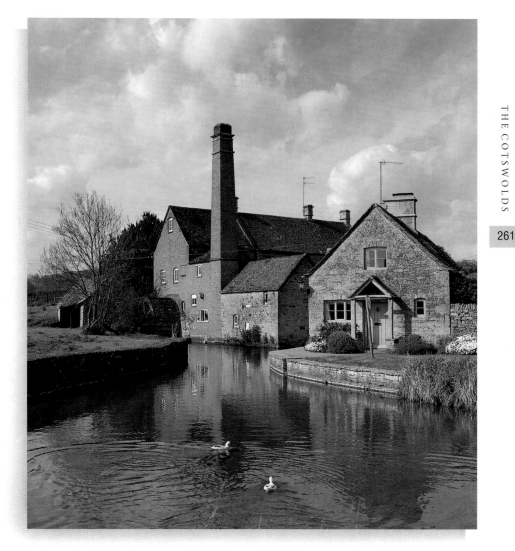

A 19th century brick-mill at Lower Slaughter.

Exhibits in the museum include superb mosaic floors depicting hunting dogs and the four seasons. Cirencester is now a thriving market town, with many elegant houses and a beautiful Perpendicular **Church of St John the Baptist.** The church was originally Norman, but during the 15th century when Cirencester was the biggest wool market in the country, some fine additions were made, financed by local wool merchants. The church is one of the finest "wool churches" in the Cotswolds.

Tetbury to the southwest of

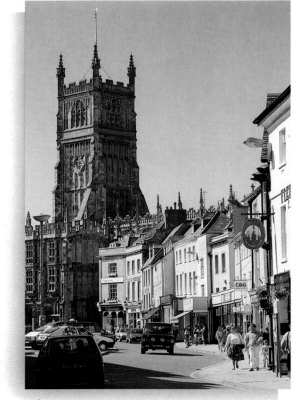

Cirencester, the capital of the Cotswolds.

man **Abbey**. One of the many Wiltshire towns which grew to prosperity through weaving, it has fine 17th and 18th century Cotswold stone houses built by the weavers. The **market cross** dates from the 16th century.

Cheltenham Spa

Cirencester, is a charming south Cotswolds market town, better known for its proximity to Highgrove, the former home of the Prince and Princess of Wales, although currently used by the Prince. Tetbury's royal connection is made clear through the string of "By Royal Appointment" plaques to be found above the doors of several local businesses, signifying that the royal seal of approval has been given to this particular shop, or to the goods which it sells.

A few miles to the east, is **Malmesbury**, an ancient town on the upper reaches of the river Avon, which is dominated by its magnificent Nor-

The Cotswolds are not only home to a profusion of beautiful villages, but also to two of England's most architecturally harmonious towns, Cheltenham Spa, and, at the extreme southern end of the Cotswolds, one of the country' most beautiful cities, Bath (see box story p.244).

When King George III brought the Royal family in 1788 to take the waters, the seal of approval was firmly placed on **Cheltenham Spa** as the most fashionable and colourful of spa towns. Cheltenham's reputation as a social and cultural centre continued to attract a constant stream of British and European nobility.

The Duke of Wellington and Queen Victoria were among the more honoured British guests, as were various French kings and Russian Grand Dukes. Visitors such as Lord Byron and Jane Austen added a literary flavour to the rich life of the town. From the 1830s, Cheltenham became a favourite place to settle for officers, after colonial duty in the army, the navy and the East India Company.

Cheltenham's classic architecture belongs to the Regency period of the 19th century, which takes its name from the period when illness forced George III to give way to his son, the future George IV, who then ruled as Regent. Grand columns, stucco-plaster, and delicate ironwork, typify Regency architecture, whose inspiration was drawn from classical Greece.

The scale and grandeur of buildings such as the **Pittville Pump Room**, the **Municipal offices** on the Promenade, **Lansdowne Crescent** and the **Queen's Hotel**, can be contrasted in size and atmosphere with the quiet elegance of small squares, ornamental fountains and exquisite villas. Most of the town's centre is listed as a conservation area of outstanding importance, and there is an ongoing programme of restoration. The Pittville Pump Room is Cheltenham's finest Regency building, and the spa waters, the only alkaline spring in Britain, can still be taken from the decorative pump in the apse of the main hall.

Many of the town's elegant lawns and gardens were laid out during the early 19th century, as part of the Regency town plan, including **Pittville Park**, **Montpellier Gardens** and **Imperial Gardens**. **Cheltenham College** and **Cheltenham Ladies College**, built of local stone, are exceptional examples of Victorian public schools, both in their harmonious architecture, and their continuing high academic standards. Gustave Holst, composer of *The Planets*, was born in Cheltenham, on Clarence Road.

Sudeley Castle

Sudeley Castle, east of Cheltenham, was once the palace of Queen Catherine Parr, the last of Henry VIII's six wives, who managed to outlive him, and who is buried in the castle chapel. Henry VIII, Anne Boleyn, Lady Jane Grey and Elizabeth I all stayed at Sudeley, as did Charles I, while Prince Rupert established the castle as his headquarters during the Civil War.

Surrounding Sudeley Castle are delightful gardens, of which the centrepiece is the Queen's Garden, named after Queen Catherine Parr, who reputedly spent many of her happiest days at Sudeley. The garden, reconstructed from an original Tudor Knot Garden, has been planted with old fashioned roses in herb-edged beds and flanked by 5 m (15 ft) high double yew hedges. For PG Wodehouse fans, Sudeley Castle was the model for *Blandings*.

William Shakespeare is without doubt the best known of all English writers, and his home town is a natural magnet for visitors from all over the world. Whether they have read his plays and sonnets or not, everyone wants to visit his birthplace and if tickets are available, see a production of one of his works at the Royal Shakespeare Theatre.

Stratford-upon-Avon dominates Warwickshire, but the county has many other attractions, chief among them the county town of Warwick and the dramatic ruins of Kenilworth Castle. The rural character of Warwickshire has become more pronounced with the creation of the West Midlands in 1974, en-

Everything's Shakespearian in Stratford-on-Avon, including the Shakespeare Hotel.

Warwickshire & West Midlands

Dressed for battle, Warwick Castle.

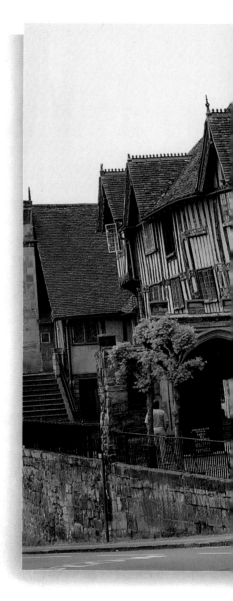

compassing the huge industrial sprawl surrounding Birmingham, England's second largest city, which behind its dull façade hides a number of unspoken treasures.

Medieval Warwick

Warwick is a pleasant town and a busy university and industrial centre, but for the visitor in search of history, the castle, the few surviving medieval buildings and the elegant Georgian houses are all grouped together within the precincts of the old city walls. The city suffered from a devastating fire in 1694, which destroyed much of the medieval architecture.

Warwick Castle, dating mainly from the 14th century, stands on the banks of the River Avon, on a site first fortified by William the Conqueror in 1068. For centuries, Warwick Castle was home to the Earls of Warwick, including Richard Neville (1428-71), known as

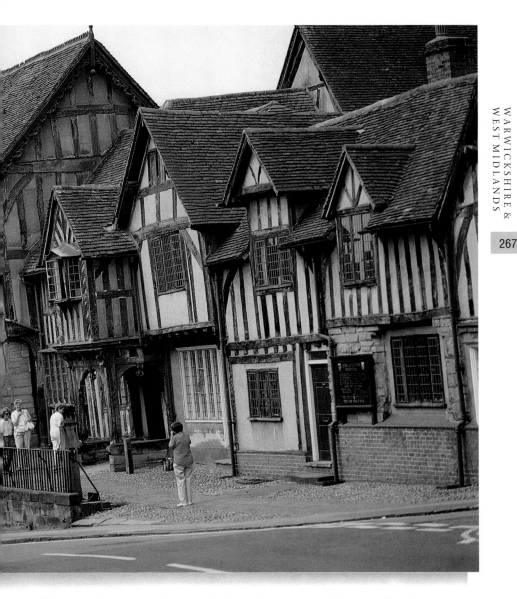

The Lord Leycester Hospital, Warwick, a remnant of the medieval town.

"the King maker". Richard III owned the castle and started new fortifications, before meeting his death at the Battle of Bosworth in 1485.

Queen Victoria dined in the castle in 1858, and planted an oak tree which can still be seen today. Of all the state rooms, the **Great Hall** is the most impressive, and in the drawing rooms are superb paintings and furniture. The

Caring for man's honour at the Lord
Leycester Hospital, Warwick.

grounds and gardens surrounding the
castle were landscaped by the great
Capability Brown.

The **Lord Leycester Hospital**, standing next to the town's West Gate, is
perhaps the most interesting building to
survive the 1694 fire. This ancient hospital was endowed in 1571 by Queen
Elizabeth I's favourite Robert Dudley,
the Earl of Leicester, as a hospital for
retired ex-servicemen and their wives,
which it still is, four centuries later. A
number of pretty, timbered buildings
are built around a tiny, central courtyard, and there is a gem of a 14th
century chapel, the tiny **Chapel of St
James**.

Modern Warwick has expanses almost as far as Coventry and there is

virtually no break between it and the
slightly faded elegance of **Royal Leam-
ington Spa.** Queen Victoria conferred
the title "Royal" on the little spa town,
after a visit to its saline spring in 1838.
You can still take the waters today at the
Royal Pump Room.

Shakespeare's birthplace, Stratford-upon-Avon.

Shakespeare sites

About 6 km (10 miles) south of Warwick is **Stratford-upon-Avon**, a pretty town

which, despite the crowds of visitors, and the thriving Shakespeare tourist industry, still retains a definite "feel" for the Bard.

Shakespeare's Birthplace, a half-

The Royal Shakespeare Company

The Royal Shakespeare Company is one of the country's leading theatre companies, specializing, though not exclusively so, in the works of their namesake.

The company has two bases, the **Royal Shakespeare Theatre** in Stratford-upon-Avon, a rather box-like looking building dating from 1932, and the Barbican Centre in London. Generally, the London company performs modern works and non-Shakespearean classics, while the Stratford based part of the company performs the plays of Shakespeare and his contemporaries.

Formerly called the Shakespeare Memorial Company in 1925 a royal charter was granted to the company, which had become by then one of the most prestigious in the country. In 1961 the director Sir Peter Hall reorganized the company, splitting it into its 2 companies. During his tenure, the Stratford company performed several plays which are still avidly remembered even today, chief among them his 1962 production of *King Lear*, and Peter Brook's spectacular 1970 production of *A Midsummer Night's Dream*, which changed people's perception of the play by doubling up certain roles, and staging it in a modern context.

In 1982, the direction of the Company passed into the joint hands of Trevor Nunn and Terry Hands, and left its former London base of The Aldwych Theatre and moved into the Barbican complex, in the City of London.

timbered house where the dramatist was born in 1564, was purchased as a national memorial in 1847, but had been a place of pilgrimage for years before that. You can see graffiti from the days when it was not considered such an anti-social crime, including the carvings left behind by the actress Dame Ellen Terry, the actor Henry Irving, and Thomas Carlyle.

In the garden are many of the plants mentioned in the plays. Next door, in the modern **Shakespeare Centre**, there is an exhibition of costumes from the BBC Shakespeare series. Besides places directly connected with Shakespeare himself, the town and its surrounding villages bear associations with many members of his family.

After finding fame and fortune in London, Shakespeare retired to Stratford in 1611, where he lived until his death in 1616. Adjoining the site of Shakespeare's last home, **New Place**, of which only the foundations survive, is **Nash's house**, where Shakespeare's

Monument to Hamlet, the Gower Memorial, Stratford.

Shakespeare's wife, Anne Hathaway's cottage, Shottery.

granddaughter lived, when married to Thomas Nash. **Hawes Croft** is an outstandingly furnished Tudor house where Shakespeare's daughter Susanna and her husband Dr John Hall lived.

The walk to **Holy Trinity Church**, where Shakespeare is buried, is a delightful one, along the banks of the River Avon. You can cross the river in a chain ferry, built in 1937, and the last surviving one in Britain. When the ferry is moored at the riverside, a chain is dropped right down to the river bed, going down to a depth of 46 m (14 feet).

Even if it were not the birthplace of Shakespeare's wife, **Anne Hathaway's Cottage**, in the village of Shottery in the western outskirts of Stratford-upon-Avon would still hold its own, for it is an architectural gem. The picturesque thatched cottage has irregular timber-framed walls, tiny latticed windows and

Journey up the River Avon, to Shakespeare's resting place, the Holy Trinity Church, Stratford-upon-Avon.

a beautiful garden.

Take the A3400 road out of Stratford to **Mary Arden's house** in the village of Wilmcote, a herring-bone timber-framed Tudor farmhouse where Shakespeare's mother lived as a child.

Although not as well-known as Anne Hathaway's cottage, it is a fascinating house, which has mercifully survived alteration. The house was occupied continuously until 1930, and is preserved in almost its original condition.

Ragley & Kenilworth

Follow the A46 out of Stratford to Alcester 1 km (2 miles) to the south of which lies **Ragley Hall**, the home of Lord and Lady Hertford. The house was built in 1680 in the Palladian style, and 70

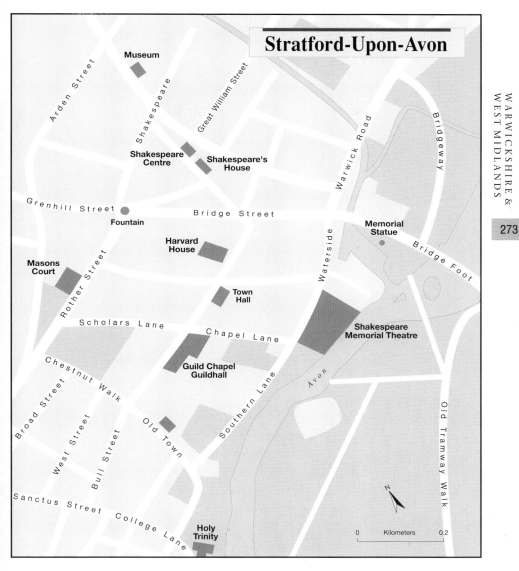

Stratford-Upon-Avon

Map labels: Museum; Arden Street; Shakespeare Street; Great William Street; Warwick Road; Bridgeway; Shakespeare Centre; Shakespeare's House; Grenhill Street; Fountain; Bridge Street; Memorial Statue; Bridge Foot; Waterside; Harvard House; Rother Street; Masons Court; Town Hall; Shakespeare Memorial Theatre; Scholars Lane; Chapel Lane; Chestnut Walk; Guild Chapel Guildhall; Avon; Southern Lane; Old Town; Broad Street; West Street; Bull Street; Sanctus Street; College Lane; Old Tramway Walk; Holy Trinity; 0 Kilometers 0.2

years later, was further embellished by beautiful plasterwork, by the craftsman James Gibbs. Of all the rooms Gibbs decorated, it is in the **Great Hall** that he excelled himself, creating the most perfect ceiling of his career. The house also has an interesting 20th century mural, on the south staircase, which depicts the present owners, their family and friends. Ragley Hall is set in 400 acres of parkland, woodland and garden, landscaped by Capability Brown.

Mid-way between Warwick and Coventry are the impressive, massive sandstone ruins of **Kenilworth Castle**. In Norman times, this was one of the

Kenilworth Castle, the backdrop to Sir Walter Scott's romantic novel.

A window to the past.

country's chief fortresses, and even to-day, it still retains an aura of invincibility. The castle was home to Simon de Montfort, John of Gaunt strengthened it, and Robert Dudley, Earl of Leicester added to it in the 16th century. The Roundheads destroyed the castle after the Civil War and as a romantic, ivy-clad ruin, it became the backdrop to one of Sir Walter Scott's novels, *Kenilworth*.

Coventry

Part of the history of **Coventry**, dating back to Saxon times, came to an abrupt halt on the night of 14 November 1940. In the biggest bombing raid of World War II, much of the city was destroyed,

Warwick Castle flies the flag of England's noble patron saint, St George.

and although a thriving new town arose out of the ashes, a great deal of ancient architecture was irreparably lost. Most of the 13th century **Coventry Cathedral** was destroyed in the bombing raid, but the skeleton that remains has been preserved as an eloquent reminder of the horrors of war, notably the **Altar of Reconciliation**. The old cathedral ruins are often the setting for major events such as the Tri-annual Mystery Plays.

Next to the ruins, the new **Cathedral of St Michael**, designed by Sir Basil Spence, has been constructed with simplicity and symbolism in mind, and it is one of the few post-war buildings to have met with near universal approval. The brilliant, kaleidoscopic colours of the vast stained glass windows, comple-

ment Graham Sutherland's avant-garde tapestry, *Christ in Glory*, which is thought to be the largest in the world.

The baptismal font of the new Cathedral is a rough boulder from the hillside above Bethlehem, where Jesus Christ was born.

Much of the ancient city has gone, but there are significant remains, including the medieval **Guildhall**, and two half-timbered Tudor almshouses, **Bond's Hospital**, and **Ford's Hospital**.

Legend claims that Lady Godiva rode naked through the streets of Coventry in the 11th century, in protest against the high taxes that her husband had imposed on the town. Today, she is still remembered and her statue in Broadgate commemorates the tale.

A Tudor-style house, Warwick.

Coventry is the home of the British Motor Car industry and the city's **Museum of British Road Transport** boasts the world's largest display of its kind, including the oldest British car and several royal cars, including Queen Mary's 1935 Daimler and King George VI's state Laundaulette.

Birmingham

Birmingham is the second largest city in England, and dominates the West Midlands. It was a major centre during the Industrial Revolution of the 18th and 19th centuries, and is still a major manufacturing and industrial centre. Dubious post-war architecture has not made it the most attractive of cities, but it is a thriving place. The modern **National Exhibition Centre** has enabled the city to play host to a number of world class exhibitions, the city also has some superb art galleries, including the **Birmingham Museum and Art Gallery**, with its outstanding Pre-Raphaelite collection, and the **Barber Institute of Fine Arts**. The Birmingham Philharmonic Orchestra also enjoys international prestige.

Leaving Birmingham, if you feel that the tangle of motorway junctions, fly-overs and under-passes gets you in a twist, you may well empathise with the name given to one of the more elaborate motorway interchanges, popularly known as the "Spaghetti Junction"!

The rounded eastern flank of England, bordered by the North Sea and The Wash, is known as East Anglia. It comprises both Norfolk and Suffolk and was at one time almost cut off from the rest of the country by fenland to the west, which has now been drained, and to the south by forest, also long since cleared. In medieval times, this area was a rich wool region, and now it is the centre of some of the most industrialized farming in the country.

Georgian architecture at Kings Lynn, Norfolk.

King's Lynn

Since the topography of Norfolk is naturally flat, colour and contrast come less from the shape of the landscape, than from the textures of the buildings, many of them built of flint, others in brown carr stone, and yet others in a mixture of timber and plaster. As you drive through

Half-timbered houses in Lavenham, Suffolk, a feature of East Anglia.

the flat Norfolk plains, there are beds of lavender, and mile after mile of reed beds, bird sanctuaries and windmills and the royal home of Sandringham.

In the west of the county, just over the border from equally flat Lincolnshire and a few miles inland from The Wash, is **King's Lynn**, formerly Bishop's Lynn, and generally referred to by the locals as simply "Lynn". The town grew up around its Saturday market, and became an important market town, with its good water transport links, either via the Great Ouse out to sea, or inland through the extensive network of canals and waterways, to the Midlands.

The town has an interesting architectural heritage, spanning the medi-

eval to the Georgian period. One of the prettiest buildings in the town is the 17th century **Custom House**, a surprisingly delicate looking building.

The **Guildhall**, with its façade of patterned flint and stone, is one of King's Lynn's oldest buildings, dating from 1421. Here you can see King John's cup, allegedly lost by the 13th century king when he was caught in a storm in The Wash.

Close to the 12th century **St Margaret's Church** is the **Hanseatic Warehouse**, which was built about 1475 and was used until 1751 as a depot for Hansa, the important North European merchant league. **True's Yard** is all that remains of King's Lynn's old fishing community of which the area known as North End was levelled in the slum clearances of the 1930s.

Once, hundreds of families lived there, within a stone's throw of their **Chapel of St Nicholas**, which still dominates the area. North End was a little community within a community, with its own boat builders, chandlers, sailmakers, pubs, bake-houses and school. Two cottages of True's Yard have been restored.

Along the banks of the Great Ouse are 16th and 17th century warehouses, large, impressive buildings which stretch from the road right down to the water's edge. Many have now been converted into restaurants and galleries, and it is worthwhile exploring them, walking through the inner courtyards down to the water's edge.

The beautiful gardens of the Sandringham Royal Estate.

Castle Acre

East of King's Lynn, 3 km (5 miles) north of Swaffham, is **Castle Acre**. Here, side by side, are the two symbols of medieval nobility, a castle for security in this world and a priory to help ensure it in the next life. The most striking feature of the ruins of **Castle Acre Priory** is the great west front of the church, a fine example of 12th century architecture, which still soars almost to its full height, and is elaborately decorated.

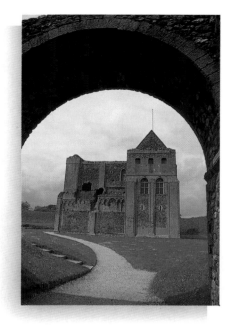

Castle Rising, once one of the most important fortifications in East Anglia.

Adjoining the west front is the splendid **Prior's Lodge** which seems more like a secular manor house than a building for monks, a reminder that the prior was also an important land-owner. The fine flint and brick gate-house survived the dissolution of the Priory in 1537. The village of **Castle Acre**, with its ruined Norman castle and 13th century **Bailey Gate** is only a short walk away.

Castle Rising & Sandringham

Two and a half km (4 miles) northeast of King's Lynn off the A149, is **Castle Rising**, once one of the most important fortifications in East Anglia. William de

Albini started building the castle in about 1138; in the 13th century, it passed to the Montalt family and in 1331 to the crown. Isabella, widow of Edward II, retired here after arranging the murder of her husband, taking residence in the castle, until her own death in 1358. The crown relinquished its hold over the castle in 1544 when it was granted to the Duke of Norfolk. Today the castle is the property of a branch of the Howard family.

The huge 12th century keep in the centre of the castle, with its walls towering to their full original height, was once one of the finest in England. It provided both an elegant residence and a defensive stronghold. There are fine views of the surrounding countryside

Holkham Hall, an 18th century Palladian-style mansion.

Sandringham House, one of Queen Elizabeth JJ's favourite retreats.

from the ramparts. Inside the castle there is a murder hole, a small hole which looks down on the main castle entrance, through which missiles could be dropped onto unwelcome arrivals.

A few miles further north is **Sandringham**, the private home of 4 gen-erations of monarchs, and, for King George V, one of his favourite places; "Dear old Sandringham, the place I love better than anywhere else in the world." The present owner, Her Majesty Queen Elizabeth II, opened the house to the public in 1977, and though the queues

Great Yarmouth harbour.

can be depressingly long, especially on weekends and holidays, it is worth the wait, for it is an interesting house, not overwhelmingly large and full of royal mementos. The dining table is set for dinner; there are family photographs everywhere and portraits of the present owners' Victorian precursors. The extensive grounds around Sandringham are beautiful and if you walk for a while, the crowds just seem to melt away.

The North Norfolk coast

The drive along the A149, from Sandringham north towards the coast, takes you through lavender fields, which from mid-June to mid-August, are a blaze of colour. The little village of **Heacham**, is the centre of the English lavender trade, the local crop being used to make the very English gifts of lavender water and soap.

Continue on the A149 travelling through the salt marshes of the north Norfolk coast to **Holkham Hall**, an 18th century Palladian-style mansion and one of Britain's most impressive stately homes, situated in a deer park of some 3,000 acres. Home to 7 generations of the Earls of Leicester, Holkham Hall is still privately owned. It has magnificent state rooms, and, the most dramatic feature of the house, a stunning alabaster entrance hall modelled on a Roman Temple of Justice. The alabaster for the hall came from Derbyshire and was

Norwich Cathedral, founded in 1096.

transported to Norfolk, by river and sea.

The Hall's grounds contain a "**Bygones museum**", an evocative collection of over 4,000 domestic and agricultural artefacts. Holkham Hall also has the novelty of the only private post office in England, **Holkham sub-Post Office**. This post office, established just over 200 years ago is unique in that successive Earls of Leicester have held the hereditary appointment of sub-post master, up to the present day. But now, any mail posted in the box does not receive the Holkham cancellation stamp

A boat outside an 18th century tide mill, Woodbridge.

for, as part of the Post Office modernization programme, Holkham mail now passes through the Norwich sorting office – probably more efficient, but not quite as interesting.

Blakeney Point

The shingle banks and shifting sand dunes of **Blakeney Point** a 2 km (3 mile) long spit, east of Sherringham, are home in summer to many species of birds. At nearby **Morston** and **Skiffkey**, there are 1,000 acres of salt marsh and inter-tidal mud flats. In July, sea lavender colours the marshes purple, and they are the breeding ground for waders whilst flocks of geese winter there.

Norwich

The coast continues round in a large, smooth sweep, with virtually no creeks and indentations, round to the popular holiday resort town of **Great Yarmouth.** Inland is the county town of Norfolk, and the largest town in the region, **Norwich**, an ancient cathedral city, and since Saxon times, the leading city of East Anglia. Norwich has a skyline that is pierced with towers and spires, more than 20 of them, including the spire of the beautiful Norman cathedral.

The city has at least 32 medieval churches and a restored castle, and some fascinating buildings, so there is lots to explore. **Strangers Hall** a rambling building with twisting stairways, dates from about 1320, but additions made in the 15th, 16th, 17th, and 18th centuries, make it the perfect architectural melting pot.

The fine building of **Norwich Cathedral** was founded in 1096, and is particularly famous for its 400 roof bosses in the vaults. The cathedral is beautifully situated at **Cathedral Close**, a large, calm and elegant area, leading down to the river.

By the river is **Pull's Ferry Watergate**, an arched gateway, built in the 15th century to guard the river approach to Norwich priory and cathedral. The gate spanned the narrow canal that led from the River Wensum to the Priory; dug before the building of the cathedral and priory in the 12th cen-

Willy Lott's cottage, Flatford Mill, was immortalized by the artist Constable.

tury, it enabled boats to carry building material right up to the site itself. Overseas cargoes would have been transshipped at Yarmouth, from sea-going ships to smaller sailing vessels.

For several centuries the canal must have been one of the important means of delivering bulky supplies to the priory. One such cargo would have been the peat cut from the numerous pits in East Norfolk, which, subsequently flooded,

are now known as the Broads (see box story p288).

After the priory was closed down at the Reformation, the ferryman's house beside the gate was built. The first ferryman was Sandling, during Queen Elizabeth I's reign, and another John Pull, lived here at the beginning of the 19th century. The arched gateway has since been known as either "Sandling's ferry" or "Pull's ferry".

The Norfolk Broads

If you imagine a triangle drawn roughly between Sea Palling on the coast, down past Great Yarmouth to Lowestoft, and inland a few miles to the east of Norwich, that is the area covered by the Norfolk Broads; 124 km (200 miles) of navigable inland waterways. The Broads are essentially shallow lakes, formed by the broadening of the River Bure and the River Yare, which connect many of the waterways. There are about 40 broads, formed out of medieval peat diggings. In the Middle Ages, the sea level was appreciably lower than it is today and the flooded excavations are today known generically as the Broads.

Individual Broads vary in size, from mere pools to the 296 acre **Hicking Broad**. Only 16 are available for public navigation, the rest are either too inaccessible, or too shallow, or are wildlife sanctuaries. The Broads are one of the country's premier wildlife habitats, home to Chinese water-deer, kingfishers, herons and grebe. The villages are famous for their hammer-beamed and thatched roof churches.

The best way of exploring the Broads is by boat, and they are deservedly popular with holidaymakers. You can hire sailing boats and cruisers of a variety of sizes and for various time durations. Only once you are on the river can you really realize the extent and beauty of the area. Trips can be organized from centres such as Wroxham, Potter Heigham and Horning.

Architectural note

As you travel around Norfolk and neighbouring Suffolk, you might be surprised to see a number of churches with round towers, a distinctive features of village churches in East Anglia. Several theories have been put forward to account for them. One suggestion is that they were originally built for defence against Scandinavian invaders, providing a secure place for the villagers and their valuables. It seems much more likely, however, that most round towers were built simply to hold the church bells, the reason for their shape being the difficulty of obtaining suitable limestone for making strong corners.

There are about 180 round towers in England, two-thirds of them are in Norfolk, and all the rest are in Suffolk. Tall square towers with flint corners were much less likely to stay up than round towers.

Bury St Edmonds

Entering Suffolk "the nicest town in the world" is surely worth a visit, for this was how William Cobbett described **Bury St Edmunds**, an ancient cathedral and market town. Bury St Edmunds takes its name from the Saxon king of East Anglia who was martyred by the Danes in AD 870, and whose remains were eventually buried in the monastery.

The town plan today remains essentially as it was laid out by Abbot Baldwin in the 11th century. Baldwin, out of wit or devotion, created a square for God, **Angel Hill**, and a square for man, the **Cornhill market place**. Angel Hill, despite the name, is actually an elegant square, laid out on the slope up from the abbey.

The **Angel Hotel**, built in 1779, is immortalised in Charles Dickens' *Pickwick Papers*. If you are looking for a cosy place for a drink, another of the

The vast open horizon of the Norfolk fens, is broken by many a windmill.

town's inns, the **Nutshell pub**, has a claim to fame, since it is reputed to be the smallest public house in Britain.

The ruins of **St Edmondsbury Abbey** are surrounded by well-kept formal gardens, in a pretty setting beside the river, an ideal place for a picnic. The abbey was originally founded in AD 633, and after St Edmund was buried there, it became an important place of pilgrimage.

It was at the High Altar of the abbey that a group of 20 rebellious barons met in 1214, to swear an oath to raise arms against King John, if he would not sign *Magna Carta* (see History box story, p 13). The town's motto "Shrine of a King, Cradle of the Law" reflects these principal events in the town's history.

Ickworth House

Nearly 2 km (3 miles) southwest of Bury St Edmonds along the A143 is **Ickworth House**, an extravagant 18th century creation.

The Ickworth estate had been in the Hervey family for some 300 years, before Frederick, Bishop of Derry and Fourth Earl of Bristol, built this striking building between 1795 and 1829, partly as a home and partly as a gallery for his collections.

The rotunda was to be His Lordship's home, and the two curving wings were to house his then extensive collections. Frederick was a larger than life character; an aristocrat, a bishop, fabu-

Tracing the steps of Constable at Flatford Mill, by the River Stour.

lously wealthy, an Irish nationalist and an inveterate traveller, after whom the Hotel Bristols chain is named. He was also a serious shopper and during his trips abroad he acquired lavish treasures. Frederick planned to exhibit these treasures at Ickworth House, together with some of the plunder that he had collected in Rome during Napoleon's 1798 campaign.

After his death, however, his son reversed the arrangements, choosing to live in the east wing and displaying in the rotunda what remained of his fa-

Norfolk flint.

ther's collection of paintings, 18th century French porcelain and silver pieces.

Immortal land

Timber and plaster buildings dating from the Middle Ages and colourful thatched cottages, are a feature of East Anglia. The village of **Lavenham** south of Bury St Edmonds is the perfect place to see this heritage, the village has 300 buildings that are listed as being of architectural and historic importance.

As you explore Suffolk, if the pretty landscape of rich farmlands, watermills and vineyards, seems somehow familiar, it may well be because you have seen pictures of it before. Two of England's best known and well loved artists, John Constable and Thomas Gainsborough were respectively from Sudbury and East Begholt, in Suffolk. One of Constable's most famous paintings *The Haywain*, was painted at **Flatford Mill** which belonged to the artist's father. The mill is now a field centre belonging to the National Trust.

The neighbouring counties of Cambridgeshire and Essex, although vastly different from each other, share many of the physical characteristics of the flat East Anglian landscape. The urban sprawl of outer London suburbia stretches into the south of Essex, yet a few miles beyond the commuter London Underground train stations, there are quiet salt marshes and county towns. The highlight of Cambridgeshire for the tourist is undoubtedly the old university town of Cambridge, but there are many other interesting towns and a pleasant landscape to enjoy.

The Great Gate at Trinity College, Cambridge.

293

Colchester

Colchester, the largest town in Essex, is Britain's oldest recorded town. In AD 43, the invading Romans chose to establish their

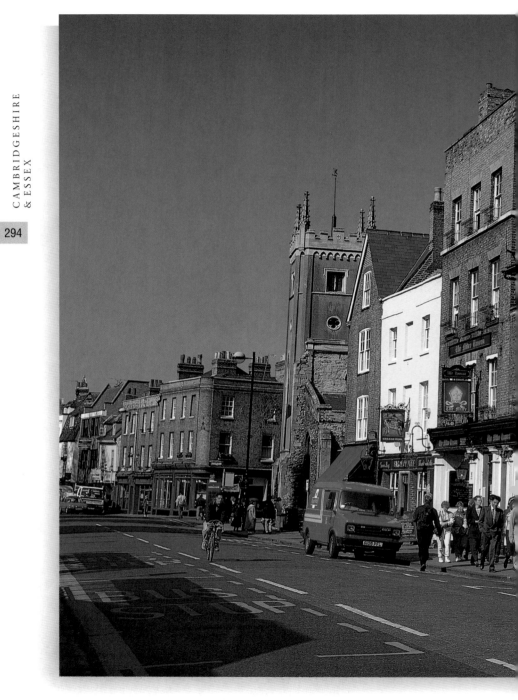

Bridge Street, Cambridge.

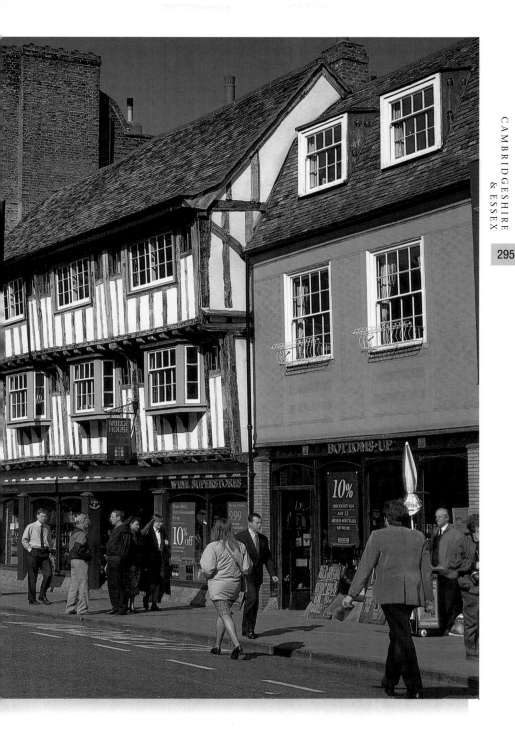

A respite from studies, punting along the River Cam, Cambridge.

town on the site of an older settlement, named *Camulodumun*. Part of the temple of the Roman emperor Claudius is still there to explore. Later, Queen Bodicea sacked the city, destroying the temple, before her rebellion was crushed. The Saxons followed the Romans, and then came William the Conqueror, who chose Colchester as the site of one of the first stone castles built to safeguard his new domain. The castle keep still re-

mains and today it houses the **Castle Museum**, containing one of the finest Roman collections in the country.

In the 16th century Protestant refugees fleeing Spanish rule in the Netherlands settled in Colchester and revitalized an ailing cloth trade. In the process, they developed the **Dutch Quarter** of the town, which lies just behind the High Street.

During the civil war, the Parlia-

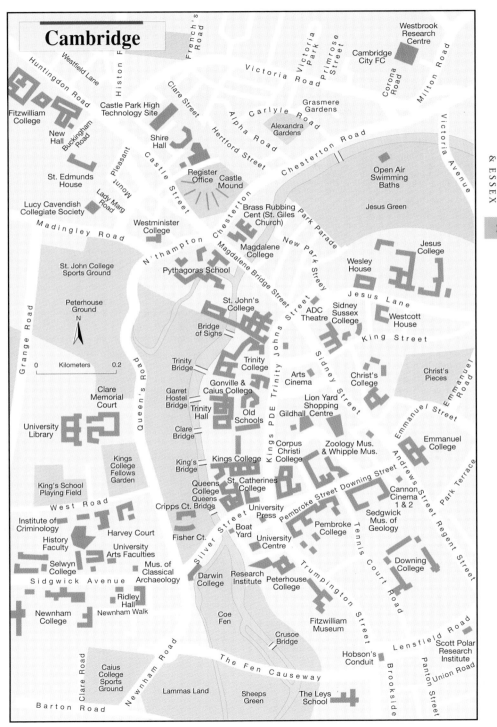

Cambridge

Westbrook Research Centre

Cambridge City FC

Victoria Park

Primrose Street

Corona Road

Milton Road

Victoria Road

French's Road

Westfield Lane

Histon F...

Clare Street

Huntingdon Road

Fitzwilliam College

New Hall

Buckingham Road

Castle Park High Technology Site

Shire Hall

Hertford Street

Alpha Road

Carlyle Road

Grasmere Gardens

Alexandra Gardens

Chesterton Road

Open Air Swimming Baths

Jesus Green

Victoria Avenue

St. Edmunds House

Pleasant

Mount

Lady Marg Road

Castle Street

Register Office

Castle Mound

Brass Rubbing Cent (St. Giles Church)

Park Parade

New Park Streey

Jesus College

Lucy Cavendish Collegiate Society

Madingley Road

Westminister College

N'thampton

Chesterton

Magdalene Bridge Street

Magdalene College

Wesley House

Jesus Lane

St. John College Sports Ground

Pythagoras School

St. John's College

Bridge of Sighs

Trinity Johns Street

Sidney Street

ADC Theatre

Sidney Sussex College

Westcott House

King Street

Christ's Pieces

Peterhouse Ground

Grange Road

N

0   Kilometers   0.2

Trinity Bridge

Trinity College

Gonville & Caius College

Garret Hostel Bridge

Clare Memorial Court

Trinity Hall

Old Schools

Arts Cinema

Lion Yard Shopping Gildhall Centre

Christ's College

Emmanuel Street

Emmanuel Road

University Library

Clare Bridge

Kings PDE

Corpus Christi College

Zoology Mus. & Whipple Mus.

Emmanuel College

Kings College Fellows Garden

King's Bridge

Kings College

King's School Playing Field

West Road

Queens College

St. Catherines College

Andrews Street

Park Terrace

Cripps Ct. Bridge

Queens

University Press

Pembroke Street

Downing Street

Cannon Cinema 1 & 2

Sedgwick Mus. of Geology

Regent Street

Institute of Criminology

History Faculty

Harvey Court

University Arts Faculties

Fisher Ct.

Silver Street

Boat Yard

University Centre

Pembroke College

Tennis Court Road

Downing College

Selwyn College

Sidgwick Avenue

Mus. of Classical Archaeology

Darwin College

Research Institute

Peterhouse College

Trumpington Street

Ridley Hall

Newnham Walk

Coe Fen

Newnham College

Crusoe Bridge

Fitzwilliam Museum

Lensfield Road

Scott Polar Research Institute

Hobson's Conduit

Brookside

Panton Street

Union Road

Clare Road

Caius College Sports Ground

Newnham Road

Lammas Land

The Fen Causeway

Sheeps Green

The Leys School

Barton Road

Cambridge

An architectural puzzle, the Mathematical Bridge, Cambridge.

If you ask an Oxford man or woman their opinion of **Cambridge**, they will probably reply facetiously, "Cambridge, where's that? Oh, you mean that place in the middle of the fens." The rivalry between the country's 2 top universities is legendary, but thankfully today it is usually reserved for sporting events, such as the Varsity rugby match or the Boat Race. When pressed, the chauvinistic Oxonian will generally admit that, after all, "that place in the fens" is rather beautiful. Cambridge is a truly delightful town, whose charms are much more on display than her rival. In Oxford, to appreciate fully the beauty of the colleges, you must push open doors, and peep into quadrangles. In Cambridge, although the colleges are private, and are usually off-limits to the general visitor during examinations, much of their beauty can be seen from and along the river. One of the glories of Cambridge is the "Backs".

The "Backs"

The "Backs" are green lawns bordering the River Cam, providing a perfect setting from which to appreciate the architecture of the colleges. The land was once a common, on which the townspeople grazed their animals, but from the 16th century onwards this land was gradually bought up by those colleges that backed onto the river, to make gardens and pleasant walks for their scholars. As the Cam winds its way past the colleges, there are scenic bridges, such as Queens College's **Mathematical Bridge**, built in 1749 on mathematical principles, and entirely without nails. In the summer, undergraduates and visitors alike turn out to punt along the river, a spectacle which usually provides much unintentional entertainment to the spectators on the bridges, as punts slowly collide, gently drift into banks and generally refuse to drift elegantly along in the intended direction.

The colleges which back onto the river are amongst the most beautiful in Cambridge: **King's College** with its stunning chapel (see box story, Arts chapter p.115), and **St John's** with its predominantly Tudor architecture and its exquisite **Bridge of Sighs**. **Trinity College** is the largest college, founded by Henry VIII in 1546, and **Queens College**, founded a whole century earlier, in 1446, has a beautiful half-timbered lodge.

As you explore Cambridge, you will find the city to be a fascinating mix of "town" and "gown", in other words, of non-University and of University life. The superb **Fitzwilliam Museum** has a collection of Old Masters, and is particularly strong in English paintings.

mentarians laid siege to the Royalist garrison for 11 weeks until the defenders were eventually starved into submission. Traces of bullet holes are still clearly

It may appear idyllic, but try your hand at punting, and you're guaranteed for fun and hard work.

visible on some of the half-timbered houses of the town.

Audley End House

In the northwest corner of the county, less than 1 km (1 mile) west of Saffron Walden, close to the Cambridgeshire border, there is a palatial Jacobean country manor house called **Audley End House**. When King James I saw Audley End, the recently completed home of Sir Thomas Howard, his Lord Treasurer, he remarked "Too large for a king - but might do for a Lord Treasurer." The king had probably contributed, unwittingly, to the building of this superb house, for in 1619 Howard was found guilty of embezzlement and sent to the Tower of London. He was released and retired to Audley End, disgraced but still in possession of his beautiful home, until his death in 1626.

One thing to remember, when visiting Audley End, which is one of the biggest houses in England, is that what we see today is barely half the original building. The house cost so much to maintain, that over half of it was demolished in the 18th century. Small wonder that James I was impressed, and not a little envious.

The house is magnificent from the very first moment you enter, with the huge wooden-panelled entrance hall leading through to the exquisite **Little Drawing Room**, designed by Robert

King's College gate, Cambridge.

Adam as a sitting room for the ladies, whilst the men lingered in the dining room. There is an alcove in the room, whose pillars had to be reset further apart, so that the voluminous skirts of the then lady of the house could fit in without being creased.

A mile or so south of Audley End is **Prior's Hall Barn** in the village of Widdington. This is one of the finest surviving medieval barns in southeast England and representative of the group of aisled barns centred on northwest Essex. It is very large and airy, with a high ceiling and surprisingly attractive woodwork inside.

Duxford air thrills

Just over the border from Essex into **Cambridgeshire** is an irresistible mu-

Cambridge students muse over May Ball encounters.

seum for flying enthusiasts, the **Imperial War Museum** in Duxford (turn off the M11 from Cambridge, at junction 10). RAF Duxford used to be a bomber base during World War I and was the Spitfire base during World War II. Duxford's hangars now house part of the collection of the Imperial War Museum and what a collection: a veteran, a Mustang, and one of the most beautiful planes ever built, Concorde. This Concorde prototype was flown into Duxford before the M11 motorway was built across the end of the runway, making it impossible now for the aircraft ever to leave Duxford by air.

The museum is not only interesting, but sheer fun, for visitors are allowed to clamber in and out of the planes and for those in search of higher things, there is a modified flight simulator, where you can head off into outer space, to do battle with inter-galactic aliens.

Architectural magnificence

About 9 km (15 miles) north of Cambridge on the A10, **Ely**, is dominated by its cathedral, which rises spectacularly out of the flat fens. The present cathedral was originally built in 1083; in 1250 the east end of the Norman building was rebuilt and in 1321 work started on the **Lady Chapel**, under the supervision of Alan de Walsingham.

The following year, the Norman

Ely Cathedral rises spectacularly out of the Cambridgeshire fens.

tower fell down and poor Alan initially did not know "where to turn or what to do". What he finally did was inspired genius. Rather than replace the tower, he built instead the **Octagon**, an enormous lantern that is acknowledged as one of the wonders of medieval engi-neering.

Travelling back towards Cambridge on the A10 is **Denny Abbey**, founded in the 12th century as a dependent priory of Ely cathedral, on what was then virtually an island in the fens. Denny Abbey was at different times home to Ben-

Cottages huddle close to the protective arms of the parish church, Cavendish, Essex.

edictine monks, Knights Templar and Franciscan nuns. The remains of the church and refectory owe their survival to their conversion to farm use.

Burghley House

Burghley House near Stamford, is the largest and grandest house of the Elizabethan age. It was built between 1565 and 1587 by William Cecil, the most trusted and able advisor to Queen Elizabeth I and the house remains a family home for Cecil's descendants.

Burghley contains one of the finest private collections of 17th century Italian paintings in the world. Over 300 great works are on display in the state rooms with remarkable wood carvings by Grinling Gibbons and his contemporaries. The house is surrounded by a large, beautiful park, landscaped by Capability Brown in the late 18th century. The herd of fallow deer is more ancient, dating from 1562. You can spend a whole afternoon walking the park.

David, Sixth Marquess of Exeter achieved, as Lord Burghley, an international reputation as a hurdler and a sportsman between 1924-33. His Olympic Gold Medal, won in the 1928 Games, and his Silver Medal, won in 1932, are displayed along with many other of his trophies. His athletic achievements were immortalised in the classic film *Chariots of Fire*.

In the geographical heart of England, with the hills of the Peak District to the north and the Cotswolds to the south, we travel eastwards from the industrialized county of Stafford, through Derby, to the east Midland Shire counties of Nottinghamshire, Lincolnshire, and Leicestershire. As we travel we will see enormous diversity, from the industrial heart of England, to vast expanses of fenland and rural hills and valleys. Historic cathedral towns and windmills break the horizon in the east, theme parks and stately homes in the west. This is one of the lesser known regions of England, but with more than its fair share of things to see.

Stamford Cathedral, Lincolnshire.

Beyond Birmingham

Britain's second biggest city, huge, sprawling **Birmingham** (see Warwickshire & the East Midlands chapter p.277) is the centre of the Midlands, but when you travel beyond the industry and the suburbs, there are a wealth of cathedrals, stately homes and quiet villages to discover. Travelling into Staffordshire, immediately north of Birmingham and the surrounding satellite industrial towns, is the peaceful cathedral city of **Lichfield**, home of the 18th century

Midlands & The Potteries

The fine interior of Lichfield Cathedral, Staffordshire.

writer Dr Samuel Johnson.

The three spires of **St Chad's Cathedral**, known as the "Ladies of the Vale", are unique in England, and they dominate the city. The cathedral has a picturesque 13th century close and hidden behind an archway in the northwest corner, is **Vicar's Close**, in whose 13th and 14th century half-timbered houses, the professional cathedral choristers, called the Vicars Choral, once lived.

Dr Johnson is not Lichfield's only famous son; Elias Ashmole (1617-83), a leading antiquarian whose collection

The "Ladies of the Vale" the 3 spires of Lichfield Cathedral, Staffordshire.

became the basis of Oxford's Ashmolean museum, was born in Breadmarket Street, as was Dr Johnson (1709-84). Johnson's contemporary David Carrick (1716-79), the greatest actor-manager of 18th century theatre, lived opposite the west gate of the cathedral. Erasmus Darwin (1731-1802) lived on the corner of the Cathedral Close.

Two miles south of Lichfield, turn off the A38 to the important Roman site of **Wall**, which, as the settlement of *Letocetum*, was a staging post on Watling Street, the principal road from London

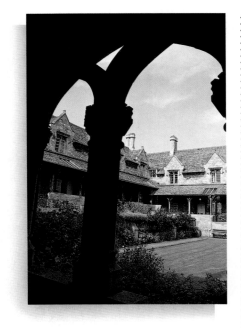

*Almhouses at the great mansion of
Burghley, Lincolnshire.*

to Chester. You can still see the remains of the hostel and the public baths, with their sequence of cold, warm and hot rooms.

West of Lichfield, at the northern tip of the Birmingham conurbation, 4 km (7 miles) north of Wolverhampton, is **Moseley Old Hall**, where King Charles II found refuge, after his escape from the Battle of Worcester. It is a pretty 17th century house with half-timbered rooms, oak panelling, fine furniture and ingenious hiding places, including that of the royal fugitive.

The Burton-on-Trent area

From Birmingham take the A38 north-

eastwards through Lichfield to **Burton-on-Trent**, made famous by the brewery industry. Follow the pungent smell of hops to the town's **Bass Museum**, probably the most comprehensive brewery museum in the world. The brewery business grew up in the town for two main reasons.

Firstly, the local water was hard, with a mineral content that proved to be ideal for the brewing of pale ale, the beer for which Burton is famed. Secondly, the town had an excellent transport network, for the Trent and Mersey canal opened in 1777, followed by the railway in 1839. Small wonder that William Bass, a carrier, passing back and forth with his wagons over the Trent bridge, came to realize the excellence of the Burton beers and decided in 1777 to buy a small brewery in the High Street.

In the museum are the stables of the Bass Shire horses, massive animals that were originally used for pulling the drays, but which are now used as very popular publicity tools. At one time, the company had over 200 horses stabled around Burton and employed its own wheelwrights and blacksmiths.

Towards the Potteries

From Burton-on-Trent, travelling west towards Stafford, you will reach **Shugborough Hall**, the ancestral home of Lord Lichfield, set in 900 acres on the edge of Cannock Chase. The beauty and wealth of the estate is largely due to the

The Potteries

Stoke-on-Trent is one of Britain's last great centres of craftsmanship and was formerly the hub of one of the country's oldest industrial conurbations, the Potteries.

In the small town of **Longton**, in the southern suburbs of Stoke-on-Trent, is the **Gladstone Pottery Museum**, which has been preserved as the only example in the Potteries of a 19th century pottery factory, complete with its cobbled yard, original workshops and huge bottle-shaped kilns. Each day there are several demonstrations which may include casting, throwing, jiggering, flower-making, decorating, modelling and hand-painting.

Also in Longton is the **Staffordshire Enamel factory**, where a Georgian craft is being revived. The origins of the English craft of enamelling on copper can be traced back to the early 18th century. In competition with the manufac-turers of the more lavish gold and enamel boxes of Europe, a thriving industry soon developed. Snuff boxes were produced, as well as bonbonnières, scent bottles, salt cellars and tea caddies. It was however the small enamel box that became synonymous with the industry. The 2 main centres of enamelling were Battersea in south London, although it existed only for 4 years, and Bilston in Staffordshire. In the late 1970s, Staffordshire Enamels® was founded, with the aim of reviving this lost English craft.

A little south of Longton, and still in the Stoke-on-Trent urban area is **Wedgwood**. In the **Wedgwood Visitors Centre**, you can see potters and decorators at work making Wedgwood® china. You can also see the very first pieces Josiah Wedgwood made, when he founded his firm in 1759.

---

efforts of two brothers: Thomas Anson (1695-1773), enlarged the existing mansion, landscaped the parkland and commissioned the building of a group of neo-classical monuments; the funds for these extensive alterations came from Thomas's brother George Anson (1697-1762), a career sailor who acquired fame and wealth by capturing a Spanish treasure galleon, and later became the first Lord of the Admiralty. Today, Shugborough is the home of the Fifth Earl, who, using the name Patrick Lichfield, is a leading professional photographer.

From Shugborough, take the A34 northwards to the urban mass of Stoke-on-Trent, 4 km (7 miles) north of which, half a mile north of the village of Biddulph, is **Biddulph Grange Garden**. This high Victorian Garden was origi-nally designed by James Bateman, and its 15 acres are divided into a number of smaller gardens, intended to house specimens from his extensive and wide-ranging collection of plants. For over 20 years from 1842, trees, shrubs and a wide variety of other plants from all over the world, were brought together at Biddulph, amid rock-work, topiary, tree stumps and an extraordinary collection of eccentric garden buildings. The result is a series of spectacularly picturesque effects and varied micro-climates. James Bateman wanted to include a world tour in his garden, so you can stroll from an Egyptian Court, past "The Great Wall of China", and through a Chinese Pagoda.

Further north from Stoke-on-Trent is an area known as **The Potteries** (see box story) which is still the centre for porcelain making and makes a fascinating visit. Another popluar destination is **Alton Towers**, on the Staffordshire-Derbyshire border, north of Uttoxeter, Britain's only world rated theme park.

There are over 125 rides and attractions, all landscaped into 500 acres, with lovely gardens. The symbol of the park is a particularly nail-biting ride called "The Corkscrew Roller-coaster", whose riders loop the loop twice under forces 3 times that of gravity.

Derby & Nottinghamshire

Heading east, the visitor crosses the southern tip of **Derbyshire**, with its county town of **Derby** and the **Royal Crown Derby porcelain factory**. The picturesque Peak District is in the north of the county (see chapter on The Northwest p331). Bess of Hardwick, a formidable lady of Tudor times and an ancestor of the Dukes of Devonshire, is buried in the vaults of **Derby Cathedral**, beneath the south aisle, whilst above is the elaborate monument she had made for herself before her death in 1607.

It is a short journey along the A52 from Derby, the county town of Derbyshire, to **Nottingham**, the capital city of Nottinghamshire. The flat plains around Nottingham were once covered with the famous **Sherwood Forest**, home to the legendary Robin Hood. **Nottingham Castle** was once home to Robin's enemy, the Sheriff of Nottingham. Eng-

land's oldest public house, **Ye Olde Trip to Jerusalem Inn**, said to date from 1189, stands at the base of Castle Rock.

Nottingham lace achieved worldwide popularity in the boom days of the textile industry around 1865. The towns abundant coal reserves provided the power for the immense machinery used in the lace making industry. A total of 130 lace making factories, a majority of which were based in Nottingham's Lace Market area, provided work for thousands of skilled workers during the 19th century.

Eastwood, just west of Nottingham is the birthplace of the novelist DH Lawrence, who was born in a tiny terrace house on 11 September 1885. Nearby, **Newstead Abbey** (7 miles north of Eastwood, on the A608), was home to another famous writer, Lord Byron.

Lincolnshire

The county of Lincolnshire is the largest of the eastern Shire counties, famous for its farming tradition. The south of the county around the Spalding and Boston areas is fenland, good soils and drainage here have enabled the growth of a fine market-garden crop.

To the north are the gently sloping and well farmed Lincolshire Wolds with their picturesque valleys and villages, centred around the pretty market town of Louth. The east coast is flat, with some well-known resorts such as **Skegness**, making the most of Lincoln-

The rich colours of autumn in the Lincolnshire countryside.

shire's sandy beaches.

Lincoln

The Romans first came to **Lincoln** in AD 48 to establish a military garrison for the forces of their ninth legion. The hilltop location provided a perfect defence position, and the iron age settlement of *Lindon* was latinized to the name of *Lindum*. In AD 96, when the strategic importance of the city declined, it was granted "colonia" status, a chartered city, providing accommodation for retired legionary soldiers. From this title of *Lindum Colonia*, the modern name "Lincoln" derives.

Lincoln Cathedral is visible to ap-

proaching travellers from up to 30 miles away, surrounded as it is by the flat Lincolnshire fens. William the Conqueror ordered the Cathedral to be built in 1072. In 1185, an earthquake razed almost the entire structure to the ground, and only the west front and the lower halves of the two western towers, survived.

In the following year, Henry II sent Bishop Hugh of Avalon to rebuild the church and in the interests of economy, the surviving Norman features were incorporated into the new, mainly Gothic structure. The fabulous 13th century **Angel Choir**, is named after the angels that decorate the windows. Bishop Hugh became a saint after his death and a large shrine was built to him at the cathedral's East End.

At the same time as he rebuilt the cathedral, Bishop Hugh of Avalon also built an imposing new **Bishop's Palace**, the remains of which are largely unaltered since Bishop Hugh of Wells completed it in the 13th century. In the south facing gardens of the ruined Palace is the most northerly vineyard in Europe, protected from the north winds by the cathedral and planted with vines donated by Lincoln's German twin town of Neustadtanderweinstrasse.

In 1068, William the Conqueror, appreciating the military value of the site earlier selected by the Romans, evicted 166 Saxon families from their homes to build his castle. Exploring the **castle** today is a potted history lesson, for within the castle precincts you can see a rare surviving copy of *Magna Carta*, as well as an Eleanor cross, one of 12 that marked the funeral procession of Queen Eleanor of Castile in 1219. A walk around the ramparts takes you from the **Observatory Tower**, with magnificent views of the city, past the huge Victorian prison complex, and the **Lucy Tower**, which was the medieval shell keep and later the Victorian burial ground for convicts.

A noticeable trend in English cities is the bringing to life of their urban and industrial heritage. Mills are being refurbished, docks are being converted, and, in the case of Lincoln, a former mental hospital has been transformed into an elegant centre. **The Lawn Complex**, which was opened in 1990, following a multi-million pound refurbishment, dates back to 1820 when it was opened as the county's first purpose-built hospital for the treatment of the mentally ill.

Today the Lawn has a large auditorium, function rooms, shops, an archaeological centre, and a conservatory, named after Sir Joseph Banks, the Lincolnshire born explorer. Banks was a close advisor to King George III and a prime initiator behind the Royal Botanical Gardens at Kew. He was appointed Chief Scientific Officer on Captain Cook's ship the *Endeavour*, on its voyage to Australia. Following the discovery of Australia, where Botany Bay was named in recognition of his achievements, Banks introduced scores of new varieties of plants into Britain.

The aptly named **Steep Hill** is the main pedestrian route between Lincoln's uphill old town and the commercial and shopping centre in the lower city. Walking down the hill take note of two special builings; the 12th century **House of Aaron the Jew** and further down the hill, the **Jew's Court**, thought to be the location of the old synagogue, which was at the heart of a flourishing medieval Jewish community. Anti-Semitic feeling in the late 13th century led to the expulsion of the Jews from England in 1290.

The Lincolnshire Fens

East of Lincoln, and standing on the

Seeded for winter, the arable fens of Lincolnshire, await the next harvest.

banks of the River Witham, **Boston** was once one of the country's leading commercial ports, the river offering a sheltered anchorage for trading ships. Today, the marshlands and mud-flats on the eastern side of Boston, towards the Wash, are important for nature conservation and provide perfect spots to see a variety of wild fowl and wading birds.

St Botolph's Church was built from profits from the wool trade. Building started in 1306 but it took until 1460 to complete the church. It is one of the largest parish churches in the country and its Tower, or "the Stump" as it is more fondly known, is an outstanding landmark, visible from as far as 12 km (20 miles) away.

During World War II, the Stump guided many airmen back to base. A climb up the tower is well worth the effort and on a clear day you can see as

Vast expanses of verdant green stretch out before you in the Leicestershire countryside.

far away as Lincoln Cathedral, 20 km (32 miles) away.

The **Guildhall Museum** dating back to 1450, is a reminder of another of Boston's historical ties, that of the Pil-

grim Fathers. It was in the Guildhall cells, on the ground floor of the museum, that William Bradford and William Brewster, were imprisoned in 1607, before their trial for their illegal

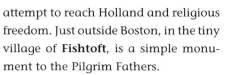

in 1819 for £1,826, and the tallest working windmill in England The five-sailed mill at **Alford**, built around 1837, has been in continuous use since it was built. Three kilometers (5 miles) north of Boston and less than $\frac{1}{2}$ km (half a mile) west of the village of Sibsey, is the **Sibsey Trader Windmill**, a rare 6-sailed windmill. On selected days throughout the year, called "milling days", the windmill is fully operational with grain being milled and flour for sale, subject, of course, to wind conditions. In the village of **Heckington**, just off the Sleaford to Boston Road (A17), there is a windmill with eight sails.

If the fens around the attractive Georgian town of **Spalding** remind you of Holland, it is not surprising, for not only are there windmills, but there are bulbs. This corner of Lincolnshire, is the centre of the country's bulb industry, especially tulips, which stretch for miles beyond the horizon. Lincolnshire's flat land is also ideal for airfields, and **Cranwell**, south of Lincoln is home to the Royal Air Force College, whilst the World War II 617 Squadron, better known as "The Dambusters" flew from **Scampton**, 3 km (5 miles) north of Lincoln.

The Wolds

The rolling hills of the Lincolnshire Wolds, centre around the Georgian market town of **Louth**. The splendid Gothic parish **church of St James**, is

attempt to reach Holland and religious freedom. Just outside Boston, in the tiny village of **Fishtoft**, is a simple monument to the Pilgrim Fathers.

Lincolnshire still has a number of working windmills. At Boston, there is the five-sailed **Maud Foster Mill**, built

The Gothic-Baroque fantasy of Belvoir Castle, Leicestershire.

famous for its (294 ft) 90 m spire. The church also contains some fine 19th century wood-carvings.

Lincolnshire's famous sons, the poet Alfred Lord Tennyson and Captain John Smith, the first governor of Virginia, both attended King Edward VI school in Louth. Tennyson's birthplace lies in the pretty wolds village of **Somersby** south of Louth, while Smith, was born at Willoughby. Animal lovers may find Louth's **cattle market** interesting, where local farmers come weekly to buy and sell cattle and sheep.

places named for and after it. Thanks to a number of stalwart Rutlanders, Rutland simply refuses to disappear.

Situated right on the border between Lincolnshire and Leicestershire, in the countryside west of Grantham, is the impressive **Belvoir Castle**, pronounced "Beever". The castle was built between 1654-68 for the Dukes of Rutland, who found their Derbyshire home, Haddon Hall too small. The house was badly damaged by fire in 1816, and the rebuilding produced a massive part-Gothic, part-Baroque fantasy.

Ashby de la Zouch Castle, in the far west of the county, near the Derbyshire border, is one of the most impressive medieval castles in the Midlands. The castle's most striking feature is the magnificent **Hastings Tower**, over 24 m (80 ft) high and named after the castle's 15th century Lord, who also built a fine chapel here, before being summarily executed by Richard III.

The castle was designed to resist siege, and the Tower was connected to the kitchens by an underground passage which can still be explored. Lord Hastings' descendents entertained royal visitors here, including Henry VII, James I and Charles I. It was for backing the Royalist side that the Tower was literally split into two, during the Civil War.

The unlucky Hastings also started to build **Kirby Muxloe Castle**, 2 $^1/_2$ km (4 miles) west of Leicester, but Richard III ensured that it was never finished, and Kirby Muxloe stands today much as Lord Hastings left it.

Leicestershire

Leicestershire is a small flat county, which has assimilated into its boundary the former county of Rutland, at one time the smallest county in England. Even though Rutland has legally ceased to exist, you will still see signs for it and

I n the west of England, 4 counties share a common border with Wales: Cheshire, Shropshire, Hereford and Worcester, and Gloucestershire, an area whose history is closely bound up with the lands to the west. This area of the western shires, embraces a number of ancient towns, charming scenery, fascinating exhibits and museums, many from the early stages of industrialization. As in every part of England, this area also offers a good number of stately homes, castles and abbeys, making for a great variety of sights to see and things to do.

■ ■ ■ ■ ■ ■ ■

Shopping in history. Chester High Street was marked out by Roman engineers in AD 79.

The Western Borders

Chester

Cheshire, the most northerly of the border counties, serves as a buffer between the industrial Midlands and Lancashire to its east, and the rural, quieter Borders, to the south. The ancient walled city of **Chester**, was the Roman fortress of *Deva*, a strategic outpost and the headquarters of the elite Valeria Victrix legion, which smashed the uprising led by Queen Bodicea.

The **city walls** were originally established by Roman legionaries to defend their fortress against attacks by ferocious Welsh tribes from across the border. Now the walls are a promenade, offering delightful views of Chester, along the entire 2-mile circuit. The walk takes visitors past the 900-year-old cathedral, the Norman **castle**, the largest Roman ampitheatre ever uncovered in Britain, and the canal in its spectacular rock cutting.

Chester flourished in the Middle Ages, when the city exported cheese, candles and salt. Cromwell's troops clashed against Royalist forces here in the English civil war, when the city suffered a 2-year siege.

Chester has a unique feature, **The Rows**, picturesque 2-tier medieval shopping galleries, lining both sides of the main thoroughfares, which were themselves marked out by Roman engineers in AD 79. **The Roodee**, once the site of the massive Roman harbour, is now a race-course, right in the centre of town, where the oldest horse races in the country take place and intriguingly, are run anti-clockwise.

To explore Chester you can walk around the city walls on your own or, throughout the summer, you can join Caius Julius Quartus, a Roman legionary in shining armour, as he escorts a wall patrol around the fortress of *Deva* - ask at the Tourist Office for details of this route march.

Historic & futuristic Cheshire

Eleven miles southeast of Chester, on a rocky crag, stand the medieval ruins of **Beeston Castle**, virtually destroyed by the Parliamentarians in the Civil War, in revenge for its loyalty to the Royalists. **Peckforton Castle**, built on a craggy hill opposite, is pure Victorian, a 19th century fantasy of what a medieval castle must have looked like. It was built between 1844 and 1851, as a functional Victorian home, but in the style of a 12th century castle.

Further east is **Northwich**, one of Cheshire's historic salt towns, which has the country's only **Salt Museum**. Cheshire is the only place in Britain where salt is produced on a large scale and the last surviving open-pan salt works is to be found on the Trent and Mersey canal, at nearby **Marston**.

The quiet little village of **Daresbury**, northwest of Northwich, is the birthplace of Charles Lutwidge Dodgson, better known as the 19th century writer Lewis Carroll. Daresbury's most famous son is remembered in a beautiful stained glass window in the village church, which features both Lewis Carroll himself and many of the characters from his best known books, *Alice's Adventures in Wonderland*, and *Alice through the Looking Glass*.

For over 400 years, silk has been woven in **Macclesfield**, east of Northwich and even today, over 9,000 metres a week are made by one firm alone. Nearby, **Gawsworth Hall** (off the A536 south of Macclesfield), is a manor house dating back to Norman times, and formerly the home of Mary Fitton, possibly the still unidentified

Statue of Charles Darwin, Shrewsbury's most famous son.

"dark lady" of Shakespeare's sonnets.

Little Moreton Hall, 2 ¹/₂ km (4 miles) south-west of Congleton (off the A34), is one of the most perfect examples of a half-timbered house in the country. Surrounded by a moat and built around a cobbled courtyard, the house is largely unfurnished, but the wainscotted long gallery, early plasterwork, wall paintings, great hall and private hall, remain as special features. Within the moated area, a formal knot garden is a recreation of a typical 17th century garden.

Figures at the 13th century Stokesay Castle, Shropshire.

A few miles to the north, and centuries apart, is **Jodrell Bank**, whose Lovell Radio Telescope is the second largest fully steerable radio telescope in the world and is as big as the dome of St Paul's, London. The telescope receives radio waves from space, 24 hours a day.

Shropshire

Shrewsbury, the county town of Shropshire, is arguably the finest Tudor town in England, with a rich architectural heritage dominated by black and white Tudor-style buildings. The two main bridges over the River Severn are still known as the **English Bridge** and the **Welsh Bridge**, reflecting centuries of border conflicts. Charles Darwin, born in Shrewsbury in 1809 is the town's most famous son.

The area around Shrewsbury is full of interesting sites. Two and half kilometres (4 miles) southeast of Shrewsbury is Attingham Park, set in landscaped grounds of 230 acres. The house was designed in 1785 for the first Lord Berwick. Attractions include the magnificent Regency state rooms, the Nash picture gallery with its collection of French and Italian paintings and a spectacular collection of Regency silver.

Continuing along the B4380 for just another mile, you will reach the site of **Wroxeter Roman City**. Between AD 58 and AD 88 there was a Roman fortress here, which acted as a military and supply base for the command of central Wales. When the army left, a civil settlement, *Viroconium*, was founded, the fourth largest city in Roman Britain. Continue along the same road to reach the multiple attractions of Iron Bridge, Coalbrookdale, Blists Hill and Coalport (see box story p.324). The peaceful ruins of the Cistercian **Buildwas Abbey**, founded in 1135, are 1 km (2 miles) west of Ironbridge. Northeast of Shrewbury off the B5062, are the ruins of the 12th century Augustinian **Haughmond Abbey**.

From Wenlock to Ludlow

Much Wenlock is a picturesque market town lying between the limestone escarpment of Wenlock Edge and the Ironbridge Gorge, in some of the most attractive countryside in Shropshire. Here are the magnificent remains of **Wenlock Priory**, a 13th century Cluniac priory.

South of Much Wenlock is the bustling market town of **Bridgnorth**. The town is divided into two, Low Town and High Town, the latter of which stands on a 656 m (200 ft) sandstone cliff. The two areas are connected by a funicular railway. The town has a fine half-timbered **Town Hall**, straddling the High Street.

The A49 road from Shrewsbury to Ludlow passes through the picturesque village of **Church Stretton**, ideal for a picnic by the stream or for the more adventurous, a walk in the mountains with the sheep. From the hills here, on a clear day, you can see the Welsh mountains.

Continuing towards Ludlow, is the beautiful 13th century fortified manor house of **Stokesay Castle**, which has hardly altered since it was built in 1281. The house was built by Lawrence of Ludlow, the leading wool merchant of his day and the tenancy of the estate was sold to him for the price of "a juvenile sparrow-hawk".

During the Middle Ages, wool was England's most important export, and the lowlands near the Welsh Border were major wool producing areas. Stokesay was therefore a convenient location for Lawrence, since it lay on the road from Ludlow, his family's place of origin, to Shrewsbury, the centre of their business.

Over the centuries the house changed families, fortunes waned and in the early 18th century the castle ceased to be occupied. By the early 19th century, the castle was in a state of disrepair. However, a few years later, as interest in Gothic architecture began to develop, Stokesay was sensitively restored.

Ludlow is often called the perfect historic town, for there are nearly 500 listed buildings here and the medieval street pattern survives almost intact. **Ludlow Castle** was begun in the late 11th century, as the border stronghold of one of the Marcher Lords, Roger de Lacy.

Ironbridge Gorge Museum

If you had ever thought that industrial history was, well, just a little bit boring, a visit to the **Ironbridge Gorge Museum** in Shropshire, will surely change your mind.

This unique UNESCO World Heritage Site is in fact not one museum, but seven, spread along the beautiful Ironbridge Gorge, 2 sq km (6 sq miles) that changed the world. There is the Iron Bridge itself and the very popular **Blists Hill Open Air Museum**, a living town of the 1890s, complete with craftsmen and workers demonstrating their skills. The **Museum of the River Visitor Centre**, the **Museum of Iron**, the **Jackfield Tile Museum**, and the **Coalport China Museum**, all give an insight into the history and manufacture of the products that made Ironbridge Gorge the birthplace of industry.

The Iron Bridge

At the end of the 18th century, **Ironbridge** was the most industrialized place in the world. This may seem somewhat hard to believe, when you see the quiet, pretty, village of today. The Iron Bridge, built between 1777 and 1781, was the first great iron bridge in the world. It has a span of just over 30 $^1/_2$ m (100 ft), spanning the Severn Gorge. It was intended from the start to be a spectacular advertizement of the skills of the Coalbrookdale ironmasters, and its construction captured the popular imagination. It was the first time that iron had played a structural role in a major civil engineering project anywhere in the world. The old furnace at Coalbrookdale had to be enlarged to produce enough iron to cast the ribs of the bridge, some of which weighed over 5 tons. Work began in November 1777, the bridge was completed in 1779 and opened to traffic on 1 January 1781. The Iron Bridge was an immediate attraction. Engineers, poets and painters came to admire it, and even during construction, engravings of the bridge were on sale to the public.

Blists Hill & the Museum of the River

The **Severn Warehouse**, built in the 1840s to house the iron products of the Coalbrookdale Company, prior to shipment down the river, and on to the world's markets, is now the Museum of the River. This interesting museum has a spectacular 12 m (40 ft) model of the Gorge as it was at exactly 1200 on 12 August 1796, when King George's cousin, William V, Prince of Orange came to visit.

On a hill overlooking the Gorge, is the Blists Hill Open Air Museum, where people in period costume ride through the streets, cast iron in the furnace, and serve you in the shops and the bank. When talking with visitors, they eschew any reference to anything later than 1890. There is only one exception; prices are quoted in Victorian as well as contemporary values. So, a cup of tea will cost 1 $^1/_2$ d (old pence) or 60p, as will a very un-Victorian Coca Cola.

A word of advice: when you visit Ironbridge, buy a "passport ticket" which admits you to all the museum sites and is valid indefinitely, until you have visited every museum, in any order, once.

Hereford & Worcester

Ludlow, lies on the border of the county of Hereford and Worcester, a county formed in 1974, by the merger of the two counties of Herefordshire and Worcestershire. The towns of **Hereford**, and **Worcester** are two attractive cathedral towns, surrounded by rich farmlands. Each town has its own individual speciality; Hereford is known for its cattle and its cider industry, while Worcester is known for its fine porcelain and its spicy Worcester Sauce, a concoction of the late 1820s.

Metal bell ringers at a shopfront in Gloucester.

Hereford Cathedral has two exceptional treasures, beyond the beauty of the early Norman building itself. In the **Chained Library** are 1,444 books, with chains attached to every front cover, the largest such collection in the world. A map of the world, the *Mappa Mundi*, on display in a special area of the cathedral, was probably made in the last 10 years of the 13th century. It is drawn on a large piece of vellum, prepared calfskin, measuring 162 $^1/_2$ by 137 cm (64 by 54 inches) and most of the space is taken up by a picture of the habitable world, drawn within a circle and shown essentially as an island.

According to the conventions of the day, the east is shown at the top of the map, and Jerusalem as the centre of the world. *Mappa Mundi*, is a wonderful depiction of the world, as it was understood (or, rather, misunderstood) by a 13th century cartographer. His imagination tends to run riot at times: in India there is a Sciapod, who shelters himself with his one large foot, from the heat of the sun, whilst the Gangines feed themselves on their only food, the scent of apples.

Closer to home, Norway is marked with a tiny figure, apparently wearing skis. The Mont St Michel in France is prominently shown, and, interestingly, Great Britain is divided into Scotland, Wales, England and Cornwall.

In 1651 Charles II used the **Worcester Commandery** as the Royalist Army headquarters, and today it is a museum

The Forest of Dean, Gloucestershire.

of the Civil War. Exactly 100 years later, the **Royal Worcester porcelain factory** was founded, and is still in production.

Worcester Cathedral, most of which dates from the 14th century, although founded centuries earlier, is currently in the middle of a £10 million restoration programme which is scheduled to last for the next 20 years.

Six kilometres (10 miles) northwest of Worcester off the A443, is the aston-ishing ruin of **Witley Court**, badly damaged by fire in 1937, but once one of the most spectacular country houses in Victorian England. Its origins may well date back to medieval times. The house was enlarged in the 17th century and then again by the Regency architect, John Nash, in the early years of the 19th century.

Queen Adelaide, widow of King William IV, lived at Witley in the 1840s,

Fine mosaics at Chedworth Roman Villa, Gloucestershire.

but the real heyday of the house came in Queen Victoria's reign, after it had been transformed into a colossal Italian-style palace for the first Earl of Dudley. The gardens were equally elaborate, with immense fountains which still survive today. Adjacent is the magnificent baroque, early Georgian, **Great Witley Church**, designed by James Gibb. The interior is an astonishing confection in white and gold, largely made of papier-maché.

At **Lower Broadheath**, almost 2 kim (3 miles) west of Worcester, is the cottage in which the composer Edward Elgar was born on 2 June 1857. It now houses a unique collection of manuscripts, photographs and memorabilia.

The three neighbouring cathedral cities of Worcester, Hereford, and Gloucester, share the annual **Three Choirs Festival**, which takes place every year in one of the three beautiful churches. Three Choirs, is also the name of a local wine, from the **Three Choirs Vineyard** at Newent, in Gloucestershire, which has revived the tradition of Gloucestershire wine making, which dates back to the 12th century. The name "Three Choirs", was chosen because the vineyard is close to the midway point between Gloucester, Hereford, and Worcester.

Gloucestershire

At **Gloucester Docks**, grain warehouses,

Tewkesbury Abbey, Gloucestershire, one of England's largest parish churches.

The English pheasant is a beautiful but shy bird, often glimpsed in the Gloucestershire countryside.

built between 1826 and 1873, are undergoing a transformation, and the whole area is now given over to galleries, shops, and the interesting **National Waterways Museum**, housed in a warehouse dating from 1873. A former corn merchant and millers warehouse now houses the **Museum of Advertising and Packaging**.

The tiny shop situated at the end of College Court, next to the cathedral gate, is the home that Beatrix Potter chose for the tailor in her children's story, *The Tailor of Gloucester*. One of the gems of **Gloucester Cathedral**, are the 14th century cloisters with their wonderful white fan-vaulting and stained glass, giving the effect of a delicate glass corridor.

Tewkesbury is in northern Gloucestershire on the border of Hereford and Worcester. The Benedictine **Abbey** was the last of the monasteries to be dissolved by Henry VIII. There has been a church on the site of the Abbey for over 1,200 years. After the dissolution, the townspeople bought the Abbey from the King for £453; thanks to them the Abbey survived and is today, one of the largest parish churches in the country.

A few miles southwest of Tewkesbury, off the A38, is a little village called **Deerhurst**, whose **Church of St Mary's**, is one of a small handful of churches which survives intact from the Anglo-Saxon period. Nearby, is a tiny Saxon chapel, called "**Oddas Chapel**", which was dedicated in 1056.

The Northwest

The industrial areas of Manchester, the Potteries, and West Yorkshire, all have one thing in common, the unspoiled landscape of the Peak District, which lies virtually on their doorsteps. Surrounded by such busy urban centres as Sheffield and Manchester, with Liverpool slightly further to the east, the 209 sq km (542 sq miles) of the **Peak District National Park** remain untouched, undeveloped, and a much appreciated breathing space for thousands of city people. In the north, the Peak District is an expanse of sombre moorlands, whilst to the south it is more pastoral in character, with dry stone walls and pretty valleys, known as "dales".

View of Chatsworth House from the River Derwent.

Exploring the Peaks

If you are a caver, potholer, or a serious walker, the Peak District is for you. There are literally

Valleys of green. Monsal Head, Derbyshire.

hundreds of caves to explore with impressive limestone features such as stalactites and stalagmites, many of them concentrated around the central region. There are a number of show-caves for the general public, but if you are looking to try out something a little more adventurous, write to the Tourist Information office in Bakewell, for details.

The **Pennine Way**, the most gruelling long distance walking trail in England, starts from **Edale** and roams for 250 miles northwards, through the Yorkshire dales and the Northumberland National Park, to the Scottish borders. Their are a number of less strenuous walks to be enjoyed in the region, again the Tourist Information Office will be able to supply details.

The Northern & Central Peaks

Perched high on a crag and surrounded by some of the most magnificent scenery in the Peak District, the ruins of **Peveril Castle** rise above the little market town of **Castleton**, about 9 km (15 miles) west of Sheffield, on the A625. Looking out from the castle's keep, with its panoramic view across the Hope Valley, it is easy to see why William Peveril, one of William the Conqueror's most trusted knights, chose this site for his fortification.

From its dramatic position on a triangular spear high above the town, Peveril commanded any approach from

Hiking the Peaks, Eyam Moor, Derbyshire.

west, east and south. The northern side was guarded by a high stone wall, which is still virtually intact. Today, the path is steep on the way up and seems almost vertical on the way down, but it does make the castle a breathtaking place to visit, literally, as well as metaphorically.

Castleton is an ideal centre for exploring the many caves in the region, some of which are natural and some the result of lead mining. The **Blue John Cavern** is the source of a very attractive semi-precious mineral, a translucent purplish-blue fluorspar, called Blue John. This area is the only place in the world where Blue John can be found, so it is interesting that vases made from it were found in the ruins of Pompeii.

Until 1974, **Peak Cavern** had been home for 300 years to a settlement of rope-makers, whose houses were built inside the entrance to the cave. In 1926, the skeletons of Bronze Age miners were found in **Treak Cliff Cavern**, with their flint implements alongside them.

South of Castleton, **Buxton** has warm springs, which the Romans discovered in AD 79, building baths there. When Mary Queen of Scots was imprisoned in Sheffield Manor, she was allowed to visit Buxton to take the waters for her rheumatism.

In 1780, the Fifth Duke of Devonshire commissioned John Carr to build **The Crescent**, and the town began to take on the aspect of a spa town, such as Bath or Cheltenham. The Crescent is still the centre of town, along with the nearby **Opera House**. Buxton became very popular in the 1860s, with the arrival of locomotives, capable of coping with the steep gradient of the surrounding hills.

The Southern Peaks

When English "foodies" think of Bakewell, rather than the charms of this pretty little Derbyshire town, they immediately think of Bakewell tarts, which are small and very sweet, iced cakes. The tart was the result of a harassed cook muddling up the recipe for a strawberry tart at the Rutland Arms Hotel, in the 1860s. She poured egg mixture over the strawberry jam instead of mixing the egg into the pastry, turning the tart into a pudding. Much to the surprise of the cook, the "tart" was so well-received,

that the disaster was instantly turned into a delicacy.

Chatsworth, almost 2 km (3 miles) east of Bakewell, has been home to the Cavendish family for nearly 450 years. It is not only one of England's most beautiful stately homes, but it also has one of the most spectacular settings - 1,000 acres of park, landscaped by Capability Brown, and a garden of over 100 acres.

The original Elizabethan house was built in 1555 by Bess of Hardwick (1527-1608), a remarkable lady who went through 4 husbands, increasing her wealth with each marriage. The house was altered by her descendents in the late 17th century, and again in the 19th century.

Chatsworth is not the biggest house in the country, but it is certainly one of the grandest, with an elegance and opulence about it more suited to a palace than a ducal residence. The **Painted Hall** is unashamedly baroque, its ceiling and walls painted with scenes from the life of Julius Caesar. There are superb paintings, furniture and antiques, and one of the real pleasures of Chatsworth, is the freedom to explore the house on your own, without being shepherded around on guided tours. The gardens are every bit as wonderful as the house, especially the 17th century **Cascade**, where each step is a different height, so that the sound of falling water varies at each point.

Travelling south into the extreme south of the Peak District, north of

Sheep finding shelter under the Cloughs, Edale.

Ashbourne, **Dove Dale**, is one of the most beautiful of the dales, a dramatic two-mile gorge in the hills, where the River Dove has washed away the limestone, to reveal cliffs, crags and caves. In Dove Dale, there is a lovely village called **Ilam**, with delightful small chalet-style houses, giving a unexpected alpine flavour to the area.

Close to Chatsworth, on the A6 south of Bakewell, is another beautiful house, **Haddon Hall**, the Derbyshire seat of the Duke of Rutland. It is England's most complete and authentic

Across the Mersey, Liverpool City

Liverpool, will always be famous the world over for *The Beatles*, the ferry across the Mersey, the Grand National and its football teams. It is a large, solid industrial town, a vigorous place, home to a humorous, quick witted people, known as "scouses", who are proud of their city's recent, distinguished history.

The waterfront

In the 19th century the port of Liverpool was the gateway to the New World. Tons of cargo arrived every day from all over the world, the main trade being cotton from America, to supply the cotton merchants and mill owners of the northwest, during the textile boom. Today, Liverpool's historic waterfront is a popular tourist attraction. Converted Victorian warehouses at the monumental **Albert Dock,** now house

the **Merseyside Maritime Museum,** which connects the region's history with the rest of the world, telling the story of the emigrants who sailed from here to start new lives in America and Australia. Next door, the **Tate Gallery,** houses the most important collection of contemporary art outside London.

Cathedrals & museums

Liverpool is a city full of contrasts, as the two magnificent, Roman Catholic and Anglican, **cathedrals** and the diversity of its museums and galleries illustrate. **Liverpool Museum** built in 1851 by the 13th Earl of Derby, contains many items of local history, while the **Walker Art Gallery,** built by the 19th century philanthropist Andrew Walker, houses one of the largest collections of fine art outside London.

medieval home, dating back to the 14th century, and is set in beautiful countryside overlooking the River Wye. A dwelling has been on the site since the 11th century *Domesday Book* survey, though the Hall, as seen today, is predominantly medieval and Tudor. Haddon Hall belonged to the Vernon family for 400 years, but in 1567, Sir George Vernon died leaving no male heir, and the Hall passed to Dorothy Vernon. In 1563, Dorothy had eloped with John Manners, the son of the Earl of Rutland. Much building work was carried out by successive generations but when a Dukedom was conferred on the Earl in 1703, Haddon was closed and not lived in for 200 years, and Belvoir Castle became the family home (see the chapter on the Midlands p317).

Thus, unlike many large country houses, Haddon escaped the alterations of the 18th and 19th centuries, through benign neglect throughout this period.

The gardens are built on 6 great stone terraces which step down the steep hillside to the river. Maintaining their 17th century structure, the gardens were replanted at the beginning of this century with a profusion of scented roses and clematis. In the tiny 14th century **chapel** there is a "squint", from which the sacristan could see the sacraments being offered and thus knew when it was time for him to ring the bell.

East of the Peaks

Six km (10 miles) east of Bakewell and

Mam Tor Edale, the dry stone walls and hills, typify the Peak District.

on the outer fringes of the Peak District, lies the former spa of the little town of **Matlock.** Opened in 1883, the **Matlock Bath Hydro** replaced the fountain bath which was built in 1786 and was demolished in 1881, because it had become too small to cope with the increasing number of visitors.

Today, the pool is still fed from the same thermal spring, with a continuous 600,000 gallons a day, at a constant temperature of 20°C. The difference today is that the pool has been transformed into an aquarium, its health-giving properties being enjoyed by a collection of carp and goldfish.

Just over 1 km (2 miles) south of Matlock, the leading role played by Derbyshire in the Industrial Revolution, is recalled today at **Cromford Mill**. The mill harnessed the abundant water power available from local rivers and waterfalls, an important force behind the Industrial Revolution.

When he set up his mill at Cromford in 1771, Richard Arkwright had no inkling that his mill was to further alter the course of industrial history, by the inauguration of the factory system. The mill site was finished by 1791, and at the same time, Arkwright developed Cromford into one of the first industrial villages, building workers' cottages, a market place and a lock-up. It was the first purpose-built town to house factory workers and a truly important one for the British economy at that time.

Hardwick & Bolsover

When Bess of Hardwick had finished building Chatsworth, she decided that her husband, the Earl of Shrewsbury, was a "knave, fool and beast" and left him, returning to her birthplace, **Hardwick Hall.** The hall lies east of the Peak District, 4 km (7 miles) west of Mansfield. Dissatisfied with the state of the house at Hardwick, she decided to build a new one, 91 metres (100 yards) from the Old Hall.

By this time Bess, was 70 years old,

The Victorian town hall of Greater Manchester.

but her energy so inspired her builder that the house was finished in 7 years.

Just 4 km (6 miles) north of Hardwich, **Bolsover Castle** looks just like a picture-book castle, thicket of battlements and domed towers rises from a wooded hill-top dominating the surrounding landscape.

Bolsover is built on the site of a genuine Norman castle though most of the present structure is a 17th century mansion. The elaborate mock medieval fortifications belong to the **Little Castle**, a romantic folly.

The urban west

The Peak District descends towards the huge urban district of **Greater Manchester**, centred around the industrial town of **Manchester**. Manchester is one

The grand civic buildings of Liverpool overlook the Mersey.

of England's finest Victorian cities, home to the Royal Northern College of Music and two international orchestras, the Hallé and the BBC Philharmonic.

The inauguration of the textile industry was one of the most important developments in the history of industrial Britain, which focused on the Northwest. Cotton imported from **Liverpool** was transported to Manchester and the the plains of **Lancashire**, where an urban spread of mill towns evolved.

The Lancashire coast stretching from Morecambe to Liverpool has a number of resorts at **Blackpool**, towering above the clean, sandy beaches. **Blackpool Tower**, is Lancashire's version of the Eiffel Tower.

The Lake District

Cumbria's dramatic scenery inspired the 19th century Romantics to verbal and artistic heights. Writers and poets such as Wordsworth, Southey, de Quincey, Coleridge, John Ruskin, and the artist Turner, all came, saw, and in many cases, stayed on in this beautiful corner of England, known universally as the Lake District. They wrote about the beauty of the lakes, dedicated poems to them, and painted them. Beatrix Potter was inspired by the countryside in which she lived, to write her delightful *Peter Rabbit* stories.

Brotherswater from Kirkstone Pass, at the entry to the Lake District.

Centuries before the lakes began to be an artistic inspiration, and then a major sporting and tourist destination, the Romans had been there, building a fort near Hardknott Pass. Then, during the Middle Ages, monks settled at Furness Abbey on the Furness Peninsula, and generations of English kings tried to subdue the troublesome Border region from strategic outposts such as **Carlisle**, at the northern tip of Cumbria.

Border territory

When the Romans built Hadrian's Wall, in an effort to keep out the troublesome Scots over the Border, the wall passed though Carlisle, *en route* to the western-

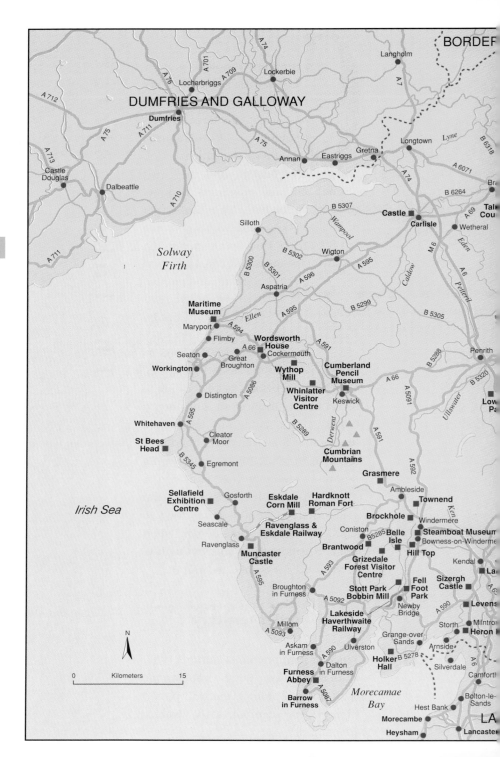

BORDER

Langholm

A74

A701

A709

A76

Locharbriggs

Lockerbie

A7

DUMFRIES AND GALLOWAY

Longtown

Lyne

B 6318

Dumfries

A75

A711

A710

Annan   Eastriggs   Gretna

Longtown

A 6071

A6071

B 6264

Bra

A712

Castle
Douglas

Dalbeattie

A713

A710

A75

Wetheral

Castle

Carlisle

Tal
Cou

A 69

M 6

Eden

A 6

Petteril

Silloth

B 5307

Wampool

*Solway
Firth*

B 5300

B 5302

Wigton

A 596

A 595

Caldew

A711

B 5301

Aspatria

B 5299

B 5305

**Maritime
Museum**

Ellen

A 595

Penrith

Maryport

A 594

A 591

B 5288

B 5320

Flimby

A 66

**Wordsworth
House**

Cockermouth

Seaton

Great
Broughton

**Cumberland
Pencil
Museum**

Low
Pa

Workington

**Wythop
Mill**

A 66

Ullswater

Distington

A 5086

**Whinlatter
Visitor
Centre**

Keswick

A 5091

Whitehaven

A 595

Cleator
Moor

B 5289

Derwent

A 591

**St Bees
Head**

B 5345

Egremont

**Cumbrian
Mountains**

A 592

Grasmere

Irish Sea

**Sellafield
Exhibition
Centre**

Gosforth

**Eskdale
Corn Mill**

**Hardknott
Roman Fort**

Ambleside

Townend

Ken

Seascale

Brockhole

Windermere

**Ravenglass &
Eskdale Railway**

Coniston

B5285

**Belle
Isle**

Steamboat Museum

Bowness-on-Winderme

Ravenglass

Brantwood

Hill Top

**Muncaster
Castle**

A 593

**Grizedale
Forest Visitor
Centre**

Kendal

La

Broughton
in Furness

**Stott Park
Bobbin Mill**

**Fell
Foot
Park**

**Sizergh
Castle**

A 6

Millom

A 5092

**Lakeside
Haverthwaite
Railway**

Newby
Bridge

A 590

Levens

A 5093

Askam
in Furness

A 590

Ulverston

Grange-over-
Sands

Storth

Miltro

Heron

N

Arnside

A 6

**Holker
Hall**

B 5278

Silverdale

Camforth

0   Kilometers   15

Dalton
in Furness

**Furness
Abbey**

A 5087

*Morecamae
Bay*

Bolton-le-
Sands

**Barrow
in Furness**

Hest Bank

Morecambe

LA

Heysham

Lancaster

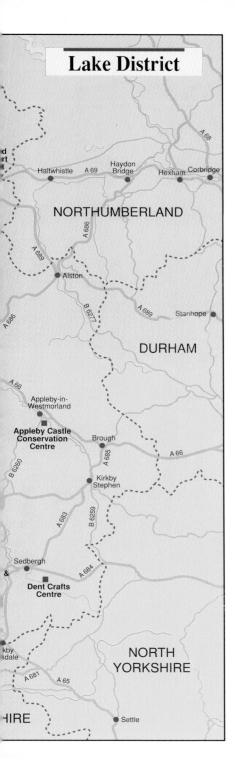

Lake District

Haltwhistle A 69 Haydon Bridge Hexham Corbridge A 68

NORTHUMBERLAND

A 686

A 689

Alston

B 6277

A 689 Stanhope

A 686

DURHAM

A 66

Appleby-in-Westmorland

Appleby Castle Conservation Centre Brough

B 6260

A 685 A 66

Kirkby Stephen

A 683 B 6259

Sedbergh

A 684

Dent Crafts Centre

kby sdale

A 681 A 65

NORTH YORKSHIRE

HIRE

Settle

Tarn Howes retreat, the Lake District.

most fort at Bowness on Solway. **Carlisle Castle** celebrated its 900th anniversary in 1992, having watched over England's frontier with Scotland since 1092, when the Normans put a massive keep on the site of a Roman fort. As an important border stronghold, Carlisle castle has been the residence of kings and various royal officials throughout the centuries. It was even the enforced home of Mary Queen of Scots in 1568. The castle was extended in the 12th century by King David I of Scotland and altered by Henry VIII. From the ramparts, there are views across the Solway Firth to Scotland.

Carlisle today is a friendly, attractive town, largely built out of mellow, red stone, and its main historic monu-

Overlooking the Lakes, the attractive Rydal Hall.

ments are the castle and the **Cathedral**, founded in 1122 as the Church of the Priory of St Mary. It became a cathedral in 1133 and has a beautiful 14th century east window. Sir Walter Scott was married in the cathedral.

The **Tullie House Museum**, opened in January 1991 after a £5 million refurbishment, is one of Britain's most innovative historic attractions, portraying

mans and on the notorious Reivers of Border history. For over 350 years, the Border country was ravaged by the lawless Reiver families who stole each others' cattle and possessions, killing and kidnapping without remorse. Their activities have given the English language such words as "bereave" and "blackmail".

From Carlisle take the A69 easterly to **Lanercost Priory**, built between 1200 and 1220. The nave of the original church has been converted into one of the prettiest parish churches in the country. Exploring the peaceful sandstone ruins today, it is difficult to remember that this secluded valley was once a highly dangerous place to live, the priory a frequent target for Scots raiding parties from across the border.

The literary lakes

The Lake District, south of Carlisle, is 340 sq km (880 sq miles) of lake and mountain-studded National Park (see box story in the Geography chapter p. 60). The Lakes vary in size from the largest and busiest, **Lake Windermere**, with steamers and ferries criss-crossing it daily, to tiny, quiet lakes like **Rydal Water**. People visit the Lake District for the scenery, for open-air activities – walking, hiking, mountaineering and sailing are some of the activities on offer – and for the literary and historic connections.

The main centres of literary pil-

Carlisle's turbulent place in border history, through images, objects and hands-on displays. The Environmental Dome speeds the visitors through the skyscape of the surrounding Border region in just 8 minutes.

The exhibition focuses on the Ro-

Isle of Man

There really is something unique about the tiny Isle of Man, off the west coast of England, and it is not only their tail-less Manx cats. This charming, popular little island has its own separate political status, for it has been a crown possession since 1828, and exercises a considerable degree of self-government. There is a Lieutenant Governor, and a unique open-air parliament, called the Tynwald.

Manx (as the locals are called) identity is complex, for the island was originally settled by Celts, then Norsemen, then the Scots, and finally the English. Sadly, the local language, Manx, is virtually defunct.

From the summit of **Mount Snaefell**, at 667 meters (2,036 ft) the highest point on the island, you can see 6 ancient kingdoms, England, Scotland, Ireland, Wales, Man itself, and, the islanders like to add, the Kingdom of Heaven.

Back to history

The Isle of Man is known today for its cats, its annual round-the-island TT motorbike race, and its railway system. The Isle of Man has its original Victorian transport system that is still used every day by the local people, and which turned 100 years-old in 1993. The **Manx Electric Railway** operates with original rolling stock, although the newest pieces are something of interlopers, since they only date from 1906. The island's capital **Douglas** lies at the hub of this vintage railway system.

The Douglas horse trams date back to 1876, forming the world's oldest horse tram service, the only time business has been halted was during the two World Wars. This unique service, with a fleet of 42 horses and 23 tram cars, runs for 2 miles along the Promenade at Douglas.

The sights

When the 23 metres (72 ft) diameter **Laxey Water Wheel** was inaugurated in 1854, it was the biggest water wheel in Europe, built to pump water from the shafts of the mines which contained lead, copper and iron ore. Throughout the year there are passenger and car ferry sailings to Douglas from Heysham and Liverpool, and seasonal services from Fleetwood, Belfast and Dublin. Off the southern tip of the island is the island of the **Calf of Man**, a bird sanctuary.

grimages are the places connected with William Wordsworth, Beatrix Potter and John Ruskin. John Ruskin's house, **Brantwood**, where he lived from 1872 to 1900, is situated on the shores of Lake Coniston. The house enjoys some of the finest lake and mountain views in England, inside which is a magnificent collection of Ruskin's drawings and watercolours.

Wiiliam Wordsworth was born in Cockermouth, to the north of Keswick, in 1770. You can visit this Georgian town house dating from 1745, where 7 rooms have been furnished in 18th century style, with personal effects of the poet.

Journeying south along the A591 from Keswick, you will reach the pretty little village of **Grasmere**, where from 1799 to 1808 William and his sister Dorothy, lived in **Dove Cottage**, until 1813 when the poet moved to nearby Rydal Mount, where he lived until his death in 1850.

In the churchyard of the 13th century **Church of St Oswald** in Grasmere, Wordsworth and many members of his family are buried. It is always easy to locate William's grave for no matter

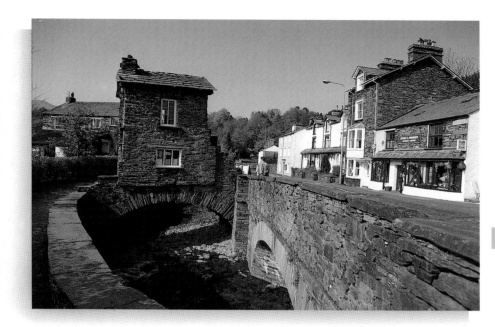

The Bridge House, Ambleside holding its own;.

what the season, there is always a bunch of daffodils on the simple stone slab, in tribute to his best known poem.

Just outside Grasmere travelling south again on the A591, overlooking tranquil **Rydal Water** is Wordsworth's home, **Rydal Mount**. The gardens were designed by the poet and both the house and gardens are open to the public. Nearby is **Rydal Hall**. Little is known about the early history of the Hall; the Le Fleming family, who claimed descent from one of William the Conqueror's knights, moved there around 1600, although a building probably existed here even earlier.

During the 20th century, the house has been a hotel and a boarding school, and now is used as a religious retreat house. The Hall is not open to the public, but the attractive formal gardens are.

The Coniston connection

West of Windemere, the A593 takes you to the beautiful and romantic valley of **Coniston**. Tennyson spent a part of his honeymoon there, in a house Turner had painted many years before. WG Collingwood moved here to live close to Ruskin, and Arthur Ransome followed soon after. Ransome made Coniston the setting for his childrens' adventure story *Swallows and Amazons*. More recently, Donald Campbell died tragically while seeking to break his own water-speed

Curious locals at Lake Windemere.

record on Lake Coniston.

Beatrix Potter land

Four km (7 miles) east of Coniston along the B5285 just outside the village of Sawrey, is **Hill Top**, where the writer Beatrix Potter stayed for intervals over 50 years from 1905 to her death in 1943. She wrote many of her childrens' stories at Hill Top, weaving her house and its pretty garden into her stories. Jemima Puddleduck laid her eggs in the rhubarb patch, which is still there, as is the clock in the house, which features in *The Tailor of Gloucester*.

In the nearby village of **Hawkshead**, where William Wordsworth ear-

lier attended the local grammar school, the **Beatrix Potter Gallery** was once the office of her husband, a solicitor called William Heelis, whom she married in 1919. The interior remains largely unaltered since Mr Heelis's day, although there is an exhibition of some of Beatrix Potter's original drawings, and illustrations from her childrens' books.

Beatrix Potter was an environmentalist long before the word was even thought of, for, using income from her *Peter Rabbit* tales, she bought farms, to stop development and keep farmers working on the land. Beatrix Potter was very influenced by her friendship with Canon Rawnsley, one of the founders of the National Trust. She built up a large estate of 14 farms, covering 4,000 acres of land, and on her death all of this passed to the National Trust, such that her property can now be enjoyed by the general public.

Ambleside

One of the prettiest and busiest little towns in the Lake District is **Ambleside**, with its distinctive **Bridge House**, which has spanned the Stock Beck since the 17th century. It connected the site of Ambleside Hall, which once stood on the hill above, with orchards and pastures on the left bank. There was a door at both ends so that the "house" could be used both as a covered bridge and a summer house.

There have been many different uses for the bridge house since then. In the 18th century when there were two water-driven mills alongside the beck, it may have been used as a counting house. In 1815 after one door had been closed up, it became a tea room and small weaving shop. In 1905 a cobbler was mending shoes downstairs and keeping his pigeons upstairs.

This unique building was being used as an antiques and gift shop in 1926, when it was bought by local subscribers for £450 and given to the National Trust for permanent preservation. In 1956 it became the very first National Trust information and recruiting centre in the country, a use which continues to the present day.

Nearly 2 km (3 miles) southeast of Ambleside at the southern end of **Troutbeck village**, is Townend, an exceptional relic of Lake District life. It was a wealthy yeoman farmer's house, built in about 1626, and contains carved woodwork, books, papers, and furniture, collected by the Brown family who lived there from that date until 1944.

Cruising the Lakes

You can walk around the lakes, and you can also sail on them, and since 1848, the classic way to view **Lake Windermere**, England's longest lake, has been to cruise on one of the steamers, all named after birds - "Swan", "Teal", and "Tern". **Lake Ullswater**, also has steamers – two pretty 19th century models which cruise up and down the Lake.

A pretty way to get to Ruskin's house, Brantwood, is to sail across Lake Coniston from Coniston pier. The National Trust runs a steam yacht gondola, which was originally launched in 1859. The *Illustrated London News* described her at the time as "A perfect combination of the Venetian Gondola and English Steam Yacht".

Kendal & environs

Everyone the world over loves chocolate, and the English are no exception. You can buy a bar of chocolate just about anywhere, anytime in England, but there are some serious hangouts for

Sailing to the mountains, White Cross Bay, Lake Windemere.

"chocoholics", some of them in the most unexpected places. In the Lake District, the busy little town of **Kendal** already has one well-known speciality to its name, Kendal Mint Cake, but it also boasts a chocolate shop for really serious chocolate fans.

The 1657 **Chocolate House** is a recreation of a series of popular 17th century chocolate houses, the first of which, according to Samuel Pepys' diary, opened in 1657. The Kendal shop is for the lover of English chocolates, as opposed to Belgian or Swiss or French

Two km (3¹/₂ miles) south of Kendal, is **Sizergh Castle**, home of the Strickland family for more than 750 years, with an impressive 14th century Pele tower. Three km (5 miles) further south, just after the turn-off onto the A590, is **Levens Hall** an Elizabethan house with a topiary garden, laid out in 1692.

The Furness Peninsula

The **Furness Peninsula** borders the Lake District National Park, and stretches from Broughton in Furness down to the Isle of Walney. The climate in this part of Cumbria is much kinder than most parts of northern England; even places 12 km (20 miles) away from the Lake District have comparably a much lower rainfall and higher temperatures.

In the pretty market town of **Ulverston**, there is a museum dedicated to Stan Laurel the famous silent-film comedian, born there on 16 June 1890. Ulverston was granted its market charter in 1280 and is still the cattle market for the area. Specialities of the region are Cumberland sausages and at the other end of the scale, Cumbria crystal, a well-known product, which is sold worldwide.

Morecambe & Lancaster

South of the lakes is Morecambe Bay, famous for its oysters. On the shore of the bay is the popular resort town of

varieties, for the chocolates are made by English specialists, and include such flavours as Earl Grey tea.

Kendal is an attractive place, full of walkers and hikers buying provisions, and it is indeed a good place to buy anything you may need for a hike, from clothing to detailed maps, and, of course, chocolate.

Morecambe with its fine sandy beach and a variety of entertainment venues. Half a kilometre (1 mile) inland from Morecambe is the medieval town of **Lancaster.** The town has a well-known Castle which still dominates the modern city of **Lancaster**, as it has done for centuries. The castle's magnificent **John of Gaunt Gatehouse** dates from the early 15th century.

Currently, most of the castle is used as a prison, but many of the 18th century rooms are open to the public. The prison is due to close in 1996 and it is hoped that the rest of the castle will then be open to the public.

Sharing the hill with the castle is the Priory **Church of St Mary**, with a history going back before the Norman conquest. It was a Priory of Benedictine monks from 1094 to 1414. The present church mainly dates from the late 14th and 15th century. Near the Priory are the remains of a **Roman bath house** which used to serve as part of an official inn outside the fort.

The former Custom House, is now the **Maritime Museum**. The **Judges' Lodging**, at the top of Church Street, was a 17th century privare house until it was used by the judges during the Lancaster Assizes.

Even up to 1975, visiting judges used to stay in the Judges House, which now houses a **Museum of Local History**. There is also a fascinating **Museum of Childhood**, which will warm your heart with its wonderful extensive collection of old dolls.

Castle Rigg stone circle under the winter snow.

357

"God's own county" is how the locals describe their large, varied and rugged county, which is one of the most dramatically beautiful ones in England. The people of Yorkshire are known for their bluntness and down-to-earth common sense and for their very strong attachment to their county. Strictly speaking, Yorkshire now comprises three different counties; North Yorkshire, South Yorkshire and West Yorkshire, which have replaced the former "ridings", or administrative divisions, of the large county. In local tradition however, the "ridings" still remain.

Young cowboys on the beach, Scarborough.

Economically in recent years Yorkshire has been hard-hit by the decline of its former industrial base. The huge mining and manufacturing belt that cuts a swathe across the southern half of Yorkshire, is faced with pit closures, reduction in industrial output, and a recession. Large towns such as Leeds and Sheffield, and smaller ones like Huddersfield, Rotherham and Barnsley, are faced with a changing future. The coal mines are closing, which has had an impact on the iron and steel industry, and associated manufacturing industries. These economic hardships have however been faced with typical Northern grit. **Leeds**, is a good example of a

Town Hall and Peace Gardens, Sheffield city centre.

town whose wealth originated from the woollen mills, but which in modern times has made great changes to adapt to the different face of economics in the 1990s (see box story p372), with some success.

York, capital of the North

King George VI once said that the history of **York** is the history of England, and as you explore the capital of the North, history is visible in every corner. There are significant remains from a diversity of historical eras; the Romans, the Vikings, the Plantagenets and the Georgians. English history comes alive effortlessly in York.

York began as a Roman fortress in AD 71, and grew into the important city of, *Eboracum*. Here Constantine the Great, the founder of Constantinople, was made Roman Emperor in AD 306. It was the Vikings who gave York its name, derived from "Jorvik" or "Yorwik", their brief, but flourishing kingdom.

York's first walls were Roman, substantial fragments of which still remain, but it is the **medieval walls**, carefully maintained and restored, which now encircle the old city, for almost 2 km (3 miles). The earth ramparts on which they stand were raised by the Romans and later by the Anglo-Danish kings of York. York uses the old word "**Minster**" – meaning a centre of Christian teaching or ministering – for the seat of its archbishop. It is of course, also a cathe-

Resting in peace in a village churchyard.

dral, containing the archbishop's "cathedra" or throne. The first Minster was built in the 7th century, and the present one is the fourth on the site. The Minster is the largest medieval structure in the United Kingdom. Work began in about 1220, and was completed 250 years later in 1472. Among the Minster's many treasures are its 128 stained glass windows, dating from the 12th to the present century.

A number of York's streets have names ending in "gate" and "bar" the Viking word for "street" and many remain unchanged from the design laid down by their medieval architects. **Bootham Bar** was the defensive bastion for the north road. **Micklegate Bar** was traditionally the monarch's en-

trance, where traitors' heads were displayed. **Monk Bar** has a portcullis still in working order while **Walmgate Bar** is the only town gate in England to have preserved its barbican, a funnel-like approach, which forced attackers to bunch together.

Situated in the heart of the city, **Clifford's Tower** was the keep of York

York Minster, one of England's largest cathedrals.

Castle, and provides one of the finest views of the city from its wall-walk. It was built by Henry III to replace the wooden keep, which in turn had replaced William the Conqueror's wooden tower, burnt down by a mob attacking besieged Jews in 1190. The present 13th century tower derives its name from Roger de Clifford, a Lancastrian leader executed in 1322, whose body hung in chains from the Tower.

The **Merchant Adventurers Hall** was built in the 1350s and is one of the finest surviving guildhalls in Europe,

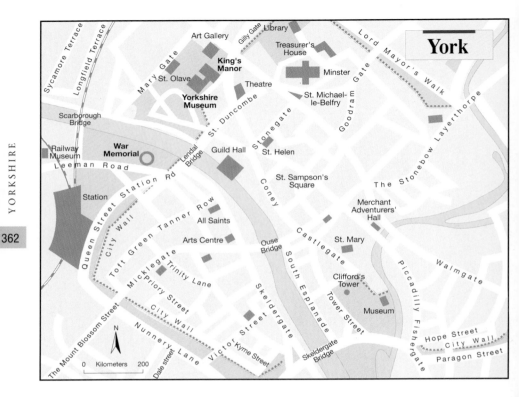

York

where merchants transacted their business and held their feasts. **The Treasurers' House** was built on the site of the Roman legionary fortress and was the residence of the Treasurers of the Minster, until 1547.

York museums

Amidst all this history, modern technology still has its place, as a visit to the excellent **Jorvik Centre** will prove. You visit this recreation of Viking York, complete with sounds and smells, in "time cars", which carry you automatically through the museum. **Castle Museum** on Tower Street recreates the life of ordi-

nary Yorkshire people in the 18th and 19th centuries, including reconstructions of streets and old shops, it is one of the country's leading folk museums. For railway buffs the **Railway Museum** near the present railway station has an excellent display of steam trains as well as hands-on exhibits.

Castle Howard

Take the A64 northeast of York to **Castle Howard**, a glorious Vanbrugh house, and the first building Sir John ever designed. His assistant on the project was Nicholas Hawksmoor, a student of Sir Christopher Wren, so it is no coinci-

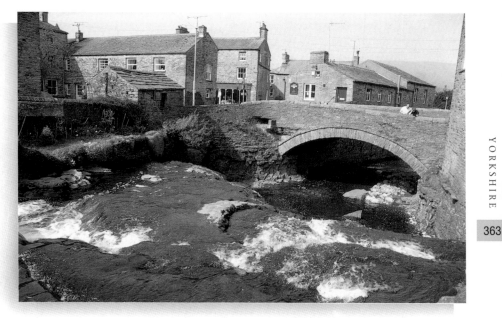

The small village of Hawes, one of Yorkshire's rural charms.

dence that the 22 metre (70 foot) high dome bears a distinct resemblance to that of St Paul's Cathedral, London. As impressive as the exterior of Castle Howard, is the interior, with its superb old masters and Italian sculpture. Even more impressive is the surrounding parkland containing Vanbrugh's last work, the **Temple of the Four Winds**.

Stretching north of York are the dales and moors for which the county is renowned. Each of the dales is different, following the course of a river and in the case of Wensleydale, giving its name to a popular English cheese. The dales and moors are peppered with abbeys and castles, set against a backdrop of grazing sheep, green hills and dry-stone walls, one of the most distinctive fea-

tures of any Yorkshire landscape. Most of the dales are generally quiet and unspoiled, that is, with the exception of areas which have been filmed in a TV series such as *Last of the Summer Wine* or *Emmerdale Farm*. These series have done alot to prmote the beauty of Yorkshire but have attracted bus-loads of noisy litter-dropping TV buffs.

Sights of the Dales

High on the fells between Wensleydale and Swaledale, are the curious "**Butter Tubs**", deep limestone potholes, whose sheer sides plummet to depths of up to 24 metres. Local legend has it that the potholes were once used as a cool store

The medieval town of Richmond was part of an ancient line of defence.

for butter, carried from the Swaledale farms, over to the market at Hawes.

Hardrow Force, just outside Hawes, is on private land and the entrance to the waterfall is through the Green Dragon Inn, in the village. Hardrow Force, at 30 metres high, is the highest single-leap waterfall in England, and it was "discovered" by the Romantic poets and artists, including Wordsworth and Turner. Naturally enough, Hardrow Force is at its most impressive after heavy rain, which, as any local will tell you, is common in the Yorkshire Dales.

Richmond

If you look at a map showing the castles and forts of Yorkshire, the defensive line is clearly visible - Richmond, Middleham, a little to the south, and to the east across to the coast Helmsley, Pickering and Scarborough castles, forming a chain across the edge of the windswept moors.

Just before you reach Scotch Corner on the A1, you will come to the junction for **Richmond. Richmond Castle** dates back to soon after the Norman Conquest, when King William was trying to secure a hold over the rebellious north. It is one of a string of fortified castles built across the northern borders of England, intended both as a defence and a deterrent to the Scots over the border, and also as a warning to the rebellious northerners themselves.

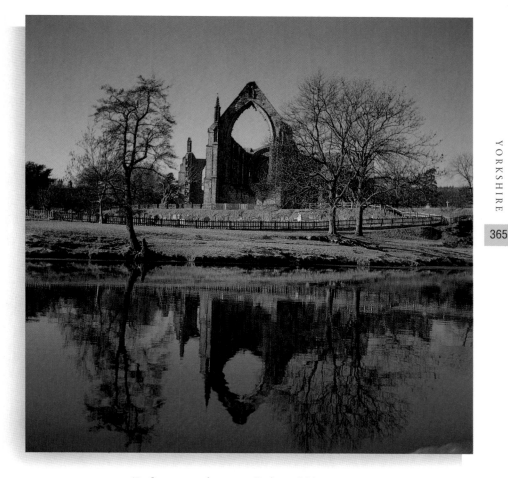

Reflections of time at Bolton Abbey.

Richmond's tiny Georgian **Theatre Royal**, with its pale green décor, dates from 1788 and is the oldest theatre in the country to survive in its original form. Yorkshire men are fiercely proud of all of their traditions and thus their very own North Yorkshire Regiment, the Green Howards, is held in great affection. The Green Howards were founded in 1688, and in their **Regimental Museum** in Richmond you can see cam-

paign trophies spanning 300 years, from 1690 to the Gulf War – including the blood-stained pistol holsters belonging to the Grand Old Duke of York of nursery rhyme fame.

To Whitby by steam train

One very pleasant way of crossing the moors is by steam train. The **North**

The haunting stolidity of Rievaulx Abbey, one of Yorkshire's finest.

Yorkshire Moors Railway has an 50 km (80 mile) route between Pickering and Grosmont near Whitby, on the coast. The line was built by the father of the railway, George Stevenson, opening in 1836 as the Whitby and the Pickering Railway, one of the world's first passenger lines. The railway line takes you across the Goathland Moors, arriving just outside **Whitby**. Whitby today is a busy fishing town and a popular holiday resort; historically it was one of Yorkshire's earliest holy places. Whitby was home to a double monastery for men and women in the 7th century, and in 664, Abbess Hilda presided over the Synod of Whitby, which decided the system for dating Easter.

Whitby is famous for its connection with the explorer Captain Cook, who lived in a little red house in **Grape Lane**, which is now a museum.

Scarborough

A few miles south down the coast is **Scarborough**, a busy and popular holiday town, its beaches huddled under the massive cliffs, which are crowned with the ruins of **Scarborough castle**, built by Henry II. The castle last came under attack during World War I, when it was shelled from the sea by German battleships. As you walk up the hill towards the castle, stop for a moment in the cemetery of the little church, and look for the grave of the novelist Anne Brontë, the least known of the three Brontë sisters, who died there in 1849.

Monasteries & abbeys

Abbeys and monasteries abound in Yorkshire. A little inland from Whitby, at the foot of the Cleveland Hills, is **Mount Grace Priory**, the best preserved Carthusian Monastery in England. Unlike other monks who lived in common, the Carthusians lived as hermits, speaking to no one and seldom emerging from their individual cells, one of which has been recently restored and furnished.

A little north of the pretty market town of **Helmsley**, at the southern point of the North Yorkshire Moors, are the peaceful ruins of the 12th century Cistercian **Rievaulx Abbey** and the 18th century **Rievaulx Terrace**, an elaborate half-mile long picnic area. The ruins of another Cistercian monastery,

Byland Abbey, are just to the south, as is the Roman Catholic **School of Ampleforth**, one of the country's leading public schools.

On the road from Helmsley to Pickering, turn off to the pretty village of **Hutton-le-Hole**. Surrounded by heather moors and with a moorland beck (stream) winding its way through the village green, the village is idyllic, being kept neatly cropped by a flock of sheep which roams freely among the cottages.

Selby Abbey, south of York, was the first monastery to be founded in the north, after the Norman conquest. It was founded in 1069 by the French monk Benedict of Auxerre, who recognized the site from a vision he had experienced in Auxerre.

The Abbey has a 14th century Washington window, high up in the choir. John de Washington was a 15th century prior, and his descendents can be traced as ancestors of George Washington. The three red stars above two red bands on a white shield, are the Washington family arms, which later became a model for the American flag, the Stars and Stripes.

One of England's most beautiful and important sites, **Fountains Abbey**, was founded by Cistercian monks in 1132 and is the largest monastic ruin in Europe. Situated on the banks of River Skell just south of Ripon, the Abbey ruins provide the dramatic focal point of the 18th Century landscape garden of Studley Royal, one of the few surviving examples of a Georgian green garden.

Picnicking beside the river at Hutton-le-Hole.

The nearby cathedral city of **Ripon** was granted its charter by Alfred the Great in 886, so not surprisingly, tradition has always been important to its people; every night, at 2100 hours, the horn blower still sets the watch.

West Yorkshire

Keighley, in the urbanized west of the county, is home to the **Keighley** and **Worth Valley Railway**, one of the country's best preserved lines. Both steam and diesel trains operate all year round, calling at 6 restored stations, one of which is **Haworth**, better known as the home of the Brontë sisters. (see box story in Arts chapter p.117)

Four km (7 miles) north of Leeds, along the A61 on the way to the elegant northern spa town of Harrogate is **Harewood House**, the home of the Lascelles family for over 200 years. It was built over a period of 13 years between 1759 and 1772.

Harewood's spectacular interior has plaster-work ceilings by the Scottish architect Robert Adam and it contains unrivalled 18th century English furniture made especially for Harewood by Thomas Chippendale, who was born only a few miles further up the Wharf Valley at Otley. The house is surrounded by 1,000 acres of parkland, gardens and woodland landscaped by Capability Brown.

Close to Harrogate is **Ripley Castle**, set in a Capability Brown landscape,

Rock-climbing on the Moors, Ilkley.

Leeds

Like so many Northern towns, Leeds appears to be a typical product of the Industrial Revolution, with grand Victorian commercial and public buildings in the centre, surrounded by a fringe of mills and working class housing, with middle class suburbs stretching out into the country beyond. Yet the first written reference to Leeds is to be found 1,000 years earlier, in the writings of the Venerable Bede in 731. The entry for Leeds in the *Domesday Book* of 1086 reveals a population of 100 to 150, settled on a manor owned by Ilbert de Lacy, a Norman baron.

The Wool heritage

Leeds owes much of its present-day appearance and prosperity to wool. The hundreds of flocks of sheep in the surrounding countryside supplied the wool for the city's mills. In the 19th century, **Armley Mill**, which has recently been renovated and turned into a working museum, was the world's largest woollen mill. In time, the merchants began to invest their city with suitably solid testimonials to their growing prosperity – a **Corn Exchange**, churches and an elaborately columned **Town Hall**.

A distinctive feature of the city's architecture is the **arcade**, a Victorian precursor of today's shopping mall, and these 19th century covered passages remain very much the way they were when they were originally built, with their mahogany shop-fronts and mosaic floors. Leeds has many arcades; Thornton's, Queen's, Victoria, Grand and Market Street, and recently, one 19th century street received 1990s-style treatment, when **Queen Victoria Street** was roofed over with Europe's largest stained glass canopy. Much of the city's industrial architectural heritage, mills, canal-side warehouses and factories, have been renovated, as the city begins to take a very obvious pride in its trading past.

The circular Corn Exchange building, dating from 1863, has been turned into a successful shopping area, with the original trading desks still in place, for the corn merchants who still trade there every Tuesday, amongst the boutiques and restaurants; adding the finishing touch, a replica of the Wright brothers' first aeroplane, the *Kitty Hawk*, hangs from the glass roof. The city's enormous **Covered Market** is being renovated, and down by the canal basin, **Granary Wharf** has been renovated, and is now home to shops, restaurants and street entertainers.

Modern museums

The splendidly imposing Town Hall is flanked by the **City Museum**, the **Art Gallery**, and the spectacular **Henry Moore Centre for the Study of Sculpture** and the **Henry Moore Trust Headquarters**, which opened in 1993, to acclaim for its architecture, and controversy over its inaugural show.

Around the City

Three miles from the city centre, on the banks of the River Aire, are the ruins of the 12th century **Kirkstall Abbey**. The Abbey Gatehouse was a private home for 4 centuries, and has now become a museum, with has an excellent recreation of a Victorian street. On the eastern edge of the city is a beautiful Tudor-Jacobean mansion, **Temple Newsam House**, home to an extensive collection of furniture made by Yorkshire's own Thomas Chippendale, and the birthplace of Lord Darnley, the short-lived husband of Mary Queen of Scots. The park is one of the city's "lungs", for, close to such a busy industrial town, there are 1,200 acres of grounds, which are the venue for summer open-air concerts. Leeds is known to music lovers as the venue for

with lakes and a deer park, and for more than 660 years, home to the Ingilbys. The village of **Ripley** owes much of its beauty to the eccentricity of Sir William

Amcotts Ingilby. On a whim, he decided to demolish the old houses and rebuild the village, modelling it on a similar one he had seen and particularly liked

The Leeds Coin Exchange, a symbol of Leed's past prosperity.

the annual **Leeds International Piano Festival**.

Leeds is also the birthplace of the chain store Marks & Spencer®, for in 1884 Michael Marks, the founder of Marks & Spencer®, first wheeled his penny bazaar barrow into Leeds market.

In 1993, Leeds celebrated the centenary of receiving its city charter. In line with the new trend of de-centralisation, the country's social security operations have been moved north from London to Leeds. In 1996, Leeds will have a new museum for the Royal Armouries; the national collection of arms and armour, is being transferred from the Tower of London, to a new purpose-built museum, on a 15 acre site at Clarence Dock on the River Aire.

in Alsace Lorraine, in France, which is why the Town Hall is called the "Hôtel de Ville".

Mother Shipton, England's most fa-mous prophetess lived 500 years ago in the time of King Henry VIII and Queen Elizabeth I. She was born in a cave besides a petrifying well in **Knaresborough**, east of Harrogate. She foretold the invasion and defeat of the Spanish Armada in 1588, and Samuel Pepys' diary records that Mother Shipton predicted the great fire of London in 1666. The cave and the petrifying well, a unique geological phenomenon, are still there and visitors come to see the cascading water turn everyday objects to stone.

Humberside

One thing Mother Shipton failed to forecast, was the re-drawing of county boundaries, to meet political and demographic pressures. Thus it was that outraged Yorkshire men saw part of southeast Yorkshire being lopped off and combined with part of northern Lincolnshire, to form the county of Humberside.

Hull is the economic centre of Humberside, and **Beverley** is its historic centre. For many years, Beverley was the county seat of the centuries old East Riding of Yorkshire, and today, it is the seat of its successor, Humberside. The **Minster** dates back to 1220. Look out for a carving of a rabbit over the sacristy door. The statue dating back to 1325 is thought to be the inspiration for the White Rabbit in Lewis Carrolls' *Alice in Wonderland*

The North East

The general description "North East" covers the four counties that stretch north from Yorkshire to the Scottish border; the large historic counties of Northumberland and County Durham, and the much smaller, more industrially oriented Cleveland, and Tyne and Wear.

Between the limestone cliffs of the North Sea coastline and the Pennine Hills and dales to the west, there is a wide variety of things to see, from Durham with its Norman cathedral and castle, to the scenery of the North Pennines; from the North of England Open Air Museum at Beamish, to Hadrian's Wall and Lindisfarne. All 4 counties have a maritime tradition and have been involved over the centuries in border disputes with their Scottish neighbours.

Durham Cathedral, overlooking the River Wear.

An ancient billboard points to Durham's historical roots.

The Prince Bishops of Durham

County Durham, also known as the land of the Prince Bishops, was once part of the ancient border kingdom of Northumbria. For centuries the powerful Prince Bishops of Durham ruled the county as a virtually independent state.

In Norman England, Northumbria was a border region, difficult to administer and the scene of constant conflict with the Scots. The King, based far away in the south of England, wanted a trusted representative who could look after this troublesome area on his behalf. Afraid of competition from local hereditary lords, he decided to give regal powers to the Bishop of Durham. The Bishop of Durham became a Prince Bishop, combining the role of churchman, politician, soldier and feudal administrator. This unique blend of civil and religious authority was to last for 8 centuries.

The Prince Bishop's territories, called the Palatinate, were extensive. They comprised land in Northumberland in-

Travel around the villages to find the true charm of England.

cluding Holy Island, and parts of North Yorkshire as well as the core area of County Durham. The Bishops ruled over this kingdom within a kingdom, with all the powers normally exercised by the King. These included administering civil and criminal law, creating their own armies, appointing their own Chancellor, minting their own money and levying their own taxes. The Prince Bishop could create his own barons, grant charters for markets and fairs, and negociate truces with the Scots.

Palatine power reached its peak in

Durham

The superb high-ceilinged interior of
Durham Cathedral.

The attractive medieval city of Durham is dominated by its Norman **Cathedral**, which was designed partly as a church of God to house the shrine of Saint Cuthbert, and partly as a castle to defend England against the fiery Scots. Founded in 1093, the cathedral soon became a major centre of Christian pilgrimage and the small town of Durham grew and prospered around it. The impressive **Castle**, dating from shortly after the Norman conquest, was home to Durham's Prince Bishops for nearly 800 years until 1836. The castle now houses **University College**, the foundation college of Durham University, the third oldest university in England, after Oxford and Cambridge universities.

The shrine of St Cuthbert

Saint Cuthbert is one of the North's most revered and best-loved Saints. After his death in 687, Cuthbert was buried on the island of Lindisfarne. Two hundred years later, the monks fled with his miraculously uncorrupt body, to escape Danish invaders. After wandering the north of England, the monks eventually settled in 995 on the naturally defensive peninsula of Durham. The original building was replaced by a white church, itself later demolished to make way for the new cathedral and shrine for Saint Cuthbert.

The cathedral's foundation stone was laid on 11 August 1093 by the Bishop of Durham in the presence of King Malcolm of Scotland. **Durham Cathedral** thus celebrated its 900th birthday in 1993. Unlike other Anglo-Norman churches, Durham's has never suffered from partial rebuilding, and is therefore the least altered, as well as one of the greatest structural achievements of the Anglo-Norman school of architecture.

The right of sanctuary

On the door of Durham Cathedral there is a "sanctuary knocker" dating from about 1140. Durham Cathedral had the right of sanctuary throughout the Middle Ages. A criminal arriving at the north door and claiming protection from the law, drew the attention of the 2 watchmen in a chamber above the door, by using the knocker.

A bell was tolled, to inform the people of Durham that sanctuary had been claimed. The fugitive was admitted and led to a railed-off

the 13th and 14th centuries when Bishop Antony Bek ruled over a virtually autonomous state, with all the trappings of royalty. After the Middle Ages, the

Prince Bishops' powers gradually declined, but it was not until 1836 that the remaining Palatinate rights and privileges were restored to the Crown. The

alcove beneath the southwest tower, where he could sleep, be fed and organize his affairs. He could choose either to stand trial or go into voluntary exile, leaving the country within 40 days, from a named port, often Hartlepool. While in the cathedral precinct, he wore a black gown with a large yellow cross on the left shoulder and on the way into exile, he carried a white wooden cross before him.

In the 15th and 16th centuries, the monks of Durham kept a record of the occasions when sanctuary was claimed; about 6 a year. Murder was the most common case and records also mention theft and debt. The Reformation, and the suppression of the monasteries under Henry VIII, brought about the abolition of many sanctuaries, and the concept of sanctuary was effectively eliminated from English Common Law in 1624.

Cathedral highlights

During the Reformation, most of the stained glass in the Cathedral, and over 30 small altars, were destroyed. Other fittings were demolished when the Scots army occupied Durham in 1640. There was further devastation and the burning of all the woodwork when 3,000 of Cromwell's prisoners, taken at the Battle of Dunbar, were imprisoned in the cathedral in 1650.

The beautiful **Chapel of the Nine Altars** was built between 1242 and 1280. The impression of soaring height was obtained by sinking the floor of the chapel below the level of the main body of the church. There were many priests in the monastery, who required room to say Mass every day, so 9 altars were provided, thus the chapel's name. In the **Galilee Chapel**, is the tomb of the Venerable Bede, author of the earliest surviving history of England.

Palatinate courts survived even longer, only being abolished in 1971.

Nowhere is the evidence of the Prince Bishops' influence stronger than in Dur-

A cyclist along the old cobbled streets of Durham.

ham, and for centuries the Norman cathedral and castle have dominated the town.

The great loop of the River Wear with its wooded gorge, provided a natural fortification and the peninsula became a defensive stronghold for the Prince Bishops. (see box story on Durham).

The North Pennines

The North Pennines straddle the counties of Cumbria, Durham and Northumberland, and give rise to the great rivers of the north, the Tees, the Tyne, the Derwent, and the Wear, all of which have their source high in the moor-

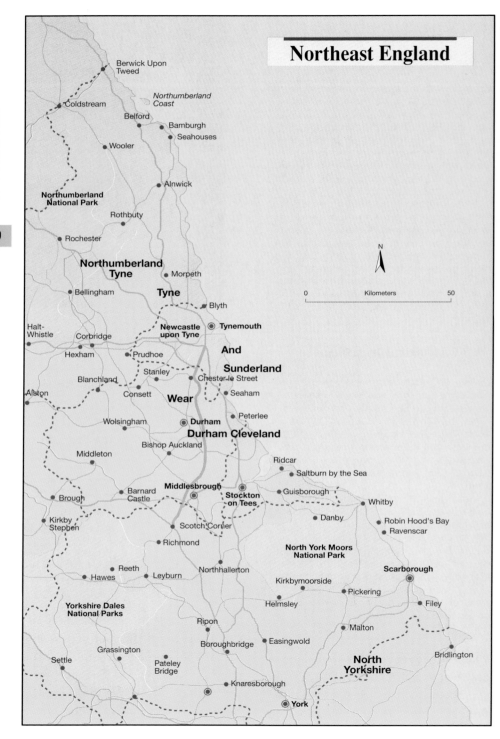

Northeast England

Berwick Upon Tweed

Northumberland Coast

Coldstream

Belford

Bamburgh

Seahouses

Wooler

Alnwick

Northumberland National Park

Rothbuty

Rochester

Northumberland
Tyne

Morpeth

Bellingham

Tyne

Blyth

Halt-Whistle

Corbridge

Newcastle upon Tyne

Tynemouth

Hexham

Prudhoe

And

Stanley

Sunderland

Blanchland

Chester-le Street

Alston

Consett

Seaham

Wear

Wolsingham

Durham

Peterlee

Durham Cleveland

Bishop Auckland

Middleton

Ridcar

Saltburn by the Sea

Brough

Barnard Castle

Middlesbrough

Stockton on Tees

Guisborough

Whitby

Kirkby Stephen

Scotch Corner

Danby

Robin Hood's Bay

Ravenscar

Richmond

North York Moors National Park

Reeth

Leyburn

Northhallerton

Scarborough

Hawes

Kirkbymoorside

Pickering

Filey

Helmsley

Yorkshire Dales National Parks

Malton

Ripon

Settle

Grassington

Boroughbridge

Easingwold

North Yorkshire

Bridlington

Pateley Bridge

Knaresborough

York

0   Kilometers   50

N

Newcastle-upon-Tyne, the bustling heart of the North East.

Raby castle, County Durham, one of England's many northern forts.

lands. Life in this part of the country was not always peaceful, and the turbulent history of this border area led first to the building of the Roman forts and Hadrian's Wall, and later to the building of a line of defensive castles.

Darlington, south of Durham, is County Durham's largest town. It is famous for the **Stockton to Darlington Railway**, the world's first public passenger railway. George Stephenson's engine *Locomotion*, which ran on the opening day in 1825, is now on display in Darlington's **Railway Centre and Museum**.

You can still ride along part of the original route by taking a train from Darlington to **Bishop Auckland**, where

Darlington Railway had begun.

To the south of County Durham are two important castles. Take the A67 westwards from Darlington to the now ruined **Barnard Castle**. The castle gave its name to the bustling market town of Barnard Castle, known as "Barney" to the locals, where Charles Dickens stayed to gather local colour for his novel *Nicholas Nickleby*. The town's **Bowes Museum** is an unexpected surprise in this rugged part of the country, for it is a grand French-style château, housing one of Britain's leading collections of European art.

Just north of Barnard Castle on the A688 is the moated 14th century **Raby Castle**, with its remodelled 18th and 19th century interior.

Hadrian's Wall

For much of the history of Northumberland, its people clung to the coast, making a living from fishing, and largely ignoring the wild interior, which even today is sparsely inhabited. The Romans considered this area to be their northern-most frontier, and built a defensive wall, **Hadrian's Wall**, across the southern part of Northumberland, probably the most spectacular memorial to the Roman empire in Britain. This barrier, stretching 45 km (73 miles) from the mouth of the Tyne in the east, to the Solway Firth in the west, was an outstanding feat of military engineering, using to full advantage the con-

Auckland Castle has for many centuries been the principle country residence of the Bishops.

Actually, the true birthplace of the railways can be found a little to the north, in **West Auckland**. On 27 September 1825, 12 wagons of coal from the Etherley Colliery at Witton Park, were hitched to George Stephenson's Locomotion Number 1, and the first train journey on the Stockton and

Rustic memories of a time gone by.

tours of the landscape. For over 250 years, it stood as Rome's northern frontier. Much of the wall still exists today and as well as the better known forts, there are many smaller sites, turrets, castles, signal towers and stretches of wall well worth visiting.

Perched on a ridge overlooking the open moorland of Northumbria, **Housesteads Fort** lies on what is deservedly the best-known part of Hadrian's Wall. The most complete example of a Roman fort in Britain, it was built as one of the 12 permanent bases to garrison the wall. You can still see the remains of all the main buildings of the fort, the headquarters, the commandant's house, barracks, granaries, hospitals and gateways, many are extremely well-preserved.

Chester's Fort is the best-preserved example of a Roman cavalry fort in the country, and the substantial remains include a bath house by the river complete with an under-floor heating system. **Corbridge**, lying south of Hadrian's Wall, at the junction of the A68 and A69 roads, was a prosperous garrison town and supply base for troops manning the frontier.

Northumberland's islands

Off the coast of Northumberland, are the barren **Farne Islands**. At high tide there are 15 islands, increasing to 28 at low tide, and they are favoured nesting grounds for seabirds, and home to the largest British colony of grey seals. The islands were first colonised in 676 by St Cuthbert who lived on Inner Farne until 685. For many years, the islands belonged to the Dean and Chapter of Durham, before passing into private hands, and in 1925 they were bought for the National Trust. They make for a wonderful place of retreat

In May 1993, the islands became a national nature reserve. Nine National Trust wardens now live on the islands for 8 months of the year, and like the monks who used to inhabitant the islands centuries earlier, they live a quiet, lonely life.

In 685, Saint Cuthbert became Bishop of Lindisfarne, living in the monastery on tiny **Holy Island**, to the north of the Farne Islands. Lindisfarne is connected to the mainland only by a narrow causeway, which is covered at high tide. On the seaward edge of this windswept island is the site of one of the most important early centres of Christianity in England.

Founded by St Aidan in the 7th century, the monastery became a place of pilgrimage after miracles were reported at St Cuthbert's shrine. It was here that the beautiful illuminated *Lindisfarne Gospels* were written rivalling in magnificence the splendid Irish *Book of Kells*. The Lindisfarne Gospels, are now kept in the British Museum The early monks were driven out by Vikings but Lindisfarne was re-established and the ruins of **Lindisfarne Priory** date from 1093.

Northumberland's castles

On a crag beside the sea, overlooking the Farne Islands, is the 12th century **Bamburgh Castle**. This rocky outcrop has been occupied for at least 2,000 years, and the present fortress was built to deter invading Scots. Almost due south of Bamburgh is **Alnwick Castle**, another border fortress which dates back to the 11th century. The rugged medieval exterior belies the richness of the interior, which was decorated in the 19th century in the classical style of the Italian renaissance.

Five km (8 miles) north east of Alnwick is **Dunstanburgh Castle**, situated on a lonely cliff top 33 m (100 ft) above the sea. Despite its isolation, Dunstanburgh has been much fought over. A Lancastrian stronghold during the War of the Roses, it was twice besieged and eventually taken by the victorious Yorkists.

Warkworth Castle, 5 km (7 $\frac{1}{2}$ miles) south of Alnwick on the A1068, towers over the river Coquet. Its 15th century keep stands within the natural defence of a horse-shoe bend of the river and dominates the surrounding landscape. The castle was begun in the 12th century, and for 6 centuries was the stronghold of the Percy family, the Earls of Northumberland. It was here that Henry Percy, the first Earl of Northumberland, plotted with his son, Harry Hotspur, to overthrow King Henry IV, a rebellion later immortalised in Shakespeare's play *Henry IV*. The attempted coup ended when Hotspur was killed at the Battle of Shrewsbury, and Percy fled to Scotland.

Newcastle–upon-Tyne

Newcastle-upon-Tyne, situated inland, on the estuary of the River Tyne, and capital of the small county of Tyne and Wear, is home to the "Geordies", the name given to the local people, who speak with an unmistakable dialect, and have a marked sense of humour.

Abundant supplies of coal and minerals made Newcastle-upon-Tyne an important industrial centre in the 19th and early 20th centuries, particularly for shipbuilding. At the turn of the century, 2 out of every 5 ships built in the world came from Tyneside, but the picture today is very different. The area is currently in the midst of an economic down-turn, and the last shipbuilding yard is fighting for its life. The **Cathedral Church of St Nicholas** has a well-known lantern tower with flying buttresses. The towns' eponymous **New Castle** of 1080 has been replaced by another new castle dating from the 12th century.

Cleveland & County Tyne

To the west of Newcastle on the A695 is medieval **Prudhoe Castle**, set on wooded hillsides overlooking the River Tyne. It commanded the principle north-south route through Northumberland and was a formidable obstacle in times of war, twice resisting attack by King William of Scotland. Although the exterior dates from the early 12th century, in the 19th century an elegant manor house was constructed within the old castle walls.

The **North of England Open Air Museum** is in **Beamish**, 5 km (8 miles) southwest of Newcastle-upon-Tyne, along the A6076 and just over 7 km (12 miles) northwest of Durham. This reconstruction of northern life in the early 1900s is set in 300 acres and uses actual buildings from across the region, including a colliery village, a town with shops and a newspaper office, a solicitors office, a teacher's house and a dental surgery, a licensed public house and stable's housing the brewery's dray horses. There is also a railway station, and a short tram ride away is the farm.

The industrial town of **Cleveland** is the home of Captain Cook, who was born in the village of **Marston** in 1728. At the age of 8 he moved to Great Ayton in Yorkshire, and later went to work first in the old village of Staithes and then in Whitby.

If you really want to have a walking holiday, the **Cleveland Way**, starts at the southern tip of the North Yorkshire Moors near Rievaulx Abbey, continues northwards through the Cleveland Hills just south of Middlesbrough and turns back along the coast to Scarborough. This walk can be very strenuous, so plan well in advance.

W hen an Englishman wants to relax, unlike his more obviously European counterparts, he does not head off to the café. More than likely he will potter around his home, tinker with his garden, walk his dog, and if all that is a little too strenuous, settle down (yes, with a cup of tea) and watch a football match on TV. The English like sport, they enjoy watching it, and even playing it. Although attitudes in society are changing rapidly, England is a country which still thinks of sport in terms of a hobby, rather than as a challenge which has to be won, at all costs.

Unlike the former Eastern bloc countries, who trained their sportsmen and women from childhood to be super-achieving athletes, the English ap-

High society and big money. Racing at Royal Ascot.

389

Sports & Recreation

The gentrified sport of Cricket.

proach is in general much more low-key. Games are to be enjoyed, and if success follows, all well and good.

Anyone for Cricket?

There is a wonderful, quotation which goes something like this: "Cricket is a game which the English, not being a spiritual people, have invented to give themselves some conception of eternity." And the fact of the matter is, that it is an extremely popular sport in England, bringing to mind as it does, the perfect – if somewhat elusive – English summer afternoon.

It has been successfully "exported" to the Indian sub-continent, the West Indies, and Australia, who England take turns to play, in various test-matches – the most famous one being that against Australia, known as The Ashes. The game has a certain aura of impenetrability around it, probably due to the rather complicated nature of its rules. How can you possibly explain to non-fluent English speakers the idea of a game where you bowl a maiden over, and are out for a duck?

Cricket is played all over the country, but unlike professional football, where the teams represent cities, in cricket the major teams represent counties, hence the name County Cricket. Boys begin to learn cricket at school, the game being particularly well cultivated in the public schools.

Wimbledon, the sporting highlight of summer for England and the world.

Wimbledon fever

The English enjoy watching tennis, appreciate the game, and are hosts to one of the world's premier tournaments, **Wimbledon** (See box story on Wimbledon p.392). As a nation however, they have not been very successful at it in recent years and indeed no English person has won the Wimbledon singles tournament since Virgina Wade took the women's title in 1977; the year of the Queen's Silver Jubilee.

Horse power

Horse racing is reputed to be Britain's oldest sport and is popular both amongst the royalty (who breed horses) and with the public at large. The big races of the sporting calendar such as the Grand National and the Derby are closely followed by much of the country, and by the bookmakers in turn.

Nineteen hundred and ninety three was an eventful year in horseracing history; the Queen's horse won the Derby and more spectacularly the **Grand National** was declared void, amidst much controversy, soul-searching and an estimated loss to the national exchequer of £6 million in tax revenues. Human error, two false starts, animal rights' protests and a bomb hoax, all conspired to make the 1993 Grand National the most jinxed ever, since its origins in 1837.

Wimbledon

The pleasant, middle-class suburb of **Wimbledon**, about 5 km (8 miles) southwest of London, takes on a completely different image in June each year, when the All-England Tennis championships take place. Wimbledon, the tennis championship, is part of the games' Grand Slam series, and is one of the world's major sporting events. Every summer, suburbia is invaded by the press, the champions, and the fans.

The first Wimbledon championship was held on one of the club's croquet lawns in 1877, and the winner was a Mr Gore. Seven years later, in 1884, a women's championship was introduced, and the men's doubles was transferred there from Oxford.

The next major change in the structure of the games came in 1913, when mixed doubles and women's doubles were introduced. Originally played by amateurs, Wimbledon was opened to professionals in 1968.

Tennis aces

In a sport like tennis, with such history and charisma, not to mention really serious money, names and statistics abound, but even so, the names of some of Wimbledon's famous players are almost the stuff of sporting legend. In 1920, Suzanne Lenglen of France became the first woman to win 3 Wimbledon championships in a single year. Eighteen years later, an American, Donald Budge, became the first man to achieve the same hat-trick.

In 1980, the Swedish player Björn Borg set a record in winning the men's singles for a fifth consecutive year. Martina Navratilova is the legendary player of the women's game, in September 1993, she announced that 1994 will be her final Winbledon singles. All eyes will as always be on Martina when in 1994 she makes a bid to again win the championship which she has already won an incredible 9 times!

Nowadays, there are also events for junior players, when people try and talent spot the potential future champions, as well as championships for senior players, when stars of earlier years play much more relaxed, friendly tennis,

secure in their former glory, and basking in the affection of the crowds. Centre Court has a capacity of 13,109 – there are approximately 10 other courts – and usually a quarter of a million spectators attend the two week competition.

The food event

Wimbledon, naturally enough, spawns many ancillary industries, everything from books and magazines to souvenirs and tee-shirts, and there is even a company that handles apartment and house rentals just for the Wimbledon fortnight. Players, coaches, and television crews need accommodation, preferably close to the tennis courts, and so local people rent out their houses for the two weeks, and go away on holiday, to escape the razzmatazz and the crazy parking, and watch the matches in peace and quiet somewhere else.

Strawberries and cream are almost as much an integral part of Wimbledon as the tennis, so perhaps a few statistics are permitted. During the two weeks of the tournament, 20 tons, or 1.5 million strawberries are consumed, all supplied from one farm in Kent. A few other statistics will explain why Wimbledon is such a social event, as well as a major sporting event. In 1993, the shopping list for the 1,500 catering staff looked something like this :

Salmon	12 tons
Sandwiches	190,000
Ice creams	110,000
Scones	150,000

And for those feeling a little thirsty :

Teas and coffees	285,000
Champagne	12,500 bottles, at an average £30 per bottle
Pimms	40,000 pints
Beer	90,000 pints

Well, after all, you do need something to wash down those 20 tons of strawberries!

A hint of sun will tempt the English out onto the beach.

This 150th Grand National fielded 39 horses, where there were 60,000 spectators at **Aintree** in Liverpool, and millions more watching on television.

Bets of £75 million were placed – the largest amount ever wagered in a single day in national gambling history – all had to be refunded! Yet, barring the 1993 fiasco, this annual race is one which particularly appeals to the British, since 19 out of the last 20 winners were bred in Ireland or Britain.

Hunting, shooting & fishing

There is an expression used to describe a certain kind of country person – "the hunting, shooting, fishing type". However picturesque the traditional red jackets, hounds and horses of fox hunters may appear, this centuries-old blood-

An Oxford rowing team practising on the River Thames.

sport arouses a considerable amount of opposition today among animal-rights activists, such that hunts are often followed by a cortége of saboteurs, who try to distract from the bait.

Fishing is in an altogether different league and come 16 March, whatever the weather, hundreds of fly-fishers set out to brave the weather, the wait and the damp, to catch trout. Angling is among the most popular participant sports in the country. Game-shooting is somewhat restricted to farming circles but you will see clay-pigeon shoots

and given that nowhere in the country is actually very far from the sea, weekends will see many city dwellers heading off to enjoy some sailing, especially on the south coast. **Cowes week** held every summer off the coast of the Isle of Wight is an international yachting gala.

The **Oxford and Cambridge boat race** is another traditional event in the annual sporting calendar attracting thousands of spectators, pundits and an international TV audience. The race is run on the Thames river from Putney Bridge east to Mortlake and only lasts about 16 minutes.

Henley is another of the river greats. At the beginning of July every year, the pretty riverside town of Henley-on-Thames in Oxfordshire is home to the world's rowing fraternity, who come to compete in the **Henley Royal Regatta**, the premier amateur regatta in England. There are several races, all raced over the same standard distance of 0.6 km (1 mile).

The **Grand Challenge Cup** was established in the first year of Henley and is for eights, that is, crews using eight oars. The **Diamond Challenge Sculls**, established in 1844, is for one man using two oars. These and the other events are all open to entries from anywhere in the world.

Henley is also part of the great traditional English society summer season, when ladies in pretty hats and men in blazers and straw-boaters turn out to watch the races - and each other, of course.

advertized in some rural areas, and many towns have their own shooting clubs.

On the river

Hardly surprising for an island race, the English love "messing about in boats"

Punting on the Backs, Cambridge's refined art of recreation.

Golf & polo

Golf is very popular in England and increasingly so. Correctly speaking Scotland is the home of golf – St Andrews golf course, being one of the best in the world – and if you are a keen golfer it would be worth your while to cross the border. However England does have a large number of golf courses and reasonably priced clubs which are generally well maintained.

The rather expensive sport of polo is the oldest equestrian sport in the world. There are around 1,500 polo players in Britain and the country's governing body, the Hurlingham Polo Association, is also the governing body for most of world polo, outside the Americas.

Kicking boots

Soccer has long been an extremely popular sport in England, every Saturday afternoon, thousands of local teams battle it out on the field, valiantly watched by a handful of loyal wives, girl-friends and mothers, whilst thousands more settle down in front of their televisions to watch the major teams play. Unfortunately the image of big league soccer has been marred in recent years by isolated amounts of hooliganism and violence which appalled 99 per cent of the English population. As a result, attendance at football matches is

A game of traditional bowls is popular in England, but so much depends on the English weather.

today overwhelmingly masculine and adult, as few women and children are willingly to run the risk of hooliganism, however unlikely it is.

Notwithstanding, the English soccer scene is thriving. Spring 1993 saw the founding of a new championship, the Premier League, with the avowed aim of fewer teams, playing fewer games, with the purpose of producing better quality football. Top players and managers are attaining almost a cult status, with players being "sold" to other clubs for record amounts of money. Generally if you buy a seat ticket and sit in the stands of the team you support, there is little danger to your safety – there are usually hundreds of police on hand and unprovoked violence is extremely rare.

If you prefer to stay indoors, matches are extremely well-covered on TV, with detailed analysis and commentary. Rugby does not command quite the same degree of frenzied loyalty from its fans, but it is still popular.

Fitness tips

Like many countries, the fitness craze took over England in the 1980s and no yuppie worth his or her salt was without a health-club membership and a sports personal-stereo. Much of the initial frenzy has abated, but there are still many keen joggers in the country, and events like the **London Marathon** attract some 20,000 runners – though not

Biking is ever popular.

all, admittedly, are locals.

If you are looking for something other than a jog whilst on holiday, or need to burn off some of your childrens' energy, a good place to go is the local leisure centre. Almost all towns will have these complexes and large towns will have several. They offer a whole host of sports; swimming, badminton, tennis, table-tennis, bowls, ice-scating... depending on their facilites, which you pay per hour to use. If your stay is more than just a few days you could enroll and learn a sport such as archery or roller-hockey, or attend step-aerobic classes – many have clubs for children if your visit coincides with the English school holidays. These centres are also a good source of information about all types of local events.

Popular hobbies

For the English themselves, the most popular hobbies are probably gardening, shopping, DIY and walking the dog. Gardening is extremely popular and the English lavish much attention on their gardens, their vegetable plots and their allotment gardens.

DIY or Do-It-Yourself, involves visiting various hardware shops and buying the equipment to do those things to your house which any sane person would pay a plumber, electrician, or an interior decorator to do. DIY is of course much cheaper, but not nearly so economical on patience and time.

The grooming of dogs is a great English hobby and every year Earls Court is host to the annual canine ritual of the **Cruft's Dog Show**, the best known dog show in England, when the most beautiful and perfectly groomed dogs do friendly battle.

Getting about & enjoying the views

England is a lovely country to enjoy on your feet, its rolling hills and dales catering to a wide range of abilities and interests. In addition to its beauty, England is a good place for walking for the simple reason that there are thousands of legal footpaths, vehemently protected

Chessington World of Adventure, one of England's colourful amusement parks.

by members of the national Ramblers Association, which allow you to enjoy the countryside from many different vantage points, along clearly defined paths. Maps of routes can be acquired from the Ramblers association, whilst local Ordnance Survey maps detailing footpaths, and various walking books can be bought from most book-shops.

The **Yorkshire Dales**, the **Peak District** and the **Lake District** are popular with serious hikers – but accessible to the novice. For variety the New Forest is a good choice for wooded scenery and the **Dorset Heritage** and **Devon** and **Cornwall Coasts** are great choices for spectacular cliff scenery. All are accessible to both the leisurely and the serious walker, depending on the route taken.

The English enjoy walking, especially if it can be combined with a visit to one of the country's stately homes or castles, a garden or a garden-centre, and, preferably, followed up by tea in a pretty village tea shop or a beer in the local pub.

Village notice boards or libraries may be able to provide you with details of locally arranged walks or tips on where to go. Check out Tourist Information centres too.

An alternative way to see the countryside, at a slightly faster pace, is to hire a bicycle and tour around. Some local bicycle shops offer bicycle hire, from mountain and racer varieties through to tandems, for the more romantically inclined.

I t was that arch-enemy of the English, Napoleon Bonaparte, who put his finger on it. The English were, he declared, a "nation of shopkeepers". He was, of course, trying to be rude, but he was also rather accurate. Historically, trading, commerce, and the desire to find ever more lucrative markets, were some of the major driving forces behind the British Empire. The intrepid explorers of the 18th and 19th centuries, who helped form what would one day be a major imperial power, were driven to colonize, partly because of the double-edged desire to locate new minerals, foodstuffs and precious stones; as well as the need to find new buyers for the manufactured goods which were being produced in increasing numbers back home. England was ever growing as an industrial power.

A maze of bargains are on offer at Camden Market, London.

Shopping in London

Today, the Empire has long since gone, but there is no shortage of shops, as befits a nation of shopkeepers, and a city like London is a major attraction for visitors and holiday shoppers. London has shops and mar-

Shopping

401

Good bargains can often be had at indoor markets

kets to suit everyone's taste, interest and price range. There are the expensive, designer shops along **Bond Street**, and the flea-markets on **Portobello Road** and **Petticoat Lane**. There is the Queen of all shops, Harrods, and the Asian markets of **Brick Lane**.

There is the former fruit and vegetable market of **Covent Garden**, in its new "avatar" as an arts and crafts style market, and the Indian supermarkets in **Southall**, where people gossip in Punjabi, buy the latest Bombay film magazines, and eat freshly made Indian sweets. There is **Carnaby Street**, the "in" place during the swinging sixties, and there is Fortnum and Mason, where, if one believes the gossip, the Queen does her food shopping.

Oxford Street

And, of course, there is **Oxford Street**, an architecturally undistinguished street in central London, running from Marble Arch eastwards to Oxford Circus, and onto the Tottenham Court Road; it is one of the world's best known shop-

Scramble your way through the goodies along Portobello road, London.

ping streets. Here you can find branches of all the main British chain stores – Marks & Spencer, Debenhams, British Home Stores, C & A, Dixons, to name but a few. There are also one-off boutiques, slightly down-market jewellery stores, fast-food restaurants, one of the biggest and busiest record and compact disc shops in the country HMV (His Majesty's Voice), and there is the colossal Selfridges department store towering over it all. There are also the crowds. Unless you absolutely thrive on wall-to-wall crowds, try and avoid Oxford Street

Whiteley's department store in a vast refurbished complex, Bayswater, London.

on Saturday afternoons and on Thursday evenings, when the area stays open for late-night shopping, which in English terms, means the rather restrained time of 2000 hours.

Saturday afternoons in the run-up to Christmas are the worst, or the best, depending on your level of crowd tolerance. The street is jammed solid with people, who have come not only to shop, but also to look at the Christmas lights and the decorated shop windows. The department stores each take a theme, and decorate their windows with toys and models illustrating it. The entire street is decorated, and there are often laser light effects at nightfall.

If you visit Oxford Street outside the most popular shopping times, although it is still very busy, you will have space to breathe, and time to look at who else is out there with you. There are endless

Every town has a range of boutiques for all ages and interests.

stalls selling postcards, imitation policemens' hats, and tee-shirts. At Christmas, these stalls often sell inexpensive wrapping paper and decorations. There are the card-trick players, trying to entice people into rapid card tricks, where they will inevitably be parted from their money in record time. There are weary-looking sandwich-men, walking bill-boards for some shop or restaurant and there are the ubiquitous vendors of "French" perfume.

Often a procession of Hare Krishna devotees, gently dances its way amongst the crowds; at Christmas, there will be a Salvation Army band out in full force; and at all times of the year there will be shoppers from all over the world: Marks & Spencer at **Marble Arch** must see more nationalities in a day than the UN Building. London is still one of the world's top shopping destinations.

Historic London shops

Holiday shopping is always fun, and when you can do it amidst historic surroundings, so much the better.

Fortnum & Mason

When residents of Mayfair describe Fortnum and Mason as their local grocer, they are actually absolutely correct, for the shop did indeed begin life in 1707 as a grocery shop. It has progressed much since those days, developing over the centuries a reputation for the variety and high quality of its food products. Although the store diversified into clothing and other items in the 1920s, the reputation of Fortnum and Mason is still largely due to its food halls, which specialize in exotic delicacies. Outside the store, on Piccadilly, there is a rather impressive clock that chimes the hours, whilst the mechanical figures of Mr Fortnum and Mr Mason, the founders, come out and bow to each other.

Harrods

Compared to Fortnum and Mason, Harrods is a relative newcomer, for it was only in 1849 that a Mr Henry Charles Harrod took over the running of another small grocery store, this time on Brompton Road. By the turn of the century business had so prospered that the shop was rebuilt, in terracotta brick, and crowned with the distinctive towers and cupolas. One of the guiding principles of Harrods® has always been excellent customer service, and at one time the store had its own bank, travel agency, booking office for theatre tickets, funeral service and pet shop.

The store was innovative for its time, introducing in the 1880s the concept of cash desks placed all over the store, for the customers' convenience, as well as offering limited credit to selected clients.

Liberty's

Liberty's on the corner of Great Marlborough Street and Regent Street, was founded in 1875, by Arthur Lasenby Liberty, the son of a draper, who had to borrow £15,000 to set up his business. From the start, the shop was an expressive outlet for Mr Liberty's enthusiasm for the decorative arts, and especially for oriental textiles: the shop specialized in silks, and within three years, was producing its own prints, based on old Indian designs.

When the Arts and Crafts Movement was in its heyday, Liberty's played a central role, through the commissioning of designs, and, of course, through selling them. The Tudor-style building was built between 1922-24, using oak and teak timbers taken from the Royal Navy's last two sailing ships. The interior is very pretty, built around a central well, with gorgeous displays of fabrics cascading down from the three floors.

Bond & Regent Streets

Leading off from Oxford Street is **Bond Street**, which starts from Oxford Street as **New Bond Street**, and joins up with Piccadilly as **Old Bond Street**. This is the street for the seriously rich shopper, for those in search of the worlds' major designer names, of antiques, old master paintings and custom-made jewellery. It is also great fun for window-shopping, even if that is the closest you will ever get to a diamond tiara from Cartier, or a solid-silver picnic set from Aspreys. Running parallel to New Bond Street is **Savile Row**, whose name is almost synonymous with good suits. **Regent Street,**

Selfridges

In 1906 an American by the name of Mr Harry Gordon Selfridge moved to London with a fortune earned through his partnership in a Chicago wholesale-retail business. He opened up a vast, temple-like department store on Oxford Street, complete with Ionic columns, and a canopied entrance. Within a short time, his partner withdrew, but after obtaining additional financial funding from a wealthy tea-broker, in 1908 he registered the shop as Selfridge and Company Ltd®. Mr Selfridge's shop window displays were much admired when the store opened, and over 80 years later, the Christmas window displays of Selfridge's are still as popular. Mr Selfridge's own story is less successful than that of his creation, for, by 1939, due to his own personal extravagance, his bankers caused him to be removed from the control of his store.

Elegant arcades

If it is raining and you feel like combining shopping and history, then head for one of London's **arcades**, an early, small-scale version of today's shopping malls. Mayfair's **Burlington Arcade** was built in 1819. Beadles patrol the arcade, and every night its gates are closed. In its beautiful surroundings and elegant shop fronts, you can shop for anything from cashmere shawls to top quality cigars.

which runs from Oxford Circus down to **Piccadilly Circus** is home to the world's best-known toy shop, **Hamleys**, as well as one of London's prettiest shops, **Liberty's**, with its mock-Tudor, timbered exterior and its unrivalled displays of fabrics. Go along for a browse, but beware of taking your children to Hamleys'; the prices are stiff.

Harrods splendour

The other great mecca of London shopping is, of course, Harrods, in **Knightsbridge**. Harrods is everything a stately department store should be: uniformed door-men to open your car door for you, a reputation for selling absolutely everything (and should your heart's desire be temporarily out of stock, Harrods will be happy to order it for you), a perfumery department whose aromas can knock you flat, and unquestionably the most gorgeous food-halls anywhere. The *art nouveau* decorations, including some stunning tiling, have been left intact, and even if you have no intention of purchasing a haunch of venison, or a pound of Darjeeling tea, or a fresh lobster, do make a pilgrimage to the food halls. Food shopping will never be the same again.

Best British buys

Although clothes from around the world are all available in England, often at good prices and if you are aiming to buy English, or British, what are the best buys? For men, Savile Row suits, Turnbull and Asser shirts, and Church's shoes are a must. If women are looking for a traditional English look, there is Jaeger, and, for parties and summer wear, Laura Ashley, now 40-years-old, is still as popular as ever. Some of the best outdoor

Harrods department store, Knightsbridge, one of London's biggest and most famous stores.

clothing – jackets and trousers to take you from a trek through the Himalayas to a hike in the Sahara – is to be found in Rohan shops.

One of the most popular beauty-care chains in the country is The Body Shop, where you can buy excellent quality toiletries, safe in the knowledge that the products have not been tested on animals, and that as much packaging as possible will be re-cycled. The Body Shop staff encourage you to bring back your empty bottles for refilling, and discourage you from taking a plastic bag.

One of the world's most famous gun makers, Holland and Holland, is based in London and though paying £35,000 for a new H & H shotgun may not be on the top of everyone's shopping list, the company has diversified into clothing and accessories, so you can acquire an expensive country look, without the guns.

Class table-ware

English porcelain is excellent, and although you will find ranges of Wedgwood, Royal Crown Derby, Coalport, and Staffordshire China in most parts of the country, it is also possible to buy directly from the factories, many of which are in the **Stoke-on-Trent** area, in the English Midlands. Cutlery from the Yorkshire town of **Sheffield** is also of excellent quality.

Shopping in the provinces, Sheffield, Orchard Square.

Decorative table mats and place mats are typically English, as is a rather unusual purchase, pot-pourri, a fragrant mixture of dried flowers, aromatic herbs and essences, which, displayed in a bowl, perfumes your room.

Whenever you visit English stately homes, just notice how often there is a bowl of pot-pourri on a chest of drawers or a coffee table. They make very popular gifts for mums.

Memorable foods

Food-wise, good buys include jams and marmalades, cheeses, and speciality biscuits such as Shrewsbury Biscuits or Kendal Mint Cake. If you are in England during the run-up to Christmas, then a Christmas pudding is always a good buy. In Soho in London, there is a shop called Simply Sausages where you can

Boutiques make their fashion statement.

buy one of the staples of the English breakfast, a "banger", as sausages are often called. But if you thought that a sausage was, well, just a sausage, think again, for this shop offers British regional sausages, international sausages, and gourmet sausages. So if you wish to experiment, skip the traditional breakfast sausage, and go for a duck with apricot and orange sausage, a steak-and-kidney sausage, or even a smoked salmon sausage.

Around the country

But shopping is not a "London only" experience, and in virtually every city in England, you will find branches of the major chain-stores. To shop at a top-of-the-range chain store, such as Marks & Spencer, is not considered at all "down market", since they have such excellent quality clothing, and the latest designs. In fact, it is almost a form of inverted snobbery to shop in chain-stores, an attitude that is probably dictated by the recession, which puts the exclusive, expensive designers out of reach of many pockets.

Whilst every town has its High Street, with a range of chain-shops, small boutiques, hairdressers, banks, cafés and restaurants; on the outskirts of many cities today are huge additional shopping centres. These hyper-market areas are where you will find furniture retailers, large toy shops, supermarkets and

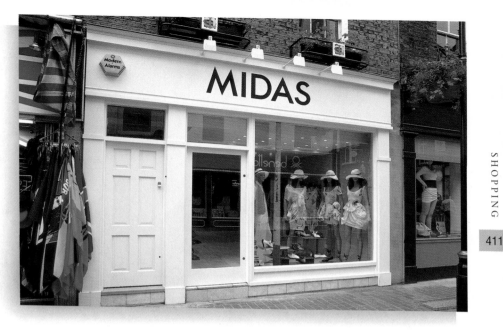

Upmarket boutiques beckon those with a surplus of cash and game for style.

DIY stores, all with their own car-parking facilities.

The Yorkshire town of Sheffield has a massive complex, the **Meadowhall Shopping and Leisure Complex**; its statistics are mind-boggling: one and a half million sq ft of floor space, over 7,000 staff, and in 1992, over 25 million visitors. Meadowhall superseded a smaller centre in Gateshead, near Newcastle, which is still nevertheless, alive and kicking.

VAT & customs

One important thing to remember, is that overseas visitors may claim back the Value Added Tax (VAT) that is included in the prices of many goods, at a rate of – at the time of writing – around 17 per cent. If you intend spending a reasonable amount in one shop, enquire about the VAT refund scheme before shopping. Usually, once all your purchases are complete, the shop will help you to fill out a VAT refund form, which you must show at Customs when you leave the country – along with the goods themselves. Not everything has VAT applied – childrens' clothing does not, for example, which is why it is such good value in England - so check first.

Do remember to leave room in your hand-baggage for those last minute airport purchases; some English chocolate, perhaps, or a bottle of English Lavender Water.

Cuisine

Someone, somewhere, once said, "The French live only to eat, whereas the English only eat to live", which was always a slightly unfair comment anyway (about the English, that is), and one that is increasingly inaccurate. If one is being scrupulously honest, well, yes, England is not one of the world's all-round gastronomic leaders. But what the English do superbly well is certain meals, and certain dishes, so when in England, it makes sense to concentrate on what they do well.

A great deal of English food is roasted, including this delicious Christmas duck.

Starting the day

And where better to start than with a full English breakfast? No self-respecting Englishman would accept a rushed, continental-style coffee and croissant,

A full English breakfast and off to a good start.

as truly deserving of the term "breakfast". A full English breakfast usually starts with fruit juice and cereals, and then moves on to a combination of fried eggs, bacon, sausage, tomatoes, mushrooms & fried bread; black pudding is another less popular tradition. Those who prefer a fishy start to the day, might like to try smoked kippers or an English speciality poached finnan haddock, served with a knob of butter.

Still feeling hungry? Good, because there is still toast and marmalade to come, and, of course, either tea or coffee. This is the sort of breakfast you will find in many of the "Bed & Breakfast" (B&B) accomodations, and it is usually well worth the money. For the average Englishman today, rising health concerns, lack of money and time, have however meant that most – when not on holiday – make do with cereals and toast, or perhaps a scrambled or boiled egg; the English do believe nevertheless, in a proper start to the day.

Lunch-break

After such a colossal start to the day, perhaps it is only to be expected that lunch is not to be regarded with the same degree of importance as it is in, say, France. That is, with the exception of Sunday lunch; another stalwart of English tradition and cooking. Roast beef with gravy, Yorkshire pudding, roast potatoes, 2 or 3 kinds of vegetables –

Hot cross buns, a delicious Easter-tide treat.

these are the classic components of the long Sunday lunch, when married children return to their parents' home for a slow, lazy meal. A word of advice: if ever you are invited to Sunday lunch at the home of Yorkshire people, prepare for one variation to the menu, for the York-shire pudding will be served, crisp and hot, on its own as a starter, and you will then get another piece of Yorkshire pudding to accompany the meat.

After this, if you still have space, there will be a traditional English dessert, such as apple pie and cream, or

English drinks

Other than the national drink, a cup of tea, the English enjoy drinking beer. Served in pints and half pints, in tall glasses or beer glasses, beer is a popular drink, particularly in pubs. In a move to get away from mas-produced beers, and back to a more traditional taste, a society called CAMRA, or the Campaign for Real Ale, encourages and promotes small, traditional breweries, and their annual guides to pubs serving "real ale", have had a significant impact on drinking habits. Another significant contribution has been made by "brew your own" kits which entail leaving jars of fermenting beer around the house, frequently to be brewed to an extremely potent state. This activity has in recent years become an extremely popular hobby.

Cider, long thought of as a "rural" drink, particularly famous in the Cornwall area, is currently enjoying a revival, and the apple-based alcoholic drink is the fastest growing sector of the UK drinks industry, with over 18 million litres (84 million) gallons consumed in 1992.

English wine

It is not widely known, but England produces wine. The Romans introduced vine-growing to England 2,000 years ago, and even managed to grow them up near their northern boundary of Hadrian's Wall. In the *Domesday Book*, over 400 vineyards were recorded. In the Middle Ages, wine-making flourished in the monasteries, until the dissolution by Henry VIII in the 16th century, and ever since, wine was imported from Europe.

After World War II, considerable research was carried out into the varieties most suited to the English climate, and one of the first vineyards to be established was the Hambledon vineyard, in 1951. By the mid-1960s a number of vineyards had been established and today, well over a 1,000 acres are in production. The vineyards are mainly in the south of the country, but vines are grown as far north as Lincolnshire and Yorkshire.

In Herefordshire there are vineyards belonging to the Bodenham English Wines group, and one feature of the vines grown there is their ability to produce full-ripened grapes, even in poor summers. This could be one of the reasons why vineyards existed in Herefordshire in Roman times.

In Sussex, near Petworth, the **Lurgashall Winery**, housed in a complex of converted 17th century and 19th century farm buildings, opened in 1985, and since then, has had several special commissions to make wines for national celebrations. Commissions include; Domesday Mead, to celebrate the 900th anniversary of the completion of the **Domesday Book**, Armada Mead, to celebrate the 400th anniversary of this famous naval victory and William and Mary

perhaps sponge pudding and custard, or an apple crumble, which all digest into a truly sleepy afternoon.

Other than this Gargantuan Sunday lunch, a mid-day meal will otherwise consist of simpler fare. Fast-food and sandwiches have inevitably taken their toll on eating habits, especially for office workers, but there is one traditional and healthy English version of fast food; in "pubs" (public houses), a popular lunch time meal is a ploughman's lunch, which consists of a thick slice of crusty bread and a generous wedge of English cheese, served with pickle and salad.

Pub-food is often advertised as "pub grub"; portions are on the whole hearty, tasty and good value for money. Hot as well as cold food is available. Nowadays pubs are quite family oriented so do not be put off if you have kids

wine and mead, in celebration of the 300th anniversary of the birth of our parliamentary system.

In addition to its wine production, the winery also produces a range of English fruit and flower wines, meads and liqueurs, using locally gathered ingredients, wherever possible; varieties range from crisp dry gooseberry wine, through to fragrant elder-flower and bramble, a wild blackberry liqueur.

The standard of English wine is steadily improving, more and more winemaker's courses are being offered to the general public, and as long as the sun shines during the summer, production should continue to improve and increase.

Sherry formalities

Sherry – a type of fortified wine – is another popular drink in England, which if you visit an English house will often be offered to you in the morning or as a pre-dinner appetizer – old people will offer it to you in the winter especially, as its high alcohol content has a warming effect. Sherry parties are also held, not to extol the virtues of sherry, but are social occasions when you are presented with a glass of sherry – you then mill around talking to people, whilst titbits of food are brought round to you.

English cheese

With the plentiful supply of fresh dairy products in England, you may well wish to sample some of the cheese. Though the selection is not on the French scale, the quality is excellent, ideal for eating with a crisp apple, bread, or savoury biscuits. In a full English dinner, biscuits and cheese will be served before the dessert. The queen of English cheeses is Stilton, a blue cheese, and other well-known varieties include Wensleydale, Cheshire, Cheddar and Double Gloucester.

A decade-long experiment with a soft French style cheese, called "Lymeswold", flopped. People did not like it, they found the name funny, and it died a quiet death – a futile attempt to change English food habits!

Pies, puddings & tarts

During your stay in England, you will be offered a whole host of pies, puddings, and tarts, which require a bit of insider-knowledge to select. It is wise to know that while a tart may well be a sweet dish, pies and puddings can be both sweet and savoury. There are apple pies and steak-and-kidney pies, Yorkshire puddings and bread-and-butter puddings – the latter is a dessert. There is a Derbyshire speciality known to everyone as a Bakewell tart, except the people from the village of Bakewell itself, who call it a pudding. There is black pudding, which is tripe; pease pudding, which is essentially a dish of boiled and mashed peas; and there is that vital component of any Christmas lunch, the Christmas pudding.

A Christmas lunch without a Christmas pudding, flambéd and served with brandy butter, is unthinkable. The ingredients are a rich mixture of sultanas, raisins, mixed fruit, suet, nuts and rum.

Roast leg of lamb with vegetables.

Heavy, aromatic and delicious, it is a disaster on the waistline.

Tea treats

English afternoon tea is famous the world over and is another of those meals that the English do really well. Tea is generally served around 1530 to 1600 hours, whereas "high tea", which is a different thing altogether, will be served a little later, around 1700 hours. Tea will consist, naturally enough, of tea, and you

Come summertime, the English love to eat alfresco.

will often be asked "Indian or Chinese, milk or lemon?", and once you have decided, you can move on to a selection of cucumber sandwiches, scones and cakes, some of which will be pies and puddings, just to confuse the issue! If you are in the extreme southwest of the country, in Devon or Cornwall, then you will be privileged to eat a clotted cream tea, which is one of the unsung stars of the English tea-table; first put jam on the scone, then top it off with a mound of fresh, clotted cream, and re-member, just refuse, totally and abso-lutely, to think about the calories!

High tea a different, more elabo-rate affair, served a little later than tea, it is a combination of an early, light dinner and tea, for in addition to the cakes and sandwiches, you will be of-fered a light meal, such as a cold meat salad. It is not normal to eat this meal in addition to dinner, but you may well be offered a light supper of hot drinks and biscuits, at around 2100, instead.

Fish-n-Chips

If you are looking for a quick, cheap but filling snack, that is truly English – as opposed to the ubiquitous, and un-Eng-lish pizzas, hamburgers and Chinese take-aways; fish-and-chips are served by thousands of take-away fish-and-chip shops all over the country. What you will find on offer, unsurprisingly, is a variety of fish, such as cod or haddock,

Cream teas are the speciality of the West country.

usually fried in batter, and chips. Although some "chippies" may well have burgers or sausages on offer, the main business of the day is, unquestionably, fish. Mushy peas (smashed peas) and baked beans, are favouite side dishes and a "chip butty" – a chip sandwich – is a popular alternative main dish. You will usually be asked "salt & vinegar?" which means would you like salt and vinegar on your chips – they are usually added in hearty amounts. English chips are much bigger and fatter than American "fries".

This is not refined or even particularly healthy cooking, but there is a very cosy feeling, especially in the winter, to carrying a bag of chips home or eating them in the car, and it is at all times a truly English experience; you will see fish-and-chip shops all over the country, and people wandering around eating them in the street. Some fish-and chip-shops also offer sit-down facilities. Arguably the best fish and chips in the country, are to be found in Yorkshire, in the small industrial town of Guiseley, just outside of Leeds, which boasts the world's largest fish-and-chip restaurant (See box story p429).

Cakes & biscuits

English cakes and biscuits come in all shapes and sizes. Cakes range from rich fruit and plum cakes, to light sponge cakes available in diverse flavours –

The world's largest fish-and-chip restaurant

If you have a head for statistics, you will be delighted with the following, which is billed as the world's largest annual shopping list:

Haddock:	264,000 lbs	(119,748 kg)
Potatoes:	660, 000 lbs	(299,369 kg)
Sauce:	20, 000 bottles	
Tea:	360, 000 tea bags	
Butter:	10,000 lbs	(4,536 kg)
Bread:	17,000 loaves	
Milk:	40, 000 pints	(22,720 l)
Sugar:	4,500 lbs	(2,041 kg)
Salt:	2,200 lbs	(998 kg)
Vinegar:	6,500 pints	(3,692 l)

Welcome to Harry Ramsden's, the largest fish and chip restaurant in the world, featured in the *Guinness Book of Records*, and serving around one million customers a year.

It all began in 1928, in **Guiseley**, just outside of Leeds, in Yorkshire, in a small wooden hut, with a capital outlay of £150. Sixty five years later, the hut is still there, as a reminder, but there are now several restaurants, where the waiter service and linen table-cloths, are a far cry from the world of humble, take-away fish and chips. Harry Ramsden's restaurant is indeed not for anyone but for the fish-and-chip conoisseur.

lemon, chocolate, orange, coconut etc. Biscuits are extremely popular in England especially for "elevenses" – coffee and biscuits at 1100 hours – and supper, and there is an enormous variety of them. The brand you buy is sometimes seen as a kind of status symbol; the Prince of Wales has recently launched a line of biscuits, produced organically on his farm, and despite a hefty price tag, they are understanderably selling like hot cakes!

Food trends & eating out

Eating out has become increasingly popular in England, which is of great advantage to you the tourist, since it has vastly improved the standard of restaurant cuisine. The English, once extremely conservative when it came to foreign cuisine, have in recent years, probably due to the increase in holidays taken abroad, become much more international in the food they enjoy when eating out. Almost every town has a French, Indian (England has probably the best Indian food outside the sub-continent), Chinese and Italian restaurant, the big cities have food from every country you can imagine; Mongolian, Nepalese, Cuban, Iranian, Indonesian, the list goes on and on.

As far as home-grown cuisine goes, the most noticeable trend is that of health food. The health craze of the 1980s has abated, but even so, there are many health-food shops and supermarkets offer a range of organically grown foodstuffs.

If you are a vegetarian you will have no problem in England, vegetarians are on the increase and every restaurant and supermarket will have a range of vegetarian dishes to choose from. Supermarkets also offer an assortment of vegetarian packed food.

Nigthlife

After a hard day in the office, or an equally hard day "doing" a major museum, or pounding the streets of an ancient cathedral city, the English office worker and the holiday maker alike, want to enjoy themselves.. Both want to let loose, have a fun evening and relax and unwind after a hard day. The options available are many and extremely diverse.

423

After dinner culture, a drink in the local pub.

Going out for a drink

For a start there is refreshment, why not go out for dinner or for a drink. Let's start with a drink. Going out for a drink, is an extremely popular social activity in England, the places to go are wine bars and pubs, where you can have a drink and people-

watch at the same time. Pubs are an integral part of the English social scene, and you will find them all over the country, from a tiny village to a large city. They are the place to head for, for a quick drink, or a lazy evening of beer and "pub grub" (food served in a pub) and easy going conversation with your neighbours.

Pubs are no longer exclusively all-male, beery places. You will see groups of women on their own, most often drinking wine, rather than beer, so never hesitate to push open that door of frosted glass, and enter the cosy, noisy atmosphere of an English pub. (see box story p.403).

Food choices

Now, after a drink, what about dinner? If you are in London or any other of the major cities, there will be a wide range of eating options, but in small villages you may well be limited to the pub itself, or to the village's only restaurant. Those in search of authentic "English" cuisine are actually far more likely to find it in a pub or an inn, whereas those in search of Italian, Indian or Chinese food, will find it available in most places, and at a variety of prices.

There are expensive Italian restaurants, pizzerias galore, and cheap and cheerful Indian and Chinese "take aways", which add a touch of spiciness, if you are finding English food rather bland. "take away" food can literally be

The Hippodrome, one of London's classier nightclubs.

taken away but if you are a connoisseur of Chinese food, for instance, you might be somewhat disappointed to find the hot taste somewhat watered down, to suit the English palate. Most English Chinese food is of the Hong Kong, Cantonese variety.

Fast food chains have made their inevitable inroads into English life, though not into the expensive London borough of Hampstead, which refused to accept a *McDonald's* on aesthetic grounds.

French restaurants are also fairly wide-spread, but tend to be more expensive than their Italian counterparts, and in London you can find virtually any cuisine that takes your fancy; excellent Japanese restaurants, Spanish, Iranian,

An English Pub

English pubs come in all shapes and sizes, from historic thatched and half-timbered buildings in sleepy country villages, to loud, raucous inner-city hang-outs. There are pubs with pretty gardens and wooden benches, and pubs where everyone spills out into the street - well, when it is sunny and warm enough, of course - and then there are others where office workers dash in for a quick half and a ploughman's. Sorry? Not clear what that last bit means? OK, perhaps it's time for a few pub translations.

What is a pub?

A "pub" is an abbreviation for public house, a place where both alcoholic and non-alcoholic drinks are served. Pubs usually have a variety of snacks on offer, and sometimes meals, which are usually served in hearty portions. Pubs can also be inns, which generally means that they are older buildings with some historical character, often former coaching inns, where travellers would stop to rest and change horses, in the days when long-distance travel was a slower affair than today. Since some of the larger pubs also offer accommodation, they are almost like small hotels.

Next, what do you do in a pub? Well, you drink, of course, but only if you are over 18 years of age. You also eat, sit and talk to friends, chat to complete strangers, listen to the juke box if there is one, or play darts or bar billiards. In long conversations with the barman or the barmaids you can put the economy to rights, solve the latest political crisis, and analyse the football results.

Pub jargon

There are a number of drinking areas in a pub; the public bar, the lounge bar, the saloon bar, the private bar, and the snug. The pub may well also have a separate restaurant or dining area and often a garden with patio, for drinking alfresco. To simplify all these categories of bars, just remember that since drinks are usually a little cheaper in the public bar, it is therefore the busiest section of a pub. This is the place where you will find the crowd, the noise and the darts' board. The lounge bar, the saloon bar and the private bar are all a bit more comfortable than the public bar, and the drinks therefore cost a little more there. The appropriately named snug is a private bar, providing a cosy and intimate atmosphere, for a small number of people.

Useful information

Many pubs are owned by a particular brewery, with which the pub has a contract, in which case the pub is known as a "tied house", and usually you will only find the beer of that particular brewery on sale. Alternatively, the pub may be privately owned, in which case it is a "free house", meaning it is free to stock beers from various different suppliers.

The current law, which dates from 1933, bans children from pubs. They are usually allowed to sit in the garden with their parents, but there is a proposal under consideration with the Home Secretary, to make some pubs "family pubs". This follows a recent move in Scotland, which has successfully opened some, though not all, pubs to families.

The most quintessentially English pub "grub", is the ploughman's lunch. This healthy meal consists of a slab of cheese, bread and butter, accompanied by tomatoes, lettuce, celery, and pickles. Accompany this by "a half" (half a pint of beer), play your favourite tune on the juke-box, and chat to the pubs frequenters, now you are well on the way to enjoying the English pub life. Cheers !

Egyptian and even Mongolian. Nothing is too outrageous, although the price may be. Chinatown, London, has an excellent range of Chinese food.

Culture scene

One of the nicest ways of spending an

evening, particularly if you are in **London**, is to go to the theatre. Londoners are spoilt for choice, for there are a wide range of theatres offering just about everything in the way of entertainment. Every night, there will be at least one opera or ballet, usually at **Covent Garden** or **The Coliseum** in St Martin's Lane.

The **Barbican**, offers excellent "serious" theatre, as do numerous other theatres in London's **West End**, where comedies, thrillers and musicals are on offer galore. Stroll along **Shaftesbury Avenue**, from busy **Piccadilly Circus** up to **Cambridge Circus** and take your pick from any number of shows.

Alternatively, go in the early afternoon to one of the half-price ticket booths, the best known one is at **Leicester Square**, and see if there are cheap tickets on offer, often for matinee performances. If you are feeling a little traditional, or nostalgic, try and see London's longest running play, the detective writer Agatha Christie's *The Mousetrap*, 40 years old in 1993, and still audiences are trying to deduce "who did it".

The Arts in the Provinces

Outside London, the choice of plays or ballet will not be so vast, but the major cities like Leeds, Liverpool, Manchester and Birmingham all have several theatres, and excellent theatre companies, and some cities such as Leeds and Ox-

West End theatres along Shaftesbury Avenue, London.

Soho in the West End of London offers all kinds of evening entertainment.

ford are often used for pre-London "test" runs of plays, so you could be lucky and see a potential smash hit in the making. The newspapers have listings of "what's on" and always remember to check for special events - the Kirov Ballet on tour, or a Chinese Opera group, or one concert by a well-known star. Tickets may not be easy to find, but it is worth a try, especially for last minute cancellations. Ask the concierge at your hotel for help.

Cinemas & nightclubs

There are cinemas galore in London, in most towns and in all cities and you will be able to see all the major American films soon after their release. Esoteric and foreign language films are a little more difficult to find, but London has a couple of cinemas where you will always be able to find a Satyajit Ray movie, or a film in its original French. For information check the newspaper listings.

Nightclubs and discotheques are another option, but since they go in and out of fashion, it is best to ask for a recommendation, before hitting the night spots. Some clubs and discos are private, some are "private", which means the man at the door exercises the right of veto as to who he will let in and who he will refuse. These bouncers also serve the useful purpose of keeping out drunkards and other less desirable types, ensuring you a peaceful evening.

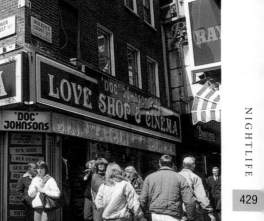

The common offerings of Soho.

Shopping, sport & museums

More and more galleries and exhibitions are staying open later, to cater for people who are at work during the day, and most museums will now have at least one night a week when they stay open very late. As a rule, nightlife in England, at least during the working week, is confined to night time and not to the wee hours of the morning. Never forget that England still has licensing hours, limiting the last orders for drinks in pubs, and as a race, the English tend to eat early anyway.

Things are gradually changing though and as more and more women work, shops are adapting their opening hours. Twenty years ago, to find a shop open at 2000 hours was rare, but now many of the large supermarket chains and department stores regularly stay open late, especially during the pre-Christmas rush when everyone is desperately shopping for presents.

In London, there are two main late night shopping areas: **Knightsbridge** stays open late on Wednesdays, and **Oxford Street** on Thursdays, this is the time when most working Londoners are able to do their shopping.

For sports' fans, another favourite thing to do, is to go and watch a football match, these are often played on midweek nights, as well as on Saturday afternoons.

TRAVEL TIPS

BUSINESS HOURS

Shops and department stores open at 0900 hours and generally stay open until 1700 or 1600 hours, though increasingly some stores stay open late, especially in large towns. Most towns will have a corner shop that is open until very late - they are often rather pricey, but that's the price of convenience. Offices are open from 0900 until 1700, whereas banks usually close around 1530 or 1600 hours.

CLIMATE & TEMPERATURE

Generally, spring and summer in England are pleasant seasons, all over the country, though you will always find that the south of the country has a gentler climate than the north. Autumn is usually beautiful, mild with just the occasional touch of frost. Winters are usually damp and cold, though it is rare for the country to experience bitterly cold weather. It sometimes snows in the winter, especially in the north of the country.

CULTURE & CUSTOMS

The English are a very polite race and expect politeness in return, though they are infinitely tolerant of genuine lapses and misunderstandings. If you are invited to an English home, you should arrive promptly at the time at which you are invited. "7.30 for 8.00" means that drinks will be served at 1930, and dinner will follow promptly at 2000. Being late is considered rude.

CUSTOMS

There are different allowances for visitors arriving from an EEC country - though these rules are likely to change with the revised rules for almost frontierless travel within Europe - so before buying any duty free items, it is important to check. Currently, the duty-free allowances for ECC travellers are; 300 cigarettes, or 150 cigarillos, or 75 cigars or 400 grams of tobacco; 5 litres of table wine plus 1.5 litres of alcohol over 22% proof or 3 litres of alcohol under 22% proof; 75 grams of perfume and 37.5 centilitres of eau de toilette. For non-ECC travellers, the allowances are 200 cigarettes, or 100 cigarillos, or 50 cigars or 250 grams of tobacco ; 2 litres of table wine plus 1 litre of alcohol over 22% proof or 2 litres of alcohol under 22% proof; 50 grams of perfume and 25 centilitres of eau de toilette.

DOMESTIC TRAVEL

In London, the options are many, the underground, or "tube" as most people call it, buses, taxis, and for some suburbs, trains. In London, it makes sense to get a Travel Card, which allows travel on the tube and the buses. Ask at any tube station for details of the various price and distance combinations. Both in London and the rest of the country, many buses are operating without a conductor, but the driver will always take the time to explain which coins are needed for a ticket.

ELECTRICITY

220 volts

FESTIVALS

There are some festivals but nothing on a countrywide basis. Check with the local tourist office, for most of the events are very much local events.

GETTING THERE

By air

London is a major airline hub, with Heathrow, Gatwick and London City airports. Stanstead, although heavily promoted as the third London airport, is a little too far away for regular commuter traffic. Given the relatively small size of the country, there is not too much domestic air travel - train or road is often as quick.

By sea
Fewer and fewer people travel by sea these days, though liners still do cross the Atlantic, sailing from Southampton to New York. There are ferries sailing every day from the west coast of England across to Ireland and the Isle of Man, from the south coast to the off-shore Isles of Scilly and the Isle of Wight, and there is very regular traffic between the various English Channel ports and the northern French coast. In peak season, there are daily ferry and Hovercraft crossings between England and France, but in the height of the summer places for cars get booked up quickly, though foot passengers should not usually have a problem. Things will be very different once the Channel Tunnel opens - at the time of writing, this is supposed to be in late 1993/early 1994.

By road
Given that the United Kingdom is an island, you can only drive into England from neighbouring Wales or Scotland, both of which have excellent motorway connections, and there are no frontier controls, of course.

By rail
Exactly the same conditions as for roads.

HEALTH
Health certificates are only necessary if you are arriving from an area where yellow fever is present.

HOLIDAYS
On the 8 main public holidays, all banks, offices, post offices and most shops and department stores are closed. This also applies on Sundays, though you will find newsagents and corner stores open at all hours.

HOSPITAL
All towns have at least 1 hospital. In case of emegency go straight to the Outpatients Department and ask for help.

MEDIA
As the home of the BBC, (British Broadcasting Company), not surprisingly radio and television are of a good standard, although you will see much criticism and soul-searching about them in the press. You can watch the BBC, the main independent channel, ITV, regional TV as well as Channel 4, largely given over to "minority" programmes. The British press varies from virtual institutions like *The Times* down to the racy, sensational tabloids at the other end of the scale. As they always seem to be engaged in cut-throat price battles, they try and scoop each other non-stop, and the Royal Family is their preferred target. In London you can find newspapers and magazines in just about any foreign language you wish.

MEDICAL ASSISTANCE
Should any problem arise, go first of all to the local chemist, and virtually every town and village in the country will have one, and ask for help there. They should be able to give you basic medicine, or, if the problem is more urgent, direct you to a doctor or hospital. Chemist chain-stores like Boots are widespread in the country, and most of them have a dispensing chemist, qualified to give advice and prescriptions. Each town, and in London, each borough will have a 24 hour chemist, so if a problem arises, and your local chemist is closed, look on the door, where the name, address and phone number of the 24 hour chemist should be displayed. If the problem is serious, head straight for the out-patients section of the nearest hospital.

MONEY & CURRENCY
The pound is divided into 100 pence. Foreign currency and travellers' cheques can be changed quickly and efficiently at banks, major hotels and exchange booths. Credit cards and personal cheques are widely used.

PASSPORTS AND VISAS
A valid passport is required, as well as a visa : only the following nationals do not need a visa - passport holders of EEC countries, of Japan, Australia, Canada, the USA, Singapore, Malaysia and New Zealand. Anyone intending to study or to work will need a different visa, and should make the appropriate enquiries before their trip.

PHOTOGRAPHY
You can photograph without any problems in England, except where it is expressly forbidden - in certain museums, for example. No-one really objects to your taking pictures of their children, though a smile always helps, but if you intend taking pictures of adults, it does help to ask permission first.

Film is widely available, and can be processed with no problem, anywhere in the country.

PLACES OF WORSHIP
Church of England and Roman Catholic churches are found in most places. Most cities have a Synagogue and a mosque.

POLICE
Every town has a police station. The emergency telephone number is 999. Police are always helpful in handling requests for directions.

POSTAL SERVICES
Post offices are open during standard business hours, which means on weekdays from 0900 to 1730 hours, until noon on Saturday, and closed on Sundays. Sub-post offices, which are often little more than a counter in a tiny shop keep similar hours. There is a 24 hour post office next to Trafalgar Square in London.

PRIVATE TRANSPORT
All the major car rental companies are present in England, and it is easy to reserve cars in advance. Very often, the rental companies have offices at the railway stations and airports, so you can walk straight off a train or a plane, and into your car. You will need your driving licence, an international licence, and, ideally, a credit card with which to pay the deposit.

PUBLIC TRANSPORT
If you travel by train, it makes sense to travel outside the rush hours. Not only will you get a seat, but you may well save money. So, if you are planning to travel on an Inter-City service, go first to the station, and enquire about cheap day returns. Most trains will have some form of catering on board, from a trolley of snacks to a sit-down restaurant.

TELEPHONE
More and more English telephone booths are being made to accept telephone cards rather than coins, so buy a card, widely on sale at post offices, or wherever you see the sign - usually in newsagents and corner shops. Telephone booths will almost certainly have information panels, giving you the access codes for both domestic and overseas dialing. Most telephones are run by British Telecom, but you will see booths for another company, Mercury. The cards are not inter-changeable.

TIME ZONES
Greenwich Mean Time

TIPPING
If a service charge in restaurants and hotels is automatically included in the bill, there is no need to tip in addition - otherwise, leave around 15%. Bell boys and porters in hotels will expect tips - roughly 20 pence per piece of luggage.

TOURS
Available in abundance in London and all the major cities, and in a range of languages, prices, and length - you can arrange just about anything from half a day at Hampton Court, to a week's trip around the Lake District.

WEIGHTS & MEASURES
England is supposed to be metric, but it isn't. That means that people still think, talk, measure and calculate in inches, feet and miles, weigh things in stones and pounds, and, of course, drink their beer in pints. So, be prepared for both systems. Some stores however, label everything in both systems.

WHAT TO WEAR
Joking apart, England does tend to experience a range of climates in a single day, so the best advice when packing, is to try and include everything from raincoats to light summery clothes. Essentials, though, remain a waterproof and a warm sweater - just in case. Remember, when dressing for sight-seeing, comfort should be your main priority. Wear comfortable shoes for all the city walking. Beach wear is only appropriate for the beach. You should have at least one smart outfit, and for men that means a jacket and tie, if you intend going to a good restaurant, a West End Show, or if you might be invited home by English people, who appreciate smartly dressed guests.

DIRECTORY

ACCOMMODATION, FROM BUDGET TO DELUXE

Room rates, unless otherwise stated, are for a single room. The mention B & B, meaning "Bed and Breakfast", indicates that a full English breakfast is included in the room rate.

AVON
BATH
Ashley Villa Hotel
26, Newbridge Road
Tel: 225-421683/428887
B & B £35-39

Brocks
32 Brock Street
Tel: 225-338374
B & B £19-20

Carfax Hotel
Great Pulteney Street
Tel: 225-462089
B & B £22-25

BRISTOL
Aaron Lodge
425 Fishponds Road
Fishponds
Tel: 0272-653132
B & B £34

Alcove
508-510 Fishponds Road
Fishponds
Tel: 0272-653886/652436
B & B £19-25

Washington Hotel
11-15 St. Pauls Road
Clifton
Tel: 0272-733980
B & B £27.50

BERKSHIRE
WINDSOR
Clarence Hotel
9 Clarence Road
Tel: 0753-864436
B & B £30

CAMBRIDGESHIRE
CAMBRIDGE
Assisi
193 Cherry Hinton Road
Tel: 0223-211466
B & B £23-28

Avimore
310 Cherry Hinton Road
Tel: 0223-410956
B & B £17-25

Christina's
47 St. Andrews Road
Tel: 0223-65855/327700
B & B £22-24

De Freville House
166 Chesterton Road
Tel: 0223-354993
B & B £16-19

CORNWALL
PENZANCE
Blue Seas Hotel
13 Regent Terrace
Tel: 0736-64744
B & B £15-17.50

Carlton Private Hotel
Promenade
Tel: 0736-62081
B & B £16.50

Chy-an-Mor Guest House
15 Regent Terrace
Tel: 0736-63441
B & B £16.50

Mount Royal Hotel
Chyandour Cliff
Tel: 0736-62233
B & B £21-24

COUNTY DURHAM
DURHAM
Lothlorien
48/49 Front Street
Witton GIlbert
Tel: 091-371 0067
B & B £15-17

Bay Horse
Brandon
Tel: 091-378 0498
B & B £26

CUMBRIA
AMBLESIDE
Compston House Hotel
Compston Road
Tel: (05394) 33272
Double B & B £31-49

Rothay Garth Hotel
Rothay Road
Tel: (05394) 34400
B & B £8.50-46.50

GRASMERE
Bridge House Hotel
Stock Lane
Tel: 05394-35425
B & B £39-43

Lake View Country House
Lake View Drive
Tel: 05394-35384
B & B £26.50

KENDAL
Burrow Hall Country Guest
House
Plantation Bridge
Tel: 0539-821711
Double B & B £45

Lane Head Country House
Hotel
Helsington
Tel: 0539-731283
B & B £35-40

WINDEREMERE
Aaron Slack Guest House
48 Ellerthwaite Road
Tel: 05394-44649
B & B £12-20

Applegarth Hotel
College Road
Tel: 05394-43206
B & B £20-35

Fir Trees Guest House
Lake Road
Tel: 05394-42272
B & B £22.50-28.50

Glenville Hotel
Lake Road
Tel: 05394-43371
B & B £17.50-22.50

The Hawksmoor Guest House
Lake Road
Tel: 05394-42110
B & B £23-35

Holly Lodge Guest House
6, College Road
Tel: 05394-43873
B & B £15-18

DERBYSHIRE
DERBY
Dalby House Hotel
100 Radbourne Street
Off Windmill
Tel: 0332-42353
B & B £17-19

Georgian House Hotel
32/34, Ashbourne Road
Tel: 0332-49806
B & B £23

DEVON
EXETER
The Edwardian
30/32 Heavitree Road
Tel: 0392-76102/54699
B & B £19-20

PLYMOUTH
Bowling Green Hotel
9-10 Osborne Place
Lockyear St, The Hoe
Tel: 0752-667485
B & B £26

Devonshire Guest House
22 Lockyer Road
Mannamead
Tel: 0752-220726
B & B £13-15

Georgian House Hotel
51 Citadel Road, The Hoe
Tel: 0752-663237
B & B £31

DORSET
BOURNEMOUTH
Alum Grange Hotel
1, Burnaby Road, Alum Chine
Tel: 0202-761195
B & B £21.37-35

WEYMOUTH
Bay Lodge
27 Greenhill
Tel: 0305-782419
B & B £21-26

Hazeldene Guest House
16 Abbotsbury Road
Westham
Tel: 0305-782579
B & B £13-15

GLOUCESTERSHIRE
CHELTENHAM
Abbey Hotel
16, Bath Parade
Tel: 0242-516053
B & B £33-35

Battledown Hotel
125 Hales Road
Tel: 0242-233881
B & B £24-26

Cleeve Hill Hotel
Cleeve Hill
Tel: 0242-672052
B & B £35-40

Knowle House
89 Leckampton Road
Tel: 0242-516091
B & B £15-17

GLOUCESTER
Bowden Hall Resort Hotel,
Bondend Lane, Upton St.
Leonard's
Tel : 0452-61412
B & B from £73.50

Denmark Hotel,
36 Denmark Road
Tel : 0452-303808
B & B from £16

Rotherfield House Hotel,
5 Horton Road
Tel : 0452-410500
B & B from £19.25

Claremont Guest House
135 Stroud Road
Tel: 0452-529540
B & B £12.50-15

GREATER MANCHESTER
MANCHESTER
Ebor Hotel
402 Wilbraham Road
Chorlton Cum Hardy
Tel: 061-881 1911
B & B £19-21

New Central Hotel
144-146 Heywood Street
Cheetham
Tel: 061-205 2169
B & B £20.50

HAMPSHIRE
PORTSMOUTH & SOUTHSEA
Abbey Lodge
30 Waverley Road
Tel: 0705-828285
B & B £15-18

Bombell Court Hotel
69 Festing Road
Tel: 0705-735915
B & B £30-36

Hamilton House
95 Victoria Road North
Tel: 0705-823502
B & B £14-16

SOUTHAMPTON
Hunters Lodge Hotel
25 Landguard Lodge
Landguard Road, Shirley
Tel: 0703-227919
B & B £20-23

Madison House
137 Hill Lane
Tel: 0703-772264
B & B £13.95-15.50

WINCHESTER
Aerie Guest House
142 Teg Down Meads (Off
Dean Lane)
Tel: 0962-862519
B & B £31-36

Number Fifty Hotel
50 Christchurch Road
St. Cross
Tel: 0962-852628
B & B £25

The Wykeham Arms
73 Kingsgate Street
Tel: 0962-853834
B & B £62.50

HEREFORD & WORCESTER
HEREFORD
Aylestone Court Hotel,
Aylestone Hill
Tel: 0432-341891
B & B £25. 00 - £40. 00

WORCESTER
Wyatt
40 Brabourne Road
Tel: 0905-26311
B & B £16-18

HUMBERSIDE
HULL
Earlesmere Hotel
76/78 Sunny Bank, Spring
Bank
Tel: 0482-473714
B & B £18.80-21.15

KENT
CANTERBURY
Castle Court
8 Castle Street
Tel: 0223-463441
B & B £16-20

Cathedral Gate Hotel
36 Burgate
Tel: 0227-464381
B & B £27.50-28.50

Ebury Hotel
New Dover Road
Tel: 0227-768433
B & B £41-46

Magnolia House
36, St. Dunstan's Ter
Tel: 0227-765121
B & B £30-35

The Canterbury Hotel,
71 New Dover Road
Tel: 0277-450551
B & B £40. 00 - £45. 00

County Hotel,
High Street
Tel: 0277-766266
B & B £72.50 - £75.50

Victoria Hotel,
59 London Road
Tel: 0227-459333
B & B £44. 00

DOVER
Beulah House
94 Crabble Hill
London Hill
Tel: 0304-201656
B & B £18-20

Castle House
10 Castle Hill Road
Tel: 0304-201656
B & B £18-30

Number One
1, Castle Street
Tel: 0304-202007
Double B & B £28-34

Walletts Court Manor
West Cliffe
St. Margarets-at-Cliffe
Tel: 0304-852424
B & B £40-55

Boston Guest House,
119 Folkestone Road
Tel : 0304-210412
B & B £15.00 - £20.00

Pennyfarthing,
109 Maison Dieu Road
Tel : 0304-205563
B & B £17.00

White Cliffs Hotel,
Waterloo Crescent, Sea Front,
Tel: 0304-203633
B & B £45. 00 - £50. 00

FOLKESTONE
The Augusta Hotel,
4 Augusta Gardens
Tel: 0303-850952
B&B £24.00-£26.00

Garden House Hotel,
142 Sandgate Road
Tel: 0303-252278
B & B £37.50

LEICESTERSHIRE
LEICESTER
Burlington Hotel
Elmfield Avenue
Tel: 0533-705112
B & B £22-25

LINCOLNSHIRE
LINCOLN
D'Isney Place Hotel
Eastgate
Tel: 0522-538881
B & B £39-53

Tennyson Hotel
7 South Park
Tel: 0522-521624
B & B £28-29

LONDON
Aber Hotel
Crouch Hill
Tel: 081-340 2847
B & B £18-25

White Lodge Hotel
1 Church Lane
Hornsey
Tel: 081-348 9765
B & B £22-24

Four Seasons Hotel
173 Gloucester Place
Regents Park
Tel: 071-724 3461
B & B £49.50

Croft Court Hotel
44 Ravenscroft Avenue
Golders Green
Tel: 081-458 3331
B & B £54

Stonehall House Hotel
35-37 Westcombe Park Road
Tel: 081-858 8706
B & B £20-22

The Diplomat
2 Chesham Street
Belgravia
Tel: 071-235 1544
B & B £64.57-83.37

Willett Hotel
17 Belgrave Road
Tel: 071-828 2972
B & B £45-58

Swiss House Hotel
171 Old Brompton Road
South Kensington
Tel: 071-373 2769
B & B £32

Wimbledon Hotel
78 Worple Road
Tel: 081-946 9265
B & B £45-48

Worcester House
28 Alwyne Road
Tel: 081-946 1300
B & B £45-49.50

Bryanston court
60 Great Cumberland Place
Tel: 071-262 3141
B & B £75

Hotel Concorde
50 Great Cumberland Place
Tel: 071-402 6169
B & B £65

Georgian House Hotel
87 Gloucester Place
Baker Street
Tel: 071-935 2211
B & B £45-50

Byron Hotel
36-38 Queensborough Ter
Tel: 071-243 0987
B & B £80-85

Park Lodge Hotel
73 Queensborough Ter
Bayswater
Tel: 071-229 6424
B & B £45-49

Pembridge Court Hotel
34 Pembridge Gardens
Tel: 071-229 9977
B & B £90-125

Chiswick Hotel
73 Chiswick High Road
Tel: 081-994 1712
B & B £64.50

Apollo Hotel
18-22 Lexham Gardens
Tel: 071-835 1133
B & B £24-30

Mentone Hotel
54-55 Cartwright Gardens
Tel: 071-387 3927
B & B £25-32

GATWICK AIRPORT (LONDON)
Barnwood Hotel
Balcombe Road

Pound Hill
Tel: 0293-882709
B & B £35

Gatwick Skylodge
London Road, County Oak
Tel: 0293-544511
B & B £38

MERSEYSIDE
LIVERPOOL
Aachen Hotel
91 Mount Pleasant
Tel: 051-709 3477
B & B £20-30

New Manx Hotel
39 Catherine Street
Tel: 051-708 6171
B & B £18.50-20

NORFOLK
NORWICH
Grange Hotel
230 Thorpe Road
Tel: 0603-34734
B & B £28-36

Marlborough House Hotel
22 Stracey Road
Thorpe
Tel: 0603-628005
B & B £16-20

NOTTINGHAMSHIRE
NOTTINGHAM
Crantock Hotel
480 Mansfield Road
Tel: 0602-623294
B & B £20-24

P & J Hotel
277-279 Derby Road
Lenton
Tel: 0602-783998
B & B £25-35

OXFORDSHIRE
OXFORD
Acorn Guest House
260 Iffley Road
Tel: 0865-247998
B & B £18-24

All Seasons Guest House
Windmill Road, Headington
Tel: 0865-742215
B & B £20-25

Combermere Guest Hosue
11 Polstead Road
Tel: 0865-56971
B & B £25-50

Cotswold House
363 Banbury Road
Tel: 0865-310558
B & B £32-35

Earlmont Guest House
322-324 Cowley Road
Tel: 0865-240236
B & B £25-30

Pickwicks Guest Huse
17 London Road
Headington
Tel: 0865-750487
B & B £28-34

River Hotel,
17 Botley Road
Tel: 0865-243475
B & B £37.50 - £55. 00

SHROPSHIRE
SHREWSBURY
Prince Rupert Hotel,
Butcher Row
Tel: 0743-236000
from £70

The Lion,
Wyle Cop
Tel: 0743-353107
from £65

Lion & Pheasant Hotel,
49-50 Wyle Cop
Tel: 0743-236288
from £23.50

Roseville Guest House
12 Berwick Road
Tel: 0743-236470
B & B £15.50-17

Sandford House Hotel
St. Julians Friars
Tel: 0743-343829
B & B £22.50

Grove Farm House
Preston, Brockhurst
Tel: 093928-223
B & B £14

The Old Farmhouse
Hillside Road
Tel: 0395-512284
B & B £18-23

SUSSEX
BRIGHTON & HOVE
Adelaide Hotel
51 Regency Square
Tel: 0273-205286
B & B £38-60

Arlanda Hotel
20 New Steine
Tel: 0273-699300
B & B £28-38

George IV Hotel
34 Regency Square
Tel: 0273-21196
B & B £30-45

Paskins Hotel
19 Charlotte Street
Tel: 0273-601203
B & B £20-22

EASTBOURNE
Bay Lodge Hotel
61/62 Royal Parade
Tel: 0323-639171
B & B £17-21

Beachy Rise
20 Beachy Head Road
Tel: 0323-639171
B & B £6-44

Chalk Farm Hotel & Restau-
rant
Coopers Hill, Willingdon
Tel: 0323-503800
B & B £27-32

Hotel Mandalay
16 Trinity Trees
Tel: 0323-29222
B & B £24-29

WARWICKSHIRE
STRATFORD-UPON-AVON
Brook Lodge
192 Alcester Road
Tel: 0789-295988
Double B & B £34-38

Courtland Hotel
12 Guild Street
Tel: 0789-292401
B & B £15-17

Craig Cleeve House
67-69 Shipston Road
Tel: 0789-296573
B & B £18.50-26

Hardwick House
1 Avenue Road
Tel: 0789-204307
B & B £16.50-23

Gravelside Barn
Binton
Tel: 0789-750502
B & B £30-40

Moonraker House
40 Alcester Road
Tel: 0789-299346
Double B & B £37-55

Twelfth Night Guest House
Evesham Place
Tel: 0789-414595
B & B £19-32

WEST MIDLANDS
BIRMINGHAM
Ashdale House Hotel
39 Broad Road
Acock's Green
Tel: 021-706 3598
B & B £25

Bridge House Hotel
49, Sherbourne Road
Acock's Green
Tel: 021-706 5900
B & B £29.37

Fountain Court Hotel
339-343 Hagley Road
Edgbaston
Tel: 021-429 1754
B & B £30-39

COVENTRY
Ashleigh House
17 Park Road
Tel: 0203-223804
B & B £15

Three Spires
62 Grosvenor Road
Tel: 0203-632596
B & B £15

Ansty Hall,
Ansty
Tel: 0203-612222
B & B from £95. 00

Croft Hotel,
23 Stoke Green
Tel: 0203-457846
B & B £27. 00 - £37. 00

Novotel Coventry,
Wilsons Lane, Longford
Tel: 0203-365000
B & B £60.50 - £64.00

YORKSHIRE
YORK
Acorn Guest House
1 Southlands Road
Bishopthorpe Road
Tel: 0904-620081
B & B £12.50-16

Arndale Hotel
290 Tadcaster Road
Tel: 0904-702424
Double B & B £44-60

Arnot House
17 Grosvenor Ter, Bootham
Tel: 0904-641966
B & B £12.50-15

Bedford Guest House
108/110 Bootham
Tel: 0904-624412
B & B £28-34

Byron House Hotel
7 Driffield Ter
The Mount
Tel: 0904-632525
B & B £25-30

Clifton Guest House
127 Clifton
Tel: 0904-634031
B & B £15

Greasmead House Hotel
1, Scarcroft Hill
The Mount
Tel: 0904-629996
Double B & B £54

Minster View
2 Grosvenor Ter
Tel: 0904-655034
B & B £14-17

AIRLINE OFFICES IN LONDON - DOMESTIC AND INTERNATIONAL

Aer Lingus
223 Regent Street, London Wl
Tel: 081-745 7017

Aeroflot
70 Piccadilly, London Wl
Tel: 071-355 2233

Air Algerie
10 Baker Street, London W1
Tel: 071-487 5903

Air Botswana
114 Tottenham Court Road,
London Wl
Tel: 071-383 3727

Air Canada
Heathrow Airport
Tel: 081-759 2636

Air China
41 Grosvenor Gardens,
London SWl
Tel: 071-630 0919

Air France
Colet Court, Hammersmith
Road, London W6
Tel: 081-742 6600

Air India
17 New Bond Street, London
Wl
Tel: 071-493 4050

Air Lanka
6 Bruton Street, London Wl
Tel: 071-439 0291

Air Malta
314 Upper Richmond Road,
London SWl5
Tel: 081-785 3177

Air Mauritius
49 Conduit Street, London Wl
Tel: 071-434 4379

Air Namibia
1 Approach Road, London
SW20
Tel: 081-543 2122

Air New Zealand
77 Fulham Palace Road,
London W6
Tel: 081-741 2299

Air U.K.
Cross Keys House, Haselett
Avenue,
Crawley,
West Sussex, RH10 HS
Reservations Linkline
Tel: 0345-666777

Air Zimbabwe
52 Piccadilly, London Wl
Tel: 071-491 0009

Alitalia Italian Airlines
205 Holland Park Avenue,
London Wl1
Tel: 071-602 7111

American Airlines
15 Berkeley Street, London Wl
Tel: 081-572 5555
Reservations Freephone
LinkLine Tel: 0800-010151

Austrian Airlines
50 Conduit Street London Wl
Tel: 071-439 1851

British Airways
156 Regent Street, London Wl
Tel: 071-434 4700

British Midland Airways
Donnington Hall,
Castle Donnington
Passenger Reservations Tel:
071-589 5599
Heathrow Airport Tel: 081-745 7321

BWIA International Airways
48 Leicester Square, London
WC2
Tel: 071-839 7155

Cathay Pacific
7 Apple Tree Yard, London
SWl
Tel: 071-930 7878

Cyprus Airways
23 Hampstead Road, London
NWl
Tel: 071-383 4831

Egyptair
296 Regent Street, London W1
Tel: 071-580 4239

El Al Israel Airlines
185 Regent Street, London W1
Tel: 071-437 9255

Finnair
14 Clifford Street, London W1
Tel: 071-629 8039

Gulf Air
10 Albermarle Street, London
W1
Tel: 071-408 1717

Iberia
130 Regent Street, London W1
Tel: 071-437 5622

Icelandair
172 Tottenham Court Road,
London W1
Tel: 071-388 5599

Japan Airlines
5 Hanover Square, London
W1
Tel: 071-629 9244

Kenya Airways
16 Conduit Street London W1
Tel: 071-409 0185

KLM Royal Dutch Airlines
Heathrow Airpot, Terminal 4
Tel: 081-750 9000

Korean Air Lines
66 Haymarket Street, London
SW1
Tel: 071-930 6513

Kuwait Airways
45 Queen's Gate, London
SW1
Tel: 071-589 4533

Lufthansa
23-26 Piccadilly, London W1
Tel: 081-750 3520

Luxair
Heathrow Airport, Terminal 2,
Tel: 081-745 4254

Malaysia Airlines
191 Askew Road, London
W12
Tel: 081-862 0770

Manx Airlines
Ronaldsway Airport,
Ballasalla, Isle of Man, IM9 9E
Tel: 071-493 0803

Middle East Airlines
48 Park Street, London W1
Tel: 071-493 5681

Nigeria Airways
12 Conduit Street, London Wl
Tel: 071-493 9726

Olympic Airways
164 Piccadilly, London Wl
Tel: 071-493 3965

Pakistan International Airlines
45 Piccadilly, London W2
Tel: 071-734 5544

Qantas
169 Regent Street, London
Wl
Tel: 081-846 0466

Royal Brunei Airlines
49 Cromwell Road, London
SW7
Tel: 071-584 6660

Sabena
36 Piccadilly, London Wl
Tel: 071-437 6960

SAS Scandinavian Airlines
52 Conduit Street, London
Wl
Tel: 071-734 4020

Saudia
171 Regent Street, London
Wl
Tel: 081-995 7777

Singapore Airlines
580 Chiswick High Road,
London W4
Tel: 081-995 4901

South African Airways
251 Regent Street, London
Wl
Tel: 071-734 9841

Swissair
Swiss Centre, Wardour Street,
London Wl
Tel: 071-439 4144

TAP Air Portugal
38 Gillingham Street, London
SWl
Tel: 071-828 2092

Thai Airways International
41 Albermarle Street, London
Wl
Tel: 071-491 7953

United Airlines
193 Piccadilly, London Wl
Tel: 081-990 9911

Virgin Atlantic
Ashdown House,
High Street, Crawley
West Sussex
Tel: 0293-747 747

**FOREIGN EMBASSIES &
HIGH COMMISSIONS IN
LONDON**
Australian High Commission
Australia House
Strand, London W1
Tel: 071-379 4334

Austrian Embassy
18 Belgrave Mews West,
London SW1
Tel: 071-235 3731

Cyprus High Commission
93 Park Street, London W1
Tel: 071-499 8272

Danish Embassy
55 Sloane Street, London SW1
Tel: 071-333 0200

Finnish Embassy
38 Chesham Place, London
SW1
Tel: 071-235 9531

German Embassy
23 Belgrave Square, London
SW1
Tel: 071-235 5033

Greek Embassy
!A Holland Park, London WII
Tel: 071-229 3850

**High Commissioner of the
Democratic Socialist Republic
of Sri Lanka**
13 Hyde Park Gardens London
W2
Tel: 071-262 1841

High Commissioner for India
India House,
Aldwych London WC2
Tel: 071-836 8484

High Commissioner for Kenya
24 New Bond Street, London
W1
Tel: 071-636 2371

**High Commissioner for New
Zealand**
New Zealand House,
Haymarket, London SW1
Tel: 071-930 8422

Icelandic Embassy
1 Eaton Terrace, London SW1
Tel: 071-730 5131

Irish Embassy
17 Grosvenor Place, London
SW1
Tel: 071-235 2171

Italian Embassy
4 Grosvenor Square, London
W1
Tel: 071-629 8200

Japanese Embassy
101 Piccadilly, London W1
Tel: 071-465 6500

Korean Embassy
4 Palace Gate, London W8
Tel: 071-581 0247

Kuwait Embassy
45 Queen's Gate, London
SW7
Tel: 071-589 4533

Luxembourg Embassy
27 Wilton Crescent, London
SW1
Tel: 071-235 6961

Malaysian High Commission
45 Belgrave Square, London
SW1
Tel: 071-235 8033

Mexico Embassy
42 Hertford Street, London W1
Tel: 071-499 8586

Morocco Embassy
97 Praed Street, London W2
Tel: 071-724 0719

Netherlands Embassy
38 Hyde Park Gate, London
SW7
Tel: 071-584 5040

Nicaragua Embassy
8 Gloucester Road, London
SW7
Tel: 071-584 4365

Pakistan Embassy
35 Lowndes Square, London
SW1
Tel: 071-235 2044

**People's Republic of China
Embassy**
5 Birch Grove, London W3
Tel: 081-993 0279

**Republic Cote d'Ivoire
Embassy**
2 Upper Belgrave Street,
London SW1
Tel: 071-235 6991

Singapore High Commission
9 Wilton Crescent, London
SW1
Tel: 071-235 8315

South African Embassy
South Africa House, Trafalgar
Square, London WC2
Tel: 071-839 2211

Swedish Embassy
11 Montague Place, London
WII
Tel: 071-724 2101
For visas
Tel: 071-724-6782

Swiss Embassy
16 Montague Place, London
WI
Tel: 071-723 0701

The Royal Thai Embassy
30 Queen's Gate, London
SW7
Tel: 071-589 0173

**United Republic of Tanzania
High Commission**
43 Hertford Street, London WI
Tel: 071-499 8951

USA Embassy
24 Grosvenor Square, London
WI
Tel: 071-499 9000

Vietnam Embassy
34 Wardour Street, London
W8
Tel: 071-434 1042

PHOTO CREDITS

Antiques of the Orient : 14, 17, 24/25
ACE/Peter Adams : 335, 337
ACE/Aitch: 338/339
ACE/Geoff Du Feu : 332
ACE/Geoff Johnson : 330
ACE/PLI : 340/341
ACE/Rolf Richardson : 333
Greg Evans : xii, xiii (top), xiv, xv, Backcover (top), 2, 3, 4/5, 8, 23, 26, 30, 38, 40, 42, 46, 49, 50, 53, 54, 57, 63, 68/69, 82, 83, 85, 86/87, 88, 89, 90, 92/93, 95, 97, 100, 102, 103, 106, 106/107, 110, 112, 114, 119, 120, 122, 128, 129, 133, 134, 136/137, 140, 141, 143, 144, 145, 147, 150, 153, 154, 157, 158, 160, 162/163, 164/165, 169, 170/171, 172, 173, 175, 180, 181, 186/187, 188/189, 190/191, 193, 196, 197, 201, 206/207, 208, 214 (top, bottom), 215 (bottom), 226, 227, 232, 233, 240, 248, 252, 254, 257, 258, 259, 260, 261, 262, 266, 266/267, 271, 281, 286, 287, 290/291, 292, 294/295, 300, 302, 304, 306, 307, 328, 342, 345, 352/353, 358/359, 360/361, 366, 388, 398, 399, 400, 402/403, 404, 405, 408, 409, 412, 414, 415, 418, 420, 426/427, 428, 429
Greg Evans/Richard Bailey : 70
Greg Evans/Dorothy Burrows : 365, 370/371
Greg Evans/Eric Carmichael : 382/383
Greg Evans/Mrs H Chapman : 116, 264
Greg Evans/Robert Clare : 75, 368/369, 393
Greg Evans/Mike Davis : 299, 301
Greg Evans/Paul Dentskevich : 424
Greg Evans/J Evans : 9
Greg Evans/Gei/J Flowerdew : 78, 239, 281, 410, 411
Greg Evans/Studio/Foto 45 : 311, 313
Greg Evans/Terry Harber : 64
Greg Evans/John Hewerding : xv (bottom)
Greg Evans/Miwako Ikeda : 187, 219, 268/269, 318
Greg Evans/K F Jervis : 217
Greg Evans/Walter F Joseph : 200, 253, 354/355
Greg Evans/Harry Lomax : 236
Greg Evans/Neil Mcallister : 62, 98
Greg Evans/Ian Murray : 250/251
Greg Evans/Ken Powell : x (bottom)
Greg Evans/Alexander Ramsay : 185
Greg Evans/N. Rivett : 256, 296
Greg Evans/Allen Roberts : 179, 246/247
Greg Evans/Robin Sandry : 56, 356
Greg Evans/M Sawyer : 303
Greg Evans/Chris Sidney : 155, 159, 161, 326, 394/395
Greg Evans/Mike South : 198, 270, 272
Greg Evans/Jackie Surtees : 378
Greg Evans/Don Sutton : x (top)
Greg Evans/Malcom Thomas : 391
Greg Evans/Tony Wadham : 202
Greg Evans/Robin Weaver : 374
Greg Evans/Monica Wells : 228/229, 422
Nigel Hicks : 1, 52, 59, 94, 125, 222, 230, 231, 241, 244, 280, 298, 396
The Image Bank : 138
The Image Bank/Michael Coyne : 45
Pateman : 12, 216, 419
Christine Pemberton : 9, 18, 34, 43, 77, 80, 121, 139, 142, 166, 176, 177, 204, 205, 207, 211, 215 (top), 218 (top & bottom), 221, 225, 268, 270, 274/275, 275, 276, 277, 278, 282 (top & bottom), 283, 284, 289, 291, 308, 314/315, 316/317, 321, 322, 325, 327, 329, 346/347, 349, 350, 360, 363, 364, 373, 376, 378, 390, 397, 402, Front & Back End
Morten Strange : 71, 72 (top & bottom), 73 (top & bottom), 74 (top & bottom), 130
Doug Traverso : 6, 16, 61, 104, 113, 115, 199, 376/377, 384/385
Bill Wassman : 430, xi (top & bottom), xiii (bottom), 146, 220, Backcover (left & right)

INDEX

INDEX

445

INDEX

447